Statistics 1
for AQA

CAMBRIDGE
UNIVERSITY PRESS

The School Mathematics Project

SMP AS/A2 Mathematics writing team David Cassell, Spencer Instone, John Ling, Paul Scruton, Susan Shilton, Heather West

SMP design and administration Melanie Bull, Carol Cole, Pam Keetch, Nicky Lake, Cathy Syred, Ann White

The authors thank Sue Glover for the technical advice she gave when this AS/A2 project began and for her detailed editorial contribution to this book. The authors are also very grateful to those teachers who advised on the book at the planning stage and commented in detail on draft chapters.

CAMBRIDGE
UNIVERSITY PRESS

University Printing House, Cambridge CB2 8BS, United Kingdom

Cambridge University Press is part of the University of Cambridge.

It furthers the University's mission by disseminating knowledge in the pursuit of education, learning and research at the highest international levels of excellence.

www.cambridge.org
Information on this title: www.cambridge.org/9780521605274

© The School Mathematics Project 2004

First published 2004
9th printing 2014

Printed in India by Replika Press Pvt. Ltd

A catalogue record for this publication is available from the British Library

ISBN 978-0-521-60527-4 Paperback

Typesetting and technical illustrations by The School Mathematics Project

Photograph on page 38 by Paul Scruton

The authors and publisher are grateful to the Assessment and Qualifications Alliance for permission to reproduce questions from past examination papers and the tables on pages 148–155. Individual questions are marked AQA.

The data on page 22 is from the National Statistics website www.statistics.gov.uk; Crown copyright material is reproduced with the permission of HMSO.

Using this book

Apart from chapter 1, which is a review of basic topics to be dipped into when needed, each chapter has the following structure.

It begins with a **summary** of what the student is expected to learn.

It then has sections lettered A, B, C, … (see the contents overleaf). In most cases a section consists of development material, worked examples and an exercise.

The **development material** interweaves explanation with questions that involve the student in making sense of ideas and techniques. Development questions are labelled according to their section letter (A1, A2, …, B1, B2, …) and answers to them are provided.

D Some development questions are particularly suitable for discussion – either by the whole class or by smaller groups – because they have the potential to bring out a key issue or clarify a technique. Such **discussion questions** are marked with a bar, as here.

K **Key points** established in the development material are marked with a bar as here, so the student may readily refer to them during later work or revision. Each chapter's key points are also gathered together in a panel after the last lettered section.

The **worked examples** have been chosen to clarify ideas and techniques, and as models for students to follow in setting out their own work. Guidance for the student is in italic.

The **exercise** at the end of each lettered section is designed to consolidate the skills and understanding acquired earlier in the section. Unlike those in the development material, questions in the exercise are denoted by a number only.

Starred questions are more demanding.

After the lettered sections and the key points panel there may be a set of **mixed questions**, combining ideas from several sections in the chapter; these may also involve topics from earlier chapters.

Every chapter ends with a selection of **questions for self-assessment** ('Test yourself').

Included in the mixed questions and 'Test yourself' are **past AQA exam questions**, to give the student an idea of the style and standard that may be expected, and to build confidence. Occasionally, exam questions are included in the exercises in the lettered sections.

Contents

1 Review: collecting and processing data 6

A Experiment or survey 6

B Sampling methods 7
random, systematic, stratified and quota sampling; questionnaire design

C Recording and presenting data 10
stem-and-leaf diagram, grouped frequency table, histogram, proportional pie chart

D Averages 15
mode, median, cumulative frequency (graph and linear interpolation), mean from frequency table (ungrouped and grouped)

E Percentiles 19
interquartile range, box-and-whisker diagram

F Secondary data 22

Mixed questions 23

2 Variance and standard deviation 24

A Measures of spread 24
variance, standard deviation

B Σ notation 26
for variance and standard deviation

C Calculating the standard deviation 27
using a calculator

D Scaling 29

E Working with frequency distributions 31
mean and standard deviation from grouped data

F Choosing measures 33
appropriateness of mode, median, mean, range, interquartile range, standard deviation, variance

3 Probability 38

A Outcomes and events 38
set notation, Venn diagram, probability of complement, addition law, mutually exclusive events

B Conditional probability 42

C Independent events 44
relation to conditional probability, multiplication law

D Tree diagrams 46
conditional probability 'in reverse'

Mixed questions 50

4 Discrete random variables 52

A Probability distributions 52

B Mean, variance and standard deviation 55

5 Binomial distribution 58

A Pascal's triangle 58
probabilities for binomial distribution with $p = \frac{1}{2}$, combinations, $\binom{n}{r}$ notation

B Unequal probabilities 62

C Using the binomial distribution 63
conditions for use, calculations using formula

D Using tables of the binomial distribution 66

E Mean, variance, standard deviation 68

Mixed questions 70

6 Normal distribution 73

  A Proportions 73
    between a given number of standard deviations
    above or below the mean, shape, symmetry

  B The normal probability distribution 77
    continuous random variable, area for
    probability, standard normal distribution, use of
    table

  C Solving problems 80
    transformation to standard normal variable

  D Further problems 83
    percentage points table

  E Other continuous distributions 86

  Mixed questions 87

7 Estimation 90

  A The sampling distribution of the mean 90
    sample statistic as estimator of a population
    parameter, unbiased estimator of population
    mean

  B Reliability of estimates 93
    standard error of the sample mean

  C Further problems 95
    sampling distribution as a normal distribution

  D The central limit theorem 98
    estimating with non-normal populations

  E Estimating the variance 101
    unbiased estimator

  F Using estimated variances 104

  Mixed questions 107

8 Confidence intervals 110

  A Estimating with confidence 110
    point estimate, standard error of the estimator

  B Confidence intervals 112
    for population with normal distribution

  C Other population distributions 117
    use of the central limit theorem

  D Using an estimated variance 119

  Mixed questions 122

9 Linear regression 124

  A The least squares regression line 124

  B Explanatory variables 128
    identifying response and explanatory
    variable, interpretation of intercept and
    gradient of regression line

  C Scaling 130

  D Residuals 131
    identification of outliers, check of
    plausibility of model

  Mixed questions 133

10 Correlation 136

  A Measuring correlation 136
    positive and negative correlation, covariance,
    product moment correlation coefficient

  B Scaling 142

  C Interpreting correlation 142
    spurious correlation, effect of outliers, non-
    linear relationships

Excel functions 147

Tables 148

  Cumulative binomial distribution function 148
  Normal distribution function 154
  Percentage points of the normal distribution 155

Answers 156

Index 186

1 Review: collecting and processing data

This is not a chapter to be worked through in the usual way. Instead, the six sections review – and provide practice in – basic statistics techniques. Use them as necessary in preparation for coursework or work in this book.

The topics covered are:

• collecting data for an experiment or survey
• recording data using a stem-and-leaf diagram or frequency table
• finding quartiles and other percentiles
• drawing a box-and-whisker diagram and histogram
• calculating different averages for a set of data
• interpreting secondary data

A Experiment or survey

Data is usually collected in response to a particular problem that needs to be investigated or to a hypothesis that needs to be tested. Examples are:

Do the levels of pollution in a reservoir comply with EU standards?

More students go to university in Scotland than in England and Wales.

Toads have larger blood corpuscles than frogs.

Which age group(s) of people are more likely to make use of the internet?

After data has been collected it can be processed and analysed. This analysis can then be used to make judgements, decisions or inferences. An **inference** is a generalised statement based on some results, for example, 'Our survey suggests that people under the age of 16 are more likely to use the internet than other age groups'.

This process often throws up new questions or may suggest an inference that needs to be tested further before we are confident about it.

Statistics is about techniques that can be used to process and analyse data and ways in which sensible inferences can be made from the analysis.

There are two ways in which data may be collected in response to a problem – by **survey** or by **experiment**. In any given situation many factors may affect the results being collected. In a survey a researcher will record factors such as the age of a person or their social status, and these can be taken into account when analysing the results. In an experiment the factors will be carefully controlled so that the factor of interest can be measured without other factors affecting the result. For example, an experiment to find out whether a new type of petrol improves car performance would need to involve a range of vehicles and testing would have to be carried out under identical conditions for all vehicles to ensure that any differences were entirely due to the new fuel.

Whether an experiment or survey is undertaken, it is important to be aware of all the factors which might affect the results. It is important that all the data is collected under the same conditions with some factors eliminated.

Exercise A (answers p 156)

1 A local newspaper wants to carry out a survey on how often people who live in a particular town go out for a meal.
What factors might affect the answers that individuals give?

2 A biology class proposes to investigate the effect of water temperature on the growth rate of tadpoles. They have 150 tadpoles and some jars with thermostats that control the temperature of the water. They decide to compare the growth rates at 10 °C, 15 °C and 20 °C.

(a) What other factors might affect the growth of the tadpoles?

(b) How can the experiment be set up to measure the effect of water temperature alone on the growth of the tadpoles?

3 Suppose you are to investigate whether the weight of a new-born baby is likely to be affected if the mother smokes during pregnancy.
Discuss the advantages and disadvantages of these methods of collecting data.

(a) Collecting appropriate data from a survey

(b) Setting up an experiment

B Sampling methods

In surveys and experiments it is very unlikely that there will be enough resources to use every member of the **population** under investigation. For this reason a **sample** of the total population is used. In choosing a sample it is important to ensure that it is **representative** of the whole population. If this is not the case it will be impossible to apply the results from the sample to the whole population.

There are three basic techniques for obtaining a sample from a population.

- **Random sampling** A sample is selected using an unbiased random method where every individual has an equal chance of being chosen. The most efficient, and unbiased, way of selecting a random sample is where you assign a number to each individual and random numbers are then used to select the sample. Random numbers are usually generated by one of these methods:

  (a) **A random number table** This consists of random digits grouped in convenient sets. To select a random number, for example in the range 1 to 250, three consecutive digits from a randomly chosen starting place are taken. If the resulting number is greater than 250 it is discarded, otherwise the individual with that number is selected. Consecutive triples of digits are chosen until the sample is the required size.

39548	45264	351
56298	27629	278
450 12	0 970 6	36
70164	2096 2 6	
40921	38786	

  →120

(b) **A calculator** Calculators usually give a random number in the range 0.000 to 0.999. You can treat the digits after the decimal point like random digits grouped in threes in a random number table.

(c) **A spreadsheet** Spreadsheets have a simple function which will generate a set of random numbers of the required size in a given range. These can be formatted to a given number of decimal places.

In random sampling the same individual may be selected more than once, but provided the population is fairly large this can be ignored and a new individual selected. The main disadvantage of random methods is that the sample obtained may over-represent certain categories of individuals.

- **Systematic sampling** A sample is taken by choosing individuals at regular intervals. Taking every tenth person on an electoral register, on which everyone appears, is an effective method of selecting a sample. However, stopping every tenth person in the street will not give a representative sample of the whole population if a cross-section of the population is not in the street that day.

- **Stratified sampling** The population is divided into categories such as age, social class and gender. The sample is then chosen so that the sample contains the same proportion of each category as does the whole population. Within the category the sample can be chosen by either a random or a systematic method. Stratified sampling is normally used by opinion poll researchers as it is much more likely to give a representative sample. Frequently a **quota sampling** method is used where researchers collect individuals of a given category as they encounter them until they have obtained the appropriate number of results for each category. Sometimes researchers will sample more from a particular category if they know that there is more variation in this category. For example, in a survey of working hours of British workers, there is likely to be a lot more variation among self-employed people than those who are employed. The researcher might therefore take a larger sample of this group and then adjust the results to reflect the actual proportions in the population.

Collecting data

Another important decision in designing a survey is how the data will be collected. In an ideal situation the research team will collect the data directly from the individuals in the sample but this may not be practicable in all situations.

If the collection method requires some effort to be made by people, for example filling in a questionnaire and posting it, a very small response is likely. In such cases only people who have strong views are likely to reply and this leads to **non-response bias**.

With any experiment or survey, it is always best to carry out a **pilot study** so that any possible problems such as bias or non-response can be resolved before the full-scale project is undertaken.

Questionnaires are often used when collecting data from people. They can be filled in by the participants or completed by a trained interviewer either face-to-face or over the telephone. The design of any such questionnaire is very important as the quality of replies and the number who respond may be affected. The following are some guidelines about the design of questionnaires.

- Explain why you are carrying out the survey.
- Do not ask for names and other personal details and assure people that the answers are confidential.
- Keep the questionnaire as short as possible and avoid unnecessary or repetitive questions.
- Do not ask sensitive questions or questions that could cause embarrassment.
- Use **closed response** questions where possible. These could involve ticking one of a range of boxes, saying whether you agree or not on a scale of 1 to 5 or just simple 'Yes' or 'No' answers. Limiting the number of answers will also make analysing the data easier but there should always be a sensible range of options and a 'Don't know' or 'Other' option.
- Do not ask for detailed information that is difficult for people to remember. Questions such as 'How many CDs did you buy last year?' may be hard to answer, even with a closed set of responses.
- Don't ask biased or leading questions such as 'Wouldn't you agree that educational standards are declining rapidly?'

Before designing a questionnaire it is important to consider what you intend to do with the data once it is collected. Questionnaires are more useful for collecting **qualitative** or **categorical** data, that is non-numerical data. This limits the type of analysis that can be carried out.

Exercise B (answers p 156)

1 A town planning department wishes to use a survey to discover what facilities may be required in a sports centre they intend to build. The following suggestions are made as to how to collect the data. What difficulties might arise with each of these methods?

(a) Place an advert in the local newspaper and ask local residents to write a letter to the council saying what they think should be included.

(b) Put boxes of questionnaires in the entrance to various local public facilities such as the library and council offices. Have another box for people to place their completed questionnaires. Leave the boxes for two weeks and collect the completed questionnaires.

(c) Ask council officers to conduct a street survey on a Saturday morning in the centre of the town with a list of questions given to each officer.

(d) Phone randomly chosen local residents on weekday evenings and ask them a series of questions.

C Recording and presenting data

Numerical data is of two types, **discrete** and **continuous**. In discrete data the possible values are separated by gaps, for example 0, 1, 2, 3, … or shoe sizes 5, $5\frac{1}{2}$, 6, $6\frac{1}{2}$, … Continuous data comes from measurement; for example, the winning time in a race could be 12.346 57… seconds, although in practice measurements can only be made to a certain degree of accuracy, so data that in theory is continuous may be recorded as discrete.

The speeds of two types of bullet were measured to the nearest $m\,s^{-1}$ in an experiment as follows.

Speed of type A ($m\,s^{-1}$)

480	493	475	471	482	487	464	516	497	485
481	471	475	498	478	487	491	489	481	493

Speed of type B ($m\,s^{-1}$)

478	463	512	503	508	497	495	482	482	474
489	490	495	503	510	501	498	470	481	486

It is difficult to compare the speeds of the types of bullets from these lists.

A simple method of organising data is to use a **stem-and-leaf diagram**. This can be drawn for a single set of data or, as in this case, back-to-back. The data above would be recorded like this.

```
          Type A           Type B
                   4 | 46 | 3
           8 5 5 1 1 | 47 | 0 4 8
       9 7 7 5 2 1 1 0 | 48 | 1 2 2 6 9
           8 7 3 3 1 | 49 | 0 5 5 7 8
                     | 50 | 1 3 3 8
                   6 | 51 | 0 2
```

Key

8	47		means 478 m s⁻¹
	49	5	means 495 m s⁻¹

Key:
$8\,|\,47\,|$ means 478 $m\,s^{-1}$
$|\,49\,|\,5$ means 495 $m\,s^{-1}$

The stem-and-leaf diagram shows that type B bullets are generally faster.

Usually when compiling a stem-and-leaf diagram it is first necessary to make a rough copy, writing the leaf values in the order they are met. Then in the final diagram they are written in order of size.

The advantage of a stem-and-leaf diagram is that no actual values are lost and since the data is written in rank order finding measures such as the median is easy. When data is wide ranging, however, stem-and-leaf diagrams are less helpful.

Another way of simplifying the data when a record of each individual item is not needed is to use a **grouped frequency table**.

There are various ways of describing the groups or **intervals**, but whatever method is used it must be clear into which interval each value has been placed. Possible intervals for the data above are 460–469, 470–479, 480–489 and so on.

This method of description is usually employed for discrete (whole-number) data as it is clear what values are contained in each group.

For continuous data use $460 \le x < 470$, $470 \le x < 480$, $480 \le x < 490$, and so on. For example, the group $460 \le x < 470$ contains values from 460 up to but not including 470.

If the first method is used for the bullet data then remember that the interval 460–469 contains values from 459.5 to 469.5, since the values have been rounded to the nearest whole number.

The number of groups to use partly depends on how big the data set is. Having too few groups will result in too much information being lost. Having too many will mean that the overall shape of the distribution will be lost.

Speed (m s⁻¹)	Frequency
460–469	1
470–479	5
480–489	8
490–499	5
500–509	0
510–519	1
Total	20

Using the first way of describing the intervals gives this frequency table for the speeds of bullets of type A.

Histograms

Bar charts of various types are a useful and common way of presenting data. However, care must be taken when the chart is drawn from a grouped frequency table.

Consider the following table and chart for the lengths of leaves on a bush.

Length (mm)	Frequency
$0 \leq x < 20$	5
$20 \leq x < 25$	5
$25 \leq x < 30$	8
$30 \leq x < 35$	2
Total	20

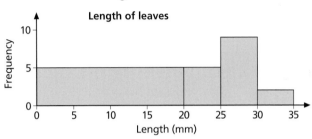

When there are uneven group sizes in a grouped frequency table, as here, a bar chart can be misleading, as it is the area of a block which is seen as the relative size of the group. It looks as though there as many leaves with lengths in the interval 0 to 5 cm as there are in the interval 20 to 25 cm. To make allowance for the different sizes of groups the **frequency density** is used instead.

For each group,   frequency density $= \dfrac{\text{frequency}}{\text{width of interval}}$

This table gives the frequency densities for the leaves.

Length (mm)	Interval width	Frequency	Frequency density
$0 \leq x < 20$	20	5	5 ÷ 20 = 0.25
$20 \leq x < 25$	5	5	5 ÷ 5 = 1
$25 \leq x < 30$	5	8	8 ÷ 5 = 1.6
$30 \leq x < 35$	5	2	2 ÷ 5 = 0.4

A bar chart can then be drawn using the frequency densities. This is called a **histogram**.

In a histogram, area represents frequency. To find the actual frequency for a particular group, you need to multiply the interval width by the frequency density for that group.

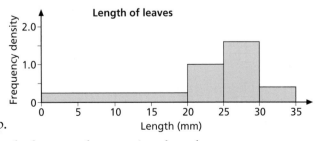

Since the intervals were written as inequalities the bars are drawn using the values 20, 25, … If the groups had been described as, say, 0–19, 20–25 …, the bars would, strictly, have to be drawn from 0 to 19.5, 19.5 to 24.5, … In reality it is often difficult to work to this degree of accuracy so the values 0, 20, 25, … may be used.

Proportional pie charts

Pie charts are useful for displaying data where there is a small number of categories, usually qualitative, and it is necessary to compare the proportions in the categories.

The colours of the 50 cars in the staff car park of a sixth-form college were recorded as follows.

Colour	Red	Black	Silver	White	Blue	Other
Frequency	6	11	8	15	6	4

The angles needed for this pie chart can be found by dividing 360° in these proportions.

Colour	Proportion	Angle
Red	$\frac{6}{50}$ = 12%	$0.12 \times 360 = 43.2°$
Black	$\frac{11}{50}$ = 22%	$0.22 \times 360 = 79.2°$
Silver	$\frac{8}{50}$ = 16%	$0.16 \times 360 = 57.6°$
White	$\frac{15}{50}$ = 30%	$0.30 \times 360 = 108°$
Blue	$\frac{6}{50}$ = 12%	$0.12 \times 360 = 43.2°$
Other	$\frac{4}{50}$ = 8%	$0.08 \times 360 = 28.8°$
Total		360°

This is the pie chart drawn with a radius of 3 cm.

Staff cars

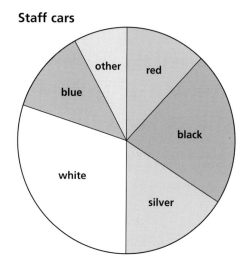

In the same survey, the 120 cars in the student car park were also surveyed and the colours noted.

Colour	Red	Black	Silver	White	Blue	Other
Frequency	35	4	24	20	28	9

Since there are more cars in this group, the size of the pie chart for students' cars can be scaled accordingly. As with histograms, it is the **areas** of the pie charts that should be proportional.

If there are k times as many people in a second group as in a first, then the area of the second circle would need to be k times the first. The radius of the first circle would need to be multiplied by $\sqrt{k}$ to give the radius of the second circle, as shown here.

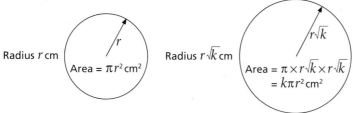

In the case of the cars data, the area of the pie chart for the student cars needs to be $\frac{120}{50} = 2.4$ times larger, so the radius needs to be increased by a factor of $\sqrt{2.4}$.

So if the radius for staff cars is 3 cm, the radius for student cars is $\sqrt{2.4} \times 3 = 4.65$ cm.

Student cars

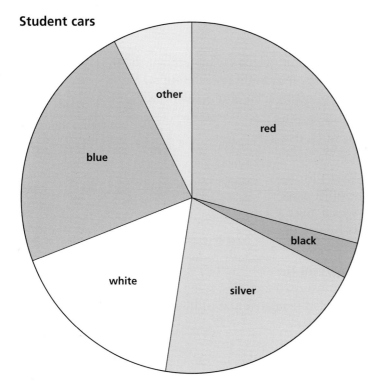

Exercise C (answers p 156)

1 The following data consists of the marks of two classes taking the same test.

Class 1 80 62 53 76 76 31 59 78 84 66 71 50 79
         69 87 64 56 65 58 78 75 60 51

Class 2 71 68 56 79 73 51 48 83 64 58 75 45 91
         80 59 34 55 73 81 62 64 69

(a) Use a back-to-back stem-and-leaf diagram to display these marks.

(b) Compare the examination marks of these two classes.

2 This histogram shows the total rainfall (in millimetres) in June for some weather stations in England.

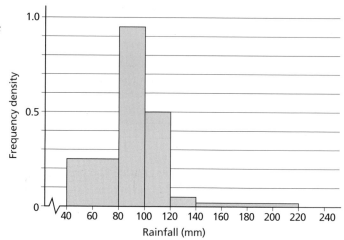

Find the actual number of weather stations recording rainfalls in these intervals.

(a) 100–120 mm

(b) 40–80 mm (frequency density = 0.25)

3 A fitness club surveys its members about which facility each of them uses most. They divide the membership into three age groups, 18–25, 26–59, 60 and over. The following table shows their results.

(a) Draw a pie chart for the 18–25 group showing the most used facilities, using a radius of 5 cm.

(b) Draw a proportional pie chart for the 26–59 group showing the most used facilities, using a radius which gives a chart that reflects the relative size of this group.

(c) Draw a proportional pie chart for the over 60 group showing the most used facilities, using a radius which gives a chart that reflects the relative size of this group.

Facility	Frequency		
	18–25	26–59	over 60
Fitness suite	12	54	4
Weights room	21	18	0
Swimming pool	8	25	21
Sauna/steam room	1	5	4
Squash court	3	18	1
Total members	45	120	30

D Averages

Sometimes it is important to represent a large data set by a few numbers that give a summary of the original set. It is useful to have a single number as the 'average' of the data. You should already be familiar with the mean, the median and the mode.

The **mode** is the value with the highest frequency and is easily identified from a frequency table. In some cases the mode is not typical of the data so it is not useful to give it. In the case of grouped data the **modal group** is the group with the highest frequency. However, which group it is will depend on how the data is grouped.

The **median** is the middle value when the data is ranked in order of size. If there is no middle value (which will happen when the number of values is even) the median is taken to be halfway between the two middle values. Since stem-and-leaf diagrams put the data into rank order they are a useful device for finding the median.

Example

These are the times, in seconds, taken by a group of students to complete a simple puzzle.

   21 34 25 18 37 27 23 35 41 29 36 47 34 25 24 52 27 19

Find the median time taken to complete the puzzle.

Solution

Put the data into a stem-and-leaf diagram.
Include a running total of the frequency.

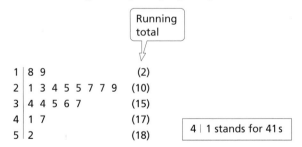

Since there were 18 students in the group, when the data are ranked the median is the average of the 9th and 10th values.

The median is therefore halfway between 27 and 29, that is 28 seconds.

Cumulative frequency

When data is recorded in a grouped frequency table, the median can be found using cumulative frequencies. The cumulative frequency is the total frequency up to a particular value.

In an experiment, 339 sunflower plants were measured six weeks after planting. The results were recorded in a frequency table, from which a cumulative frequency table can be drawn up.

Height (cm)	Frequency
3–6	10
7–10	21
11–14	114
15–18	105
19–22	54
23–26	35

Height (cm)	Cumulative frequency
up to 6	10
up to 10	10 + 21 = 31
up to 14	31 + 114 = 145
up to 18	145 + 105 = 250
up to 22	250 + 54 = 304
up to 26	304 + 35 = 339

From the cumulative frequency table there are two possible methods of finding the median.

- **Using a cumulative frequency graph** Each cumulative frequency is plotted against the maximum value of the interval. The median can then be read from the graph.

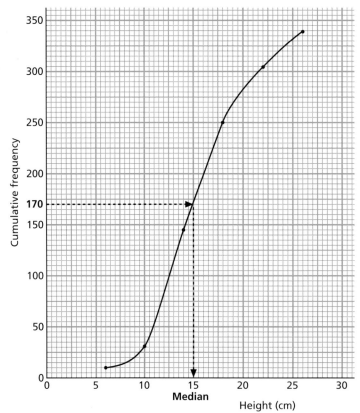

(Strictly, the maximum values of the intervals are 6.5, 10.5, … because the measurements have been rounded. But 6, 10, … have been used here and are sufficiently accurate for an approximate technique.)

- **Using linear interpolation**

  The shape of the cumulative frequency graph between the known points is not known for certain. If it is assumed to be a straight line between each pair of points, then the median can be estimated directly from the cumulative frequency table, without drawing the graph.

  The method is called **linear interpolation** and can be used in other circumstances to estimate a value between two known values.

  For the sunflower data:

  The median is the 170th value, which is between the points (14, 145) and (18, 250).

  In fact it is $\dfrac{170 - 145}{250 - 145}$ of the distance between 145 and 250,

  which is $\dfrac{25}{105}$ or $\dfrac{5}{21}$ of the distance between 145 and 250.

  Using similar triangles the median is $14 + \dfrac{5}{21} \times 4$

  $$= 14.95 \, \text{cm}$$

  Since it is only an assumption that the points are connected by a straight line, this is still an approximation.

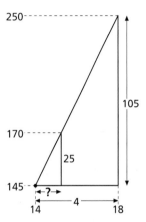

The mean

The **mean** is the most commonly used of the measures of average. Sigma notation is useful for describing it (and other statistical calculations).

If a data set of size n has values $x_1, x_2, x_3, x_4, \ldots, x_n$, then the mean can be calculated by

$$\text{Mean} = \frac{\sum x_i}{n} \qquad (\sum \text{ means 'add together'.})$$

The mean of a set of data values is given the symbol $\bar{x}$.

Calculators usually have a statistical mode where the values of $\sum x_i$, n and $\bar{x}$ are given when a set of data is entered.

When discrete data is presented in a frequency table, the mean can be calculated directly from the frequency table by multiplying each value x_i by its frequency f_i, summing to get $\sum x_i f_i$, and dividing the result by n.

This table shows the number of cabbage white caterpillars found on 50 cabbage leaves.

Number on leaf (x_i)	Frequency (f_i)
0	8
1	11
2	16
3	9
4	5
5	0
6	1

$$\text{Mean} = \frac{\sum x_i f_i}{n}$$

$$= [(0 \times 8) + (1 \times 11) + (2 \times 16) + (3 \times 9) +$$
$$(4 \times 5) + (5 \times 0) + (6 \times 1)] \div 50$$

$$= 96 \div 50 = 1.92$$

When data is grouped in a frequency table, the mean can be found approximately by multiplying the mid-points of the intervals by the frequencies.

This is the sunflower heights data from earlier in this section.
The mid-points are found from half the sum of the two end-points of the interval*, $(3 + 6) \div 2 = 4.5$ and so on.

Height (cm)	Mid-interval (x_i)	Frequency (f_i)	$x_i f_i$
3–6	4.5	10	45
7–10	8.5	21	178.5
11–14	12.5	114	1425
15–18	16.5	105	1732.5
19–22	20.5	54	1107
23–26	24.5	35	857.5
	Total	339	5345.5

Estimate of mean $= \dfrac{5345.5}{339} = 15.8\,\text{cm}$

Exercise D (answers p 157)

1 In an aptitude test, 20 people were asked to do a jigsaw puzzle.
The times taken, in seconds, by 19 of them were recorded as follows.

   46 13 53 78 49 51 52 104 58 63 34 43 52 72 40 75 45 48 75

(a) Find the mean and median for this data.
Which value do you think is more representative of the data?

(b) The twentieth person gave up after 148 seconds.
What would the mean and median change to if this result was included?

2 At a supermarket the time was measured from when each customer arrived at a checkout until they had finished being served.
The results are recorded in this table.

(a) Find the cumulative frequencies and use interpolation to find the median time at the checkout.

(b) Calculate an approximation for the mean using 11 as the mid-interval value for the last group.

(c) Because of a fault in the cash register, a customer in the survey recorded as being at the checkout for 7 minutes was in fact there for 25 minutes.
How does this affect the answers to (a) and (b)?

Time (t min)	Frequency
$0 \le t < 2$	8
$2 \le t < 4$	14
$4 \le t < 6$	23
$6 \le t < 8$	35
$8 \le t < 10$	20
$t \ge 10$	4

---

* In some cases, such as ages, this rule does not apply. An interval of 30–39 years would include ages from 30 to just under 40, so the mid-interval value would be 35.

E Percentiles

The 60th **percentile** of a set of data is the value which has 60% of the population below it. Percentiles can be read from a cumulative frequency graph or found by linear interpolation.

This cumulative frequency graph shows the heights of a group of 140 girls.

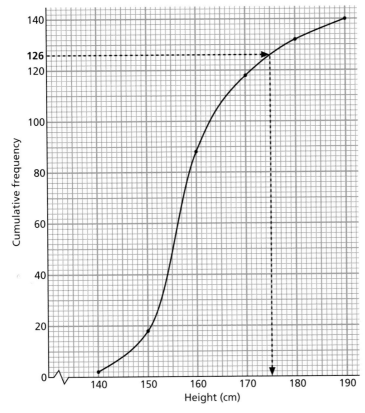

The 90th percentile is the height of the 126th (90% of 140) person in rank order. From the graph this can be seen to be a height of 175 cm.

This tells us that approximately 90% of the girls were shorter than 175 cm and consequently only 10% were taller than 175 cm. This could be a useful fact in clothing or building design.

Two percentiles that are particularly useful are the 25% percentile (the **lower quartile, LQ**) and the 75% percentile (the **upper quartile, UQ**). The difference between these is called the **interquartile range (IQR)**. The interquartile range is the range within which the middle 50% of a set of data lies. It is a useful measure of how spread out a set of data is as it is not affected by a few extreme values.

In the above example the lower quartile is given by the 35th value which, from the graph, is about 153 cm.
The upper quartile is given by the 105th value which, from the graph, is about 164 cm.

The interquartile range is $164 - 153 = 11$ cm.

This is the data for the speed of bullets met in section C. Since there are 20 results, the median is the average of the 10th and 11th results, that is 492.5.

Type B bullet speeds

46 3	(1)	
47 0 4 8	(4)	
48 1 2 2 6 9	(9)	
49 0 5 5 7 8	(14)	
50 1 3 3 8	(18)	
51 0 2	(20)	46	3 represents 463 m s^{-1}

A **box plot** or **box-and-whisker diagram** is a pictorial representation of data using the median, the quartiles and the maximum and minimum values. This box plot shows the reaction times (in hundredths of a second) of a group of people.

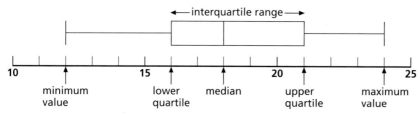

A set of data with a symmetrical distribution has a symmetrical box plot.

In the next example, 25% of the data is in the shaded part. We say the data is positively skewed.

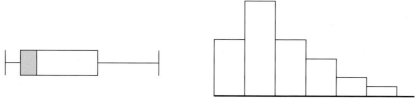

Box plots can be drawn against a horizontal or a vertical scale. They are particularly useful for displaying more than one set of data for comparison.

This diagram shows the reaction times for a group of adult males and females.

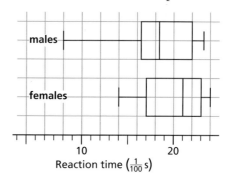

Various pieces of information can be gained from the diagram, for example:

• Males had a shorter median reaction time (0.185 s as opposed to 0.21 s).

• Females had a slightly wider interquartile range so their reaction times are more varied.

- Both distributions are asymmetrical.
- The male distribution is skewed with a long tail towards the shorter reaction times. 25% of males had a reaction time shorter than 0.165 s.

Exercise E (answers p 157)

1 This table shows the lengths of stay in a hospital after a heart attack for 149 males and 48 females.

Length of stay (days)	Number of males	Number of females
0–5	40	16
6–10	58	16
11–15	39	7
16–20	6	3
21–25	4	3
25–30	2	3

(a) Find the cumulative frequencies for the length of stay for the males and use this to draw a cumulative frequency graph.

(b) Use your graph to find for the males

  (i) the median length of stay   (ii) the interquartile range

  (iii) the length of stay beyond which only 20% of them stay at the hospital

(c) Use linear interpolation to find the median and interquartile range of the length of stay of the females.

(d) Compare the length of stay in the hospital for males and females after a heart attack.

2 These box plots show the distributions of students' marks in three tests A, B, C.

(a) In which test are the marks highest, on average?

(b) In which test are the marks most spread out, on the whole?

(c) Which test has the highest proportion of candidates getting between 30 and 45 marks?

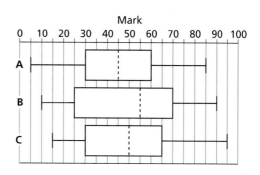

F Secondary data

The term 'raw data' is used for the actual data collected in a survey or experiment. If you have collected this data yourself then it is **primary data**. **Secondary data** is raw or summarised data that has been collected by somebody else. Secondary data can be found from various sources and is increasingly available on the internet. It may be possible to carry out a statistical investigation wholly or partly using secondary data.

If you want to make use of secondary data in your own investigation, you need to know how the data was collected. The source of the data should also be acknowledged.

Exercise F (answers p 157)

The following data is from the Office for National Statistics (ONS) website.

Offenders found guilty of, or cautioned for, indictable offences: by sex, type of offence and age, 2002

England and Wales	Rates per 10 000 population				
	10–15	16–24	25–34	35+	Total
Males					**(thousands)**
Theft and handling stolen goods	86	183	104	17	131.5
Drug offences	18	159	62	9	84.1
Violence against the person	31	77	32	9	51.8
Burglary	29	49	21	2	30.4
Criminal damage	13	18	7	2	12.5
Robbery	6	14	4	0	7.2
Sexual offences	3	4	3	2	5.0
Other indictable offences	11	102	59	12	69.0
All indictable offences	196	606	292	53	391.5
Females					
Theft and handling stolen goods	51	67	32	6	50.1
Drug offences	2	15	9	1	9.8
Violence against the person	11	12	5	1	9.5
Burglary	3	3	1	0	2.1
Criminal damage	2	2	1	0	1.6
Robbery	1	1	0	0	0.9
Sexual offences	0	0	0	0	0.1
Other indictable offences	3	20	13	2	14.4
All indictable offences	74	119	61	12	88.6

Source: National Statistics website: www.statistics.gov.uk

1 Why are 'Rates per 10 000 population' used in this table rather than actual frequencies?

2 How do you think this data was collected?
Is the source likely to be reliable?

3 Draw a composite bar chart of the male rates for each type of crime using separate bars for each age group.

4 (a) Draw a pie chart showing the type of crimes for the males, based on the total offences. Use a radius of 5 cm.

(b) Draw a pie chart for the type of crimes committed by females, based on the total offences. Use a radius such that the area of the pie chart reflects the different total number of offences committed by females.

Mixed questions (answers p 158)

The ages of people going to see two films at a cinema one evening were recorded as:

Smash and Grab

Age	Frequency
0–15	28
16–24	47
25–39	32
40–59	15
60+	1

Celtic Dream

Age	Frequency
0–15	29
16–24	45
25–39	52
40–59	37
60+	24

Note that the age group 0–15 extends to the day before someone's 16th birthday.

Use an upper limit of 80 for the last group when answering the following questions.

1 Draw a histogram for each of the films.

2 Draw a pie chart for each of the films using a radius of 4 cm for *Smash and Grab*. Use a radius for *Celtic Dream* which reflects the different total number of people who watched this film.

3 Calculate the median age and the interquartile range for each of the films.

4 The oldest person to watch *Smash and Grab* was 62 and the youngest 12.
The oldest person to watch *Celtic Dream* was 85 and the youngest 6.
Use this information and your answer to question 3 to draw box and whisker diagrams for the two films using the same scale.

5 Calculate an estimate for the mean age of people going to see each of the films.

6 Compare the distribution of ages going to see each of these films.
Which of the diagrams you drew in questions 1, 2 and 4 is most useful in answering this question?

2 Variance and standard deviation

In this chapter you will learn
- how to find the variance and standard deviation of a set of data
- how variance and standard deviation are affected by linear scaling
- how to choose appropriate measures of average and spread

A Measures of spread (answers p 159)

The mean and median are both used to give a central or 'typical' value for a
set of data. However, on their own they give an incomplete picture of the data.
For example, the two sets of data shown in these two frequency diagrams
have the same mean but are otherwise very different.

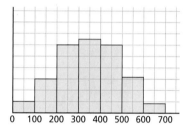 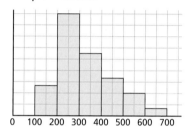

One way of getting a better picture of the distribution of the data is to calculate
a measure of spread. One such measure is the interquartile range (IQR), which
tells us the range of the 'middle half' of the data.

The median and quartiles can be shown in a
box-and-whisker diagram.

The interquartile range is dependent on only
some of the data. The original data values could
be changed in a number of ways without affecting
the median and IQR. We need an alternative
measure of spread that uses all the data if we
want something more sensitive.

Heights of a group of people

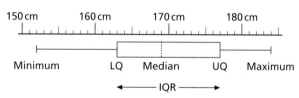

Some students compared the lengths of laurel leaves on a hedge bordering their
school to see if there was a difference between those inside and those outside the school.
They took some leaves from the hedge inside the school and some from the outside.
These are the lengths of their leaves, measured in centimetres.

Outside	7.9	6.1	7.2	6.0	7.8	7.5	6.3	8.1	7.3	7.4	6.5
Inside	8.5	6.4	7.3	5.7	7.1	6.6	7.4				

This is a dot plot of these results.

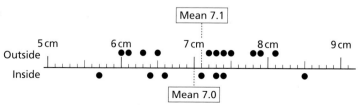

A1 From the dot plot, which leaves appear to have a wider spread, those inside the school or those outside?

Instead of using the interquartile range we can consider the **deviation** of each length from the mean of its group.

For the outside leaves, the deviation of the smallest leaf from the mean is $6.0 - 7.1 = -1.1\,\text{cm}$.
Notice that this deviation is negative because the length is less than the mean.

A2 Find the deviation from the mean of each of the other outside leaves.
Suppose it is suggested that the sum of all the deviations could be used as a measure of the spread of the outside leaves.
What is wrong with this suggestion?

A3 Find the sum of the deviations from their mean of the lengths for the inside leaves. Does the same thing happen? Can you explain why?

There are two possible ways of using the deviations to measure spread.

• Ignore the sign of the deviations and then add.

• Square the deviations (to get all positive values) and then add.

The first of these is more difficult to handle mathematically, so the second is generally used.

The deviations of the outside leaves are $0.8, -1.0, 0.1$, and so on.
Squaring them gives $0.64, 1, 0.01$, and so on.

A4 Calculate the sum of the squared deviations for each group of leaves.
Is this a useful measure of spread to compare the two sets of data?

To allow for the fact that the two groups have different numbers of items, the sum of the squared differences is divided by the number of items.
This measure is called the **variance**.

A5 Calculate the variance of each group of leaf lengths.
Which group does the variance suggest has the greater spread?

Because the deviations were squared, the units of the variance are cm^2.
It would be more useful to have a measure of spread in the same units as the data.
By taking the square root of the variance we arrive at a measure called the **standard deviation**.

A6 Calculate the standard deviation of each group of leaf lengths.

Example 1

Calculate the mean and standard deviation of the ages of seven children at a holiday playgroup. These ages are 1, 2, 2, 3, 5, 6 and 9 years.

Solution

The mean is $(1 + 2 + 2 + 3 + 5 + 6 + 9) \div 7 = 4$ years

The sum of the squared deviations of the ages from the mean is
$(1 - 4)^2 + (2 - 4)^2 + (2 - 4)^2 + (3 - 4)^2 + (5 - 4)^2 + (6 - 4)^2 + (9 - 4)^2 = 48$

Variance $= \frac{48}{7} = 6.86$ Standard deviation $= \sqrt{6.86} = 2.62$ years (to 2 d.p.)

Exercise A (answers p 159)

1 The numbers of eggs laid by some hens each day in a 10-day period were

    4 3 0 1 6 1 3 3 2 4

Find the mean and standard deviation of the number of eggs laid.

2 Find the mean and standard deviation of these temperatures, in °C, measured at two-hourly intervals starting at midnight.

    7.2 5.3 4.8 5.8 8.4 12.5 15.6 17.5 16.0 10.4 8.1 6.9

3 A group of young rats was split into two groups and each group was given a different diet. This table shows the weight gains, in grams, of the two groups after 8 weeks.

Diet A	24	18	52	41	27	35	24	26	30	25		
Diet B	7	19	68	13	34	64	25	38	29	45	31	14

Find the mean and standard deviation for each group. Comment on the results.

B Σ notation (answer p 160)

The definitions of mean, variance and standard deviation can be expressed using the symbol Σ (sigma), which means 'sum of ...'.

Suppose the data consists of n values: $x_1, x_2, x_3, \ldots, x_n$.

The mean is denoted by $\bar{x}$ ('x bar').

To calculate $\bar{x}$, we add the values and divide by n. This is written $\bar{x} = \dfrac{\Sigma x_i}{n}$.

'Σx_i' means 'the sum of all the values of x'.

The sum of all the squared deviations from the mean is written $\Sigma(x_i - \bar{x})^2$.

K   So the definitions of variance and standard deviation are

$$\text{variance} = \frac{\Sigma(x_i - \bar{x})^2}{n} \qquad \text{standard deviation} = \sqrt{\frac{\Sigma(x_i - \bar{x})^2}{n}}$$

The standard deviation is denoted by s or s_x.

The variance is usually denoted by s^2 or s_x^2.

Calculators and spreadsheets

Scientific calculators nearly always have keys for obtaining the mean and standard deviation. The mean is usually denoted by $\bar{x}$ or occasionally μ.

The standard deviation is sometimes denoted by σ_n. A calculator will probably also have a σ_{n-1} key; this will be dealt with later.

B1 Find out how to obtain the mean and standard deviation of a set of data on your calculator using the examples in exercise A.

A spreadsheet will also find the mean (AVERAGE(range of cells) in Excel) and standard deviation (STDEVP(range of cells) in Excel).

C Calculating the standard deviation

So far you have used this formula for the standard deviation: $\quad s_x = \sqrt{\dfrac{\Sigma(x_i - \bar{x})^2}{n}}$

This is an inefficient method for calculating the standard deviation. The data has to be used first to calculate the mean, then each value has to have the mean subtracted from it. A calculator would need a lot of memory to complete this process unless everything was entered twice.

The difficulty arises in finding $\Sigma(x_i - \bar{x})^2$.

We have to calculate this: Multiplying each term out gives this:

$$(x_1 - \bar{x})^2 \qquad\qquad x_1^2 - 2\bar{x}x_1 + \bar{x}^2$$
$$(x_2 - \bar{x})^2 \qquad\qquad x_2^2 - 2\bar{x}x_2 + \bar{x}^2$$
$$(x_3 - \bar{x})^2 \qquad\qquad x_3^2 - 2\bar{x}x_3 + \bar{x}^2$$

$$\cdot \qquad \cdot \qquad\qquad \cdot \qquad \cdot \qquad \cdot$$

$$\cdot \qquad \cdot \qquad\qquad \cdot \qquad \cdot \qquad \cdot$$

$$\cdot \qquad \cdot \qquad\qquad \cdot \qquad \cdot \qquad \cdot$$

$$(x_n - \bar{x})^2 \qquad\qquad x_n^2 - 2\bar{x}x_n + \bar{x}^2$$

Adding the terms gives $\Sigma(x_i - \bar{x})^2 \qquad \Sigma x_i^2 - 2\bar{x}\Sigma x_i + n\bar{x}^2$

However, since $\bar{x} = \dfrac{\Sigma x_i}{n}$, we can replace Σx_i in the middle term of the second expression by $n\bar{x}$.

This gives $\quad \Sigma x_i^2 - 2\bar{x}n\bar{x} + n\bar{x}^2$
$$= \quad \Sigma x_i^2 - 2n\bar{x}^2 + n\bar{x}^2$$
$$= \quad \Sigma x_i^2 - n\bar{x}^2$$

This gives a more efficient formula for the standard deviation:

$$s_x = \sqrt{\dfrac{\Sigma x_i^2 - n\bar{x}^2}{n}}$$

A slightly simpler form of the formula at the foot of the previous page is

$$s_x = \sqrt{\frac{\sum x_i^2}{n} - \bar{x}^2}$$

This is the form used by a calculator as it requires only three memories to keep running totals of n, $\sum x$ and $\sum x^2$. Calculators usually have keys to display these totals and it is useful to write them down so that you and others can check your results. If data is later changed these totals can be altered without having to re-enter all the data in order to recalculate the mean and standard deviation.

Exercise C (answers p 160)

Where possible, use the statistical functions on your calculator, showing the steps you take.

1 The numbers of peas in 14 pods were as follows.

    2 3 3 4 5 5 5 6 7 8 8 9 9 10

Find the mean and standard deviation of the number of peas in a pod.

2 Fifteen sacks of potatoes were taken from a lorry and weighed to the nearest kilogram:

    49 52 47 53 55 48 50 50 54 52 51 52 49 50 53

Calculate the mean and standard deviation of these masses.

3 Twenty-five students in a class weigh themselves in kilograms and the values are confidentially recorded. The teacher tells them that $\sum m = 1245$ and $\sum m^2 = 62\,820$. Find the mean and standard deviation of the students' masses.

4 The heights (h) of 10 seedlings were measured in centimetres and calculations gave $\sum h = 85.6$ and $\sum h^2 = 742.96$.

(a) Find the mean and standard deviation of the heights of the seedlings.

(b) It was later found that one length of 8.6 cm was entered incorrectly as 6.8 cm. Find the correct mean and standard deviation of the heights.

5 Five people in a lift have a mean mass $\bar{x} = 70$ kg. The standard deviation of their masses is 10 kg.

(a) Find their total mass, $\sum x$, and find $\sum x^2$.

(b) A man weighing 80 kg leaves the lift. Calculate the mean and standard deviation of the masses of those remaining.

6 30 pears in a tray have a mean mass of 105 g and a standard deviation of 6.1 g.

(a) Calculate the total of the squared deviations of the masses from their mean.

(b) Another tray contains 20 pears with mean mass 105 g and standard deviation 8.4 g. Find the total of the squared deviations from the mean for all 50 pears in the two trays, and hence the standard deviation for those pears.

D Scaling (answers p 160)

D1 The dot plot below shows the data set 0 3 3 5 6 7 in black.
This data has a mean of 4 and standard deviation 2.3.
The white dots show the same values with 10 added to each one.

What do you think the mean and standard deviation of the data with
10 added will be? Check your answer with a calculator or spreadsheet.

D2 This dot plot shows the original data doubled.

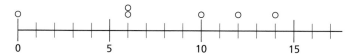

What do you think the mean and standard deviation of this set will be?
Check with a calculator or spreadsheet.

If the data values $x_1, x_2, x_3, x_4, \ldots, x_n$ each have a number b added to them,

$$\text{mean} = \frac{((x_1 + b) + (x_2 + b) + (x_3 + b) + \ldots + (x_n + b))}{n}$$

$$= \frac{\Sigma x_i + nb}{n}$$

$$= \frac{\Sigma x_i}{n} + \frac{nb}{n}$$

$$= \bar{x} + b$$

$$\text{standard deviation} = \sqrt{\frac{\Sigma((x_i + b) - (\bar{x} + b))^2}{n}}$$

$$= \sqrt{\frac{\Sigma(x_i - \bar{x} + b - b)^2}{n}}$$

$$= \sqrt{\frac{\Sigma(x_i - \bar{x})^2}{n}}$$

$$= s_x$$

D3 Prove that when all the numbers in a data set are multiplied by a,
the mean and standard deviation are also multiplied by a.

K In general if a variable x is transformed using a linear transformation $y = ax + b$
where a and b are constants, then

$$\bar{y} = a\bar{x} + b \quad \text{and} \quad s_y = as_x$$

Example 2

A teacher marks a test out of 30. The mean mark is 21.5 and the standard
deviation is 6.4. On the end-of-term report a mark out of 100 must be given,
so the teacher decides to multiply all the marks by 3 and add on 10.
What are the mean and standard deviation of the marks out of 100?

Solution

For the marks out of 30, $\bar{x} = 21.5$ and $s_x = 6.4$

For the marks out of 100, mean $= 3 \times 21.5 + 10 = 74.5$
$$\text{s.d.} = 3 \times 6.4 = 19.2$$

Exercise D (answers p 160)

1 A student measures the resistance of a piece of wire, repeating the experiment
six times to validate her results. Her results are:

   Resistance (ohms) 54.2 53.7 55.0 53.7 54.0 54.6

   (a) Find the mean and standard deviation of the readings.

   (b) She discovers that, to compensate for faulty equipment, each reading
   should be increased by 10%.
   Write down the new mean and standard deviation.

2 A teacher's class has 32 pupils with a mean age of 14.0 years and a standard
deviation of 0.25 years.
Write down the mean and standard deviation of the ages of the same 32 pupils
exactly two years later.

3 The temperature is recorded at twelve London weather stations on a given day.
The mean recorded temperature is 12 °C, with a standard deviation of 0.5 °C.

   The formula for F, the temperature in degrees Fahrenheit, in terms of C,
   the temperature in degrees Celsius, is

   $$F = 1.8C + 32$$

   Write down the mean temperature and the standard deviation in degrees Fahrenheit.

4 The marks in a test have mean 33 and standard deviation 4.2.
They are to be scaled linearly using the formula $y = ax + b$, where x is
a given mark in the test and y is the corresponding scaled mark, so that
the scaled marks have a mean of 50 and a standard deviation of 10.

   (a) Find a and b.

   (b) Peter gets 40 marks in the test. What is his scaled mark?

E Working with frequency distributions (answers p 160)

In a set of data some values may be repeated several times.
The following are the numbers of visits made to a doctor in a 6-month period by a group of twenty of her patients.

0 1 5 2 1 5 3 3 2 4 3 6 2 3 1 0 1 0 3 2

This data can be recorded in a frequency table.
To find the mean and standard deviation requires Σx_i and Σx_i^2 to be calculated from the data.

No. of visits	Frequency
0	3
1	4
2	4
3	5
4	1
5	2
6	1
Total	20

When calculating Σx_i the value 3 must be included in the sum five times. Therefore a far quicker way to find Σx_i is to multiply each of the values by its frequency and sum these products.

Similarly in calculating Σx_i^2 each value of x_i^2 will be included in the sum a number of times given by its frequency.

K If each value x_i has an associated frequency f_i, then the mean and standard deviation can be calculated by

$$\bar{x} = \frac{x_1 f_1 + x_2 f_2 + \ldots + x_n f_n}{n} = \frac{\sum x_i f_i}{n} \quad \text{and} \quad s_x = \sqrt{\frac{\sum x_i^2 f_i}{n} - \bar{x}^2}$$

E1 Calculate the mean and standard deviation of the number of visits to the doctor. A spreadsheet can be used to do this.

E2 Find out how to enter data from a frequency table into your calculator to calculate the mean and standard deviation.

The table refers to the number of shots played in each of fifty rallies between two tennis players before and after a coaching session. Only the grouped data for the length of each of the fifty rallies is recorded, not the original results.

Number of shots in rally	Number of rallies Before coaching	Number of rallies After coaching
1–10	32	5
11–20	12	20
21–30	3	15
31–40	2	3
41–50	1	5
51–60	0	2
Total	50	50

Using the mid-interval value as representative of the length of rally in the group, a 'before coaching' table can be produced as below.

Taking each of the rallies in the 1–10 group as having 5.5 shots, the total number of shots played for these 32 rallies is **estimated** to be $5.5 \times 32 = 176$.

The values of Σx_i and Σx_i^2 can now be found, as before, by multiplying each mid-interval value and mid-interval value squared by the group's frequency.

Group	Mid-interval value	Frequency before coaching
1–10	5.5	32
11–20	15.5	12
21–30	25.5	3
31–40	35.5	2
41–50	45.5	1

E3 Use a calculator to find the mean and standard deviation of the rally length before and after coaching. Comment on the results.

Note that the mean, variance and standard deviation calculated from a grouped frequency table are only estimates. The assumption is that the data is reasonably evenly spread within each group. Using more groups of a smaller size will lead to better estimates.

Exercise E (answers p 160)

1 This table shows the time it takes in minutes for students at a school to travel to school.

Time taken (min)	Frequency
0–14	124
15–29	205
30–44	141
45–59	87
60–89	18

   (a) Find an estimate of the mean and standard deviation of the time it takes students to get to school.

   (b) How accurate do you think the estimate is? What could have been done when recording the data to obtain a more accurate estimate from a grouped table?

2 In a statistical investigation of the works of Charles Dickens, a student recorded the lengths of a number of sentences randomly chosen from one of his novels.

   The results are shown in this table.

Number of words	Frequency
1–5	2
6–10	7
11–20	46
21–30	27
31–40	19
41–50	7
50+	2
Total	110

   (a) Calculate estimates for the mean and standard deviation of the number of words per sentence in this sample. Assume that the upper limit of the last interval is 60.

   (b) Give two reasons why these estimates might be inaccurate.

3 A projected population distribution of England and Wales for the year 2025 is given in this frequency table.

Age group (years)	Frequency (thousands)
0–14	9 928
15–29	9 953
30–44	10 075
45–59	9 808
60–74	8 989
75–89	4 289
90–99	469

   (a) Age is a special case as the 15–29 group includes people up to the day before their 30th birthday. The mid-interval value for this group is therefore 22.5. Find the mid-interval values for each of the other groups.

   (b) Estimate the total population in 2025.

   (c) Calculate an estimate of the mean and standard deviation of the age of the population in 2025.

   (d) In 1986 the mean age was 38.1 years with standard deviation 22.9 years. Comment on the differences between the age distribution for 1986 and the projected distribution for 2025.

F Choosing measures (answers p 161)

(Before working through this section, you may wish to revise the topics of cumulative frequency, median and interquartile range, which are dealt with on pages 15 to 17 and 19.)

There are two basic reasons for finding and quoting an 'average' value: to summarise a set of data by giving a 'representative' value, or to make comparisons. The choice of which measure to use may be guided by features of the data or by what the result will be used for.

F1 This table shows the annual wages, in thousands of pounds, of the workers in a factory.

(a) (i) Estimate the median wage of these workers.

(ii) Estimate the mean wage of these workers.

(b) Which of these two measures do you think is more representative of the wages at this factory?

Annual wage w (£000)	Frequency
$10 \leq w < 15$	42
$15 \leq w < 20$	75
$20 \leq w < 25$	48
$25 \leq w < 30$	35
$30 \leq w < 40$	18
$40 \leq w < 60$	10
$60 \leq w < 80$	6
$80 \leq w < 120$	2

The median wage is the wage of the 'middle-earning' worker. The mean wage is found by adding up the wages of all the workers and sharing out the total equally between the workers. In a pay dispute, the parties may use different measures to justify their case.

There are two commonly used measures of spread: standard deviation and interquartile range. In cases where the data is to be compared with a theoretical model (you will be studying some of these in later chapters) the standard deviation (or variance) is used. In other situations there may be reasons for preferring the interquartile range.

F2 A group of 80 students took part in an experiment in which they were given a geometrical puzzle to solve. The time taken by each student was recorded.

A grouped frequency table of the results is given here.

What feature of this data makes it impossible to estimate with confidence the mean and standard deviation of the times taken to solve the puzzle?

Time, t s	Frequency
$0 < t \leq 20$	6
$20 < t \leq 40$	13
$40 < t \leq 60$	23
$60 < t \leq 80$	18
$80 < t \leq 100$	10
$100 < t \leq 120$	6
$t > 120$	4

F3 The puzzle-solving data is reproduced here, but this time the last interval is given as '$120 < t \le 140$'.

Time, t s	Frequency
$0 < t \le 20$	6
$20 < t \le 40$	13
$40 < t \le 60$	23
$60 < t \le 80$	18
$80 < t \le 100$	10
$100 < t \le 120$	6
$120 < t \le 140$	4

(a) Draw a cumulative frequency graph and use it to find

    (i) the median   (ii) the interquartile range

(b) Suppose that the last interval in the table had been given as '$120 < t \le 150$'.

    (i) How would this change affect the cumulative frequency graph?

    (ii) How would it affect the median and the interquartile range?

    (iii) How would the change affect estimates of the mean and standard deviation calculated from mid-interval values?

The median and interquartile range are unaffected by extreme values at either end of the range of data. If extreme values are regarded as relatively unimportant compared with the main body of the data, then interquartile range may be a better measure of spread.

In the puzzle-solving experiment, it is possible that timing stopped after 120 seconds, so that any student who had not solved the puzzle by then was recorded as '> 120'. However, even without knowing the times for these students, it is still possible to find the median time and the interquartile range.

When the distribution of data is symmetrical there is usually little difference between the mean and median, and the measures of spread will give a similar picture when comparing two sets of data. However, if the data set is skewed or there are extreme values at the ends, called outliers, the mean and standard deviation will be affected. There are two arguments:

- Since the median and IQR are less affected by values at the extremes of a distribution they are more appropriate in cases where such values may occur.

- As the mean and standard deviation include all the values they are more 'sensitive' measures and give a better picture of the whole data set.

Users of statistics are sometimes guilty of choosing a measure that shows the result they would like to be true. In practice it is best to use one or both sets of measures but point out any limitations of the measures in the light of the data.

The tables opposite highlight the advantages and disadvantages of the different measures.

Measure of average	Advantages	Disadvantages
Mode	With data such as clothes sizes the mode is a useful statistic, since it is the 'most popular' size. The modal group is also useful with grouped data.	The mode is of no use with small data sets and in some cases does not give a central value. The modal group will depend on how the data was grouped initially.
Median	It is not unduly influenced by one or two extreme values or outliers.	It is insensitive as it does not use the whole data set and is governed by only a small section of the data in the middle. Calculators are difficult to program to find the median.
Mean	It uses the whole data set and thus represents every item of data. Its calculation can easily be written as a mathematical formula and calculators can easily be programmed to find it.	It can be greatly affected by a small number of outliers.

Measure of spread	Advantages	Disadvantages
Range	It shows the full extent of the spread of the data and is needed for a box-and-whisker diagram.	It is dependent only on the most extreme values.
Interquartile range	It is not unduly influenced by one or two extreme values or outliers. Useful statements can be made about a single set of data such as 50% of the data lie within the IQR.	It is insensitive as it does not use the whole data set and is governed by one or two data values. Calculators are difficult to program to find the IQR.
Standard deviation and variance	They use the whole data set and thus represent every item of data. Their calculation can easily be written as a mathematical formula and calculators can easily be programmed to find them. They are most useful in comparing two sets of data with the same measurements.	They can be greatly affected by one or two outliers. For a single set of data the standard deviation gives little useful information.

Key points

- The variance is the mean of the squared deviations from the mean of every value. The standard deviation is the square root of the variance. (p 25)

- The standard deviation can be found by

$$s_x = \sqrt{\frac{\sum (x_i - \bar{x})^2}{n}} \quad \text{or} \quad s_x = \sqrt{\frac{\sum x_i^2}{n} - \bar{x}^2}$$

  The second formula is easier for calculation. (pp 26–28)

- When data values have associated frequencies the mean and standard deviation can be found by

$$\bar{x} = \frac{\sum x_i f_i}{n} \quad \text{and} \quad s_x = \sqrt{\frac{\sum x_i^2 f_i}{n} - \bar{x}^2}$$

  When the data is grouped, the mid-interval value of the group can be used as the x-value for that group to obtain estimated values of the mean and standard deviation. (p 31)

- When a constant b is added to every item in a set of data, the mean also increases by b but the standard deviation is unchanged. (p 29)

- If each value in a data set is multiplied by a, then the mean and standard deviation are also multiplied by a. (p 29)

Test yourself (answers p 161)

1 The systolic blood pressures of a group of boys in a class are measured as follows, in millimetres of mercury (mmHg).

141 132 132 109 92 107 102 104 97 163 86 98 91 106 157

(a) Find the mean and standard deviation of the boys' blood pressures.

(b) 14 girls in the same class also have their blood pressure measured. The girls' blood pressures were found to have mean 106.8 mmHg and standard deviation 18.9 mmHg. Compare the results for the boys and girls.

2 The marks of ten students on a test were found to have a mean of 71 and a standard deviation of 7.

(a) (i) Find the total of the ten marks, $\sum x$.

(ii) Show that the value of $\sum x^2$ is 50 900.

(b) When the marks were checked it was discovered that one of the marks was incorrect. A mark given as 79 should have been 97. Calculate the mean and standard deviation of the corrected marks. AQA 2002

3 A chef prepares 10 meals using portions of meat bought in a shop.

The masses, x grams, of the 10 portions of meat are such that
$$\Sigma x = 2000 \text{ and } \Sigma x^2 = 409\,000$$

(a) Find the mean and standard deviation of these masses.

(b) Deduce the mean and standard deviation of the costs of the portions of meat, given that the meat costs 2 pence per gram.

(c) Each meal costs £1 in addition to the cost of the meat.
Write down the mean and standard deviation of the total cost of a meal.   AQA 2002

4 The wingspans of some butterflies of a certain tropical species were measured in millimetres. The results are shown in this table.

Find estimates for the mean and standard deviation of the wingspans of this species.

Wingspan (mm)	Frequency
50–59	3
60–69	8
70–79	12
80–89	9
90–99	4
100–109	1

5 A small firm wishes to introduce an aptitude test for applicants for assembly work. The test consists of a mechanical puzzle. The assembly workers, currently employed, were asked to complete the puzzle. They were timed to the nearest second and the times taken by 35 of them are shown below.

Time to complete puzzle (s)	Frequency
20–39	6
40–49	8
50–54	7
55–59	5
60–69	9

(a) Draw a cumulative frequency diagram of the data and estimate the median and interquartile range.

(b) Calculate estimates of the mean and standard deviation.

(c) In addition to the data in the table, five other assembly workers completed the puzzle but took so long to do it that their times were not recorded. These times all exceeded 100 seconds.
Estimate the median time to complete the puzzle for all 40 assembly workers.

(d) The firm decides not to offer employment to any applicant who takes longer than the average time taken by the assembly workers who took the test.

(i) State whether you would recommend the median or mean to be used as a measure of average in these circumstances. Explain your answer.

(ii) Write down the value of your recommended measure of average.   AQA 2001

3 Probability

In this chapter you will learn how to
• find the probability of combinations of events
• use conditional probabilities

A Outcomes and events (answers p 162)

The study of probability developed quickly in the seventeenth century in connection with games of chance. Since then the ideas of probability have been applied in many areas of science, including physics and biology.

One of these areas of application is genetics, the study of how attributes of parents (such as sex, eye colour, susceptibility to diseases, and so on) are passed on to their offspring.

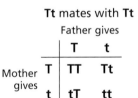

One inherited attribute of humans is being able or not being able to roll the tongue. This is something you either can or can't do – there is no 'halfway' stage.

The genetic information passed on by a parent can be thought of as either T (yes) or t (no). Every person has two parents, so a person's genetic make-up can be either TT or tt or Tt.

A person who is TT will be able to roll the tongue and a person who is tt will not. Geneticists have found that T is 'dominant', so a person with T can roll their tongue.

When two people mate and produce offspring, each parent gives the offspring one of its two letters. If a parent is TT they will give T and if they are tt they will give t. If the parent is Tt, they are equally likely to give T or t.

What happens when two Tt people mate is shown in the table on the right.

There are four **equally likely outcomes** for the offspring:

  TT, Tt, tT, tt

Because T is dominant, the offspring will be able to roll the tongue for three of these outcomes:

  TT, Tt, tT

Tt mates with Tt

Father gives

	T	t
Mother gives T	TT	Tt
t	tT	tt

These outcomes are said to be **favourable** for the **event** 'the offspring can roll the tongue'.

The probability that the offspring will be able to roll the tongue is

$$\frac{\text{number of favourable outcomes}}{\text{total number of equally likely outcomes}} = \tfrac{3}{4}.$$

The formula above for the probability of an event is generally applicable.
The first step in applying it is to identify the equally likely outcomes.

Some of the examples in this chapter are based on an ordinary pack of cards.
The cards are split into four 'suits': clubs (♣), diamonds (♦), hearts (♥), spades (♠).
In each suit the 13 cards are Ace, numbers 2–10, Jack (J), Queen (Q) and King (K).
The Jacks, Queens and Kings are called 'court cards' (or 'picture cards').

There are 52 cards altogether. If a card is picked at random (which means that all
the cards are equally likely to be chosen), there are 52 equally likely outcomes.

Let C stand for the event 'a court card is chosen'.
The number of outcomes favourable to C is denoted by n(C).

A1 What is the value of n(C)?

A2 Let D be the event 'a diamond is chosen'. What is the value of n(D)?

The events C and D can be shown in a **Venn diagram**.

Think of the rectangle as containing all the cards in the pack.
The circle labelled C contains the court cards.
The circle labelled D contains the diamonds.

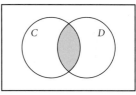

$C \cap D$ shaded

The shaded intersection of C and D contains the cards that
are both court cards and diamonds (J♦, Q♦, K♦).
This set of cards is denoted by $C \cap D$ ('C and D').
n($C \cap D$) = 3.

A3 The overlapping circles C and D divide the rectangle
into four 'compartments'. The number of outcomes
in each compartment can be written on the diagram.
What are the three missing numbers here?

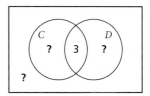

The shaded part of the diagram on the right shows the event
called the 'union' of C and D, denoted by $C \cup D$ ('C or D').
It contains all the outcomes favourable to the event 'the card
chosen is either a court card or a diamond'. (This includes
cards which are both.)

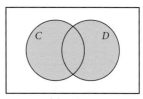

$C \cup D$ shaded

A4 What is the value of n($C \cup D$)?

The shaded part of this diagram shows the event 'the card
chosen is not a court card'. This event, called the **complement**
of C, is denoted by C'.

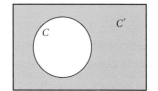

A5 What is the value of (a) n(C') (b) n(D')

K To summarise the notation: if A and B are any two events,
A' is the event 'A does not happen',
$A \cap B$ is the event 'A and B both happen',
$A \cup B$ is the event 'either A or B (or both) happens'.

This Venn diagram shows the event C defined on the previous page, together with its complement C'.

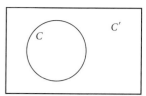

There are 52 equally likely outcomes when a card is picked at random from the pack.

The probability of C is denoted by $P(C)$. $P(C) = \dfrac{n(C)}{52} = \dfrac{12}{52} = \dfrac{3}{13}$

D **A6** Find the value of $P(C')$.
Verify that $P(C') = 1 - P(C)$.

Use a Venn diagram or otherwise to explain why, for any event A,
$P(A') = 1 - P(A)$.

A7 The diagram shows the two events C and D defined previously.

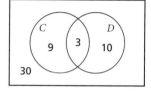

(a) Find the value of   (i) $P(C \cap D)$ (ii) $P(C \cup D)$
(b) Verify that $P(C \cup D) = P(C) + P(D) - P(C \cap D)$.
(c) Use a Venn diagram to explain why, for any two events A and B,
$$P(A \cup B) = P(A) + P(B) - P(A \cap B)$$

The diagram shows two events A and B which have no outcomes in common. (In other words, A and B can't both happen together.) A and B are called **mutually exclusive events**.

(An example is A: 'the chosen card is a club';
B: 'the chosen card is a heart'.)

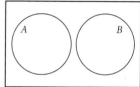

mutually exclusive events

A8 (a) If A and B are mutually exclusive, what is the value of $P(A \cap B)$?
(b) What can you say about $P(A \cup B)$ when A and B are mutually exclusive?

K For any events A, B: $P(A') = 1 - P(A)$ (1)
$$P(A \cup B) = P(A) + P(B) - P(A \cap B) \qquad (2)$$
If $P(A \cap B) = 0$, then A and B are mutually exclusive and
$$P(A \cup B) = P(A) + P(B) \qquad (3)$$

Example 1

In a college, the percentage of students who study history is 35%. The percentage who study maths is 50%. The percentage who study neither history nor maths is 30%. A student is chosen at random. Find the probability that the student studies

(a) either history or maths
(b) both history and maths
(c) only one of the two subjects

Solution

(a) 30% of students study neither H(istory) nor M(aths), leaving 70% that study either H or M. So $P(H \cup M) = 0.7$

(b) Use the equation $P(H \cup M) = P(H) + P(M) - P(H \cap M)$:
$$0.7 = 0.35 + 0.5 - P(H \cap M), \text{ from which } P(H \cap M) = 0.15$$

(c) $P(\text{only one of the subjects}) = P(H \cup M) - P(H \cap M)$
$$= 0.7 - 0.15 = 0.55$$

You could also use a Venn diagram, showing the probabilities in each compartment. Start with 0.3 outside both circles. The completed diagram is shown on the right.

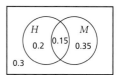

Exercise A (answers p 162)

1 Alan picks a number at random from the set 1, 2, 3, 4.
Beth picks a number at random from the set 1, 2, 3.
Colin picks a number at random from the set 1, 2.

   (a) List all the equally likely outcomes of the three choices.

   (b) Find the probability that the three numbers picked are

      (i) all the same   **(ii)** all different

2 In a college, 50% of students study maths and 35% study science.
55% of students study either maths or science.
A student is picked at random. Find the probability that the student studies

   (a) both maths and science   **(b)** only one of the two subjects

3 In a raffle, 1000 tickets are sold, numbered from 1 to 1000. One winning ticket is picked at random. Find the probability that the winning number is

   (a) a multiple of 5

   (b) a multiple of 5 but not a multiple of 20

   (c) a multiple of 4 or a multiple of 5

4 A box contains cubes of different colours and materials. If a cube is taken out at random, the probability that it is red is 0.25, the probability that it is red or wooden is 0.8, and the probability that it is both red and wooden is 0.2.
Find the probability that the ball is

   (a) neither red nor wooden   **(b)** wooden   **(c)** wooden but not red

*5 A school offers three languages for GCSE: French, German and Spanish.
All students are required to study at least two of these languages.
90% of students study French and 70% study German. 5% study all three languages.

   A student is picked at random. Find the probability that the student studies

   (a) French and German   **(b)** Spanish

B Conditional probability (answers p 162)

Suppose a pack contains these 12 cards: $\boxed{1}\boxed{2}\boxed{3}\boxed{4}\boxed{5}\boxed{6}\boxed{7}\boxed{8}\boxed{9}\boxed{10}\boxed{11}\boxed{12}$

A card is picked at random.

Let E be the event 'the number chosen is even'.
Let L be the event 'the number chosen is less than 6'.

The two events are shown in the Venn diagram on the right, together with the individual cards.

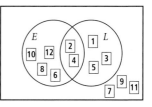

B1 Find   **(a)** P(L)   **(b)** P(E)   **(c)** P($L \cap E$)

Suppose someone picks a card at random and tells us the number is even.

The set of equally likely outcomes is now reduced to the set for E: $\boxed{2}\boxed{4}\boxed{6}\boxed{8}\boxed{10}\boxed{12}$

Of these cards, the only ones favourable to the event L are those in $L \cap E$: $\boxed{2}\boxed{4}$

So the probability of L given that E has happened $= \dfrac{n(L \cap E)}{n(E)} = \dfrac{2}{6} = \dfrac{1}{3}$

The probability of L given E is written P($L|E$). It is called a **conditional probability**.

P($L|E$) can also be expressed in terms of probabilities.

Let N stand for the total number of cards in the pack. (In this example, $N = 12$.)

$$P(L|E) = \frac{n(L \cap E)}{n(E)} = \frac{\dfrac{n(L \cap E)}{N}}{\dfrac{n(E)}{N}} = \frac{P(L \cap E)}{P(E)}$$

B2 Verify that the formula $P(L|E) = \dfrac{P(L \cap E)}{P(E)}$ gives the same result $\left(\dfrac{1}{3}\right)$ as before.

 For any pair of events A, B,

$$P(B|A) = \frac{P(A \cap B)}{P(A)} \qquad (4)$$

B3 **(a)** What does P($E|L$) mean, in words?   **(b)** Find the value of P($E|L$).

B4 Define G as the event 'the number chosen is greater than 4'. Find

     (a) P($G|E$)   **(b)** P($E|G$)   **(c)** P($G|L$)   **(d)** P($L|G$)

B5 Define M as the event 'the number chosen is a multiple of 3'.
     L is defined as before.

     (a) Draw the Venn diagram for M and L, showing each individual card.

     (b) Find   **(i)** P($M|L$)   **(ii)** P($L|M$)

Example 2

Dawn has a collection of photos. This table shows the number of photos in each of four categories.

	People	Places
Glossy	44	36
Matt	26	14

Dawn picks a photo at random.

(a) Given that the photo is glossy, what is the probability that it shows people?

(b) Given that the photo shows places, what is the probability that it is matt?

Solution

(a) There are $44 + 36 = 80$ glossy photos altogether. So $P(\text{people}\,|\,\text{glossy}) = \frac{44}{80} = 0.55$.

(b) There are $36 + 14 = 50$ photos of places altogether. So $P(\text{matt}\,|\,\text{places}) = \frac{14}{50} = 0.28$.

Example 3

In a library, 40% of books are paperbacks. 80% of all the books in the library are fiction. 25% of all the books are paperback fiction. A book is chosen at random.

(a) Given that the book is a paperback, what is the probability that it is fiction?

(b) Given that a book is fiction, what is the probability that it is a paperback?

Solution

(a) $P(\text{fiction}\,|\,\text{paperback}) = \dfrac{P(\text{fiction and paperback})}{P(\text{paperback})} = \frac{0.25}{0.4} = 0.625$

(b) $P(\text{paperback}\,|\,\text{fiction}) = \dfrac{P(\text{paperback and fiction})}{P(\text{fiction})} = \frac{0.25}{0.8} = 0.3125$

Exercise B (answers p 162)

1 A card is drawn at random from this pack.

| 1 | 2 | 3 | 4 | 5 | 6 | 7 | 8 | 9 | 10 | 11 | 12 |

(a) Given that the card is black, what is the probability that the number on it is even?

(b) Given that the number on the card is even, what is the probability that the card is black?

2 This table shows the percentages of stamps of different types in Bharat's collection.

	UK	Foreign
Used	36%	24%
Unused	14%	26%

Bharat picks a stamp at random from the collection.

(a) What is the probability that the stamp is used?

(b) Given that the stamp is used, what is the probability that it is foreign?

(c) Given that it is a UK stamp, what is the probability that it is unused?

3 30% of the pages in a book have a picture on them. 10% have a map. 3% have both a picture and a map.

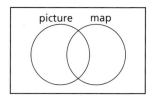

(a) Copy this Venn diagram and write the percentage of pages in each part.

A page is picked at random.

(b) Given that the page has a picture, what is the probability that it also has a map?

(c) Given that the page has a map, what is the probability that it also has a picture?

(d) What is the probability that the page has neither a map nor a picture?

(e) Given that the page does not have a picture, what is the probability that it does not have a map?

4 Students at a college study **two** subjects from this list: painting, sculpture, ceramics. 45% of the students study painting and sculpture, 30% study painting and ceramics and the rest study sculpture and ceramics.

A student is chosen at random.

(a) Given that the student studies painting, what is the probability that they also study ceramics?

(b) Given that the student studies ceramics, what is the probability that they also study sculpture?

5 Each student in a college studies one and only one of the three languages French, German and Spanish. The percentage breakdown of the students by gender and by language studied is given in the table.

	French	German	Spanish
Male	30%	8%	6%
Female	21%	18%	17%

A student is picked at random.

(a) Given that the student is female, what is the probability that she studies French?

(b) Given that the student studies either German or Spanish, what is the probability that the student is male?

C Independent events (answers p 162)

C1 Suppose you pick a card at random from this pack. `1` `2` `3` `4` `5` `6` `7` `8` `9` `10` `11` `12`

Define the events E and M as follows:
   E: the number picked is even M: the number picked is a multiple of 3

(a) Find the following probabilities.

   (i) $P(M)$ (ii) $P(E)$ (iii) $P(M|E)$ (iv) $P(E|M)$

(b) Comment on your results and what they mean.

Two events are called **independent** if knowing that one has happened makes no difference to the probability of the other.

The events M and E in question C1 are independent, because $P(M|E) = P(M)$. It is also true that $P(E|M) = P(E)$.

In general, two events B and A are independent if $P(B|A) = P(B)$.

By replacing $P(B|A)$ by the equivalent expression $\dfrac{P(A \cap B)}{P(A)}$ from equation (4) on page 42,

we can state the condition for independence as: $\dfrac{P(A \cap B)}{P(A)} = P(B)$

$$\Rightarrow \quad P(A \cap B) = P(A) \times P(B)$$

K   Two events A and B are independent when $P(A \cap B) = P(A)P(B)$ (5)

Example 4

This table shows the numbers of male and female students studying and not studying art in a college. A student is picked at random. Are the events 'the student is male' and 'the student studies art' independent?

	Male	Female
Art	27	48
Not art	83	92

Solution

There are 250 students altogether of whom 110 are male, so $P(\text{male}) = \frac{110}{250} = 0.44$.

There are 75 art students altogether, so $P(\text{art}) = \frac{75}{250} = 0.3$.

27 students are both male and study art, so $P(\text{male and art}) = \frac{27}{250} = 0.108$.

$P(\text{male}) \times P(\text{art}) = 0.44 \times 0.3 = 0.132$. This is not 0.108, so the events are not independent.

Exercise C (answers p 162)

1   This table shows the numbers of male and female students studying and not studying maths at a college. A student is chosen at random.

	Male	Female
Maths	72	58
Not maths	48	22

(a) Find the probability that the student studies maths.

(b) Given that the student is male, find the probability that the student studies maths.

(c) Show that studying maths is not independent of the gender of the student.

2   Jo and Kay are each thrown a ball. The probability that Jo catches hers is 0.3. The probability that Kay catches hers is 0.4. The two events are independent. Find the probability that

(a) Jo and Kay both catch

(b) at least one of the two girls catches

3 A rugby club has three categories of membership – adult, social and junior. The number of members in each category, classified by gender, is shown in the table.

	Adult	Social	Junior
Female	25	35	40
Male	95	25	80

One member is chosen, at random, to cut the ribbon at the opening of the new clubhouse.

(a) Find the probability that:

    (i) a female member is chosen

    (ii) a junior member is chosen

    (iii) a junior member is chosen, given that a female member is chosen

(b) V denotes the event that a female member is chosen.
    W denotes the event that an adult member is chosen.
    X denotes the event that a junior member is chosen.

    For the events V, W and X,

    (i) write down two which are mutually exclusive

    (ii) find two which are neither mutually exclusive nor independent;
        justify your answer

AQA 2003

D Tree diagrams (answers p 163)

A dice is rolled and a coin tossed. This table shows the equally likely outcomes for the pair of results.

		Dice					
		1	2	3	4	5	6
Coin	Head	H, 1	H, 2	H, 3	H, 4	H, 5	H, 6
	Tail	T, 1	T, 2	T, 3	T, 4	T, 5	T, 6

The table shows that $P(\text{head on coin}) = \frac{1}{2}$, $P(6 \text{ on dice}) = \frac{1}{6}$ and $P(\text{head and } 6) = \frac{1}{12}$.

So $P(\text{head and } 6) = P(\text{head}) \times P(6)$. It follows that 'head' and '6' are independent events. (This is what we would expect, as the dice and the coin do not affect each other.)

The possible outcomes can also be shown in a **tree diagram**.

Probabilities are multiplied along the branches as shown.

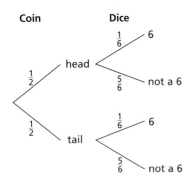

$P(\text{head and } 6) = \frac{1}{2} \times \frac{1}{6} = \frac{1}{12}$

$P(\text{head and not a } 6) = \frac{1}{2} \times \frac{5}{6} = \frac{5}{12}$

$P(\text{tail and } 6) = \frac{1}{2} \times \frac{1}{6} = \frac{1}{12}$

$P(\text{tail and not a } 6) = \frac{1}{2} \times \frac{5}{6} = \frac{5}{12}$

Where outcomes are not independent, the conditional probabilities are written on the branches.

From equation (4) on page 42 it follows that $P(A \cap B) = P(A) \times P(B|A)$

So the multiplication rule still applies.

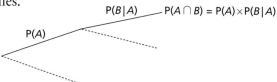

D1 An athlete has to jump over two hurdles.
The probability that he clears the first is 0.7.
If he clears the first, the probability that he clears the second is 0.6.
If he doesn't clear the first, the probability of clearing the second is 0.2.

(a) Copy and complete the tree diagram.

(b) What is the probability that the athlete

    (i) clears both hurdles

    (ii) clears the first but not the second

    (iii) clears the second but not the first

    (iv) clears neither hurdle

(c) Find the probability that the athlete

    (i) clears at least one hurdle

    (ii) clears exactly one hurdle

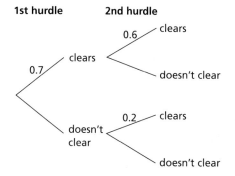

D2 A box contains 3 red and 2 green counters. A counter is taken at random from the box and is **not** replaced. Then a second counter is taken at random.

(a) What is the probability that the first counter is red?

(b) Given that the first counter is red, what is the probability that the second counter is red?

(c) Given that the first counter is green, what is the probability that the second counter is red?

(d) Draw a tree diagram. Use it to find

    (i) the probability that both counters are red

    (ii) the probability that exactly one counter is red

    (iii) the probability that both counters are green

D3 A box contains 3 dark chocolates, 2 milk chocolates and 1 white chocolate. Three chocolates are taken from the box at random, one after the other, without replacement. Find the probability that

(a) all three chocolates are dark chocolates

(b) none of the chocolates is a milk chocolate

The results obtained from a tree diagram calculation can be used to calculate a conditional probability 'in reverse'. The next example shows how.

Example 5

A trainee has two tests, A and B. The probability of passing A is 0.8.
If the trainee passes A, the probability of passing B is 0.9.
If they fail A, the probability of passing B is 0.6.

(a) Find the probability of passing B.

(b) Find the probability of passing at least one of the tests.

(c) Given that a trainee passes B, find the probability that they pass A.

Solution

(a) The tree diagram is drawn on the right.

$$\text{P(pass } B) = \text{P(pass } A \text{ and pass } B) + \text{P(fail } A \text{ and pass } B)$$
$$= 0.8 \times 0.9 + 0.2 \times 0.6 = 0.84.$$

(b) 'Pass at least one' is the complement of 'fail both'.
So P(pass at least one) = 1 − P(fail both).

P(fail both) = $0.2 \times 0.4 = 0.08$.
So P(pass at least one) = $1 - 0.08 = 0.92$.

Alternatively, add P(pass A, pass B), P(pass A, fail B), P(fail A, pass B).

(c) *Use the formula for conditional probability (page 42, equation (4)).*

$$\text{P(pass } A \,|\, \text{pass } B) = \frac{\text{P(pass } A \text{ and pass } B)}{\text{P(pass } B)}$$

Use the tree diagram to find P(pass A and B). *You have already found* P(pass B) *in* (a).
P(pass A and B) = $0.8 \times 0.9 = 0.72$. P(pass B) = 0.84 from (a).
So P(pass $A\,|\,$pass B) = $\frac{0.72}{0.84} = 0.857$ (to 3 s.f.).

[Tree diagram: 0.8 pass A — 0.9 pass B, 0.1 fail B; 0.2 fail A — 0.6 pass B, 0.4 fail B]

Exercise D (answers p 163)

1 A pack contains cards numbered 1, 2, 3, 4, 5.
A card is picked at random and not replaced;
then another card is picked.
Copy and complete the tree diagram and find
the probability that the numbers chosen consist
of one odd and one even.

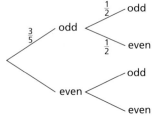

2 A pack contains six cards numbered 1 to 6.
A card is taken at random and not replaced; then a second card is taken.
Find the probability that at least one of the numbers is greater than 3.

3 Two letters are posted on the same day.
Letter A is sent by first-class post and has a probability of 0.9 of being delivered the next day.
Letter B is sent by second-class post and has a probability of only 0.3 of being delivered the next day.

(a) Find the probability that

    (i) both letters are delivered the next day

    (ii) neither letter is delivered the next day

    (iii) at least one of the letters is delivered the next day.

(b) Given that at least one of the letters is delivered the next day, find the probability that letter A is delivered the next day.   AQA 2003

4 The experience of a commuter is that her train is cancelled with probability 0.02. When it does run, it has probability 0.9 of being on time.
This information is shown on the tree diagram.

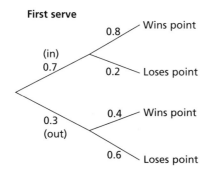

(a) Find the probability that the train runs on time.

(b) Given that the train is **not** on time, find the probability that it has been cancelled.   AQA 2001

5 A tennis player is allowed two serves. The probability that a particular player's first serve will be in is 0.7. She has probability 0.8 of winning the point when her first serve is in. Otherwise, her probability of winning the point is only 0.4. This information is shown in the tree diagram.

First serve

0.8 — Wins point
(in) 0.7
0.2 — Loses point

0.3 (out)
0.4 — Wins point
0.6 — Loses point

(a) Find the probability that she wins a point when she is serving.

(b) Given that she does win this point, find the probability that her first serve was in.   AQA 2002

The method you have been using to calculate a conditional probability 'in reverse' can be expressed in symbols.

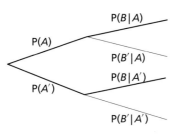

$$P(A|B) = \frac{P(A \cap B)}{P(B)}$$

$$= \frac{P(B|A)P(A)}{P(B|A)P(A) + P(B|A')P(A')}$$

Key points

- Notation: A' means 'not A'
  $A \cap B$ means 'A and B'
  $A \cup B$ means 'A or B (or both)' (p 39)

- $P(A') = 1 - P(A)$ (p 40)

- $P(A \cup B) = P(A) + P(B) - P(A \cap B)$ (p 40)

- If A and B are mutually exclusive, then $P(A \cup B) = P(A) + P(B)$ (p 40)

- $P(B|A)$ means the conditional probability of B given A. (p 42)

- $P(B|A) = \dfrac{P(A \cap B)}{P(A)}$ so $P(A \cap B) = P(A)\,P(B|A)$ (p 42)

- If $P(A \cap B) = P(A)\,P(B)$, then A and B are independent (and vice versa) (p 45)

Mixed questions (answers p 163)

1 Following a flood, 120 tins were recovered from Dharmesh's corner shop. Unfortunately the water had washed off all the labels. Of the tins, 50 contained pet food, 20 contained peas, 35 contained beans and the rest contained soup.

(a) Dharmesh selects a tin at random. Find the probability that it

    (i) contains soup

    (ii) does not contain pet food

(b) Dharmesh selects two tins at random (without replacement). Find the probability that

    (i) both contain peas

    (ii) one contains pet food and the other contains peas

(c) Dharmesh selects three tins at random (without replacement). Find the probability that one contains pet food, one contains peas and one contains beans.

(d) Find the probability that Dharmesh will have to open more than two tins before she finds one which does not contain pet food. AQA 2002

2 Shahid, Tracy and Dwight are friends who all have birthdays during January. Assuming that each friend's birthday is equally likely to be on any of the 31 days of January, find the probability that

(a) Shahid's birthday is on January 3rd

(b) both Shahid's and Tracy's birthdays are on January 3rd

(c) all three friends' birthdays are on the same day

(d) all three friends' birthdays are on different days AQA 2002

Test yourself (answers p 163)

1 For training purposes, a bank monitors telephone calls made by Arif, Belinda and Charles. Their calls are recorded. However, due to incorrect use of the equipment, some of the recordings are inaudible. The 95 calls made during a particular week are summarised in the table.

	Audible	Inaudible
Arif	17	13
Belinda	10	15
Charles	23	17

The head of the monitoring service decides to listen to one of the telephone calls chosen at random.

(a) Write down the probability that the chosen call was

    (i) made by Arif and inaudible   (ii) not made by Arif

    (iii) inaudible   (iv) made by Arif given that it was inaudible

(b) If three different telephone calls are chosen at random, find the probability that they were made by

    (i) Arif   (ii) the same person   AQA 2001

2 A bottle bank consists of three containers, one each for green, brown and clear bottles. A notice requests people using the bottle bank to place bottles in the appropriate container. However some mistakes are made.

This table summarises where the last 200 bottles taken to the bank were placed. For example, 15 brown bottles were incorrectly placed in the container for green bottles.

		Colour of bottle		
		Green	Brown	Clear
	Green	85	15	5
Container	Brown	4	45	6
	Clear	1	5	34

(a) One of the 200 bottles is chosen at random. Find the probability that the chosen bottle is

    (i) green and correctly placed in the green container

    (ii) placed in the correct container

    (iii) placed in the correct container given that the bottle is clear

(b) Three of the 200 bottles are chosen at random without replacement. Find the probability that

    (i) the first bottle chosen is green   (ii) all are green

    (iii) two are green and one is brown   AQA 2002

3 In a group of students 60% are female and 40% are male. A third of the female students study Spanish but only a quarter of the male students study Spanish.

A student is chosen at random from the group.

(a) (i) Show that the probability that the chosen student is female and studies Spanish is 0.2.

    (ii) Calculate the probability that the chosen student studies Spanish.

(b) Given that the chosen student does study Spanish, calculate the conditional probability that the chosen student is female.   AQA 2002

4 Discrete random variables

In this chapter you will learn
- what is meant by 'discrete random variable' and 'probability distribution'
- how to find the mean, variance and standard deviation of a discrete random variable

A Probability distributions (answers p 164)

'Senet' is a board game known to have been played in ancient Egypt.
Instead of dice, four 'sticks' are thrown. Each stick is rounded on
one side and flat on the other. The score depends on the number of
sticks that land flat side up.

Number of flat sides up	0	1	2	3	4
Score	5	1	2	3	4

Score 3

It is impossible to tell, just from the shape, what is the probability of a stick
landing flat side up, although 'flat side up' seems more likely than 'curved side up'.

The only way to get an estimate of the probability is by experiment:
throw the stick many times and find the **relative frequency** of flat side up.

In such an experiment a stick was thrown 100 times and landed flat side up
70 times. This gives 0.7 as an estimate of the probability of landing flat side up.
The probability of landing curved side up is thus estimated as 0.3.

These estimates can be used to find the probability of each of the five scores.
Assume that each stick falls independently of the others, either F (flat side up)
or C (curved side up). We can list all the different possible ways the four sticks
could land:

> FFFF   (only outcome with 4 flat sides up)
> FFFC   FFCF   FCFF   CFFF   (outcomes with 3 flat sides up)
> FFCC   FCCF   CCFF   FCFC   CFCF   CFFC   (with 2 flat sides up)
> and so on

A1 Complete this list of all the possible outcomes for the four sticks.

The sixteen outcomes are not equally likely. For example, the probability of
getting FFFF is $0.7 \times 0.7 \times 0.7 \times 0.7$ (because the four sticks fall independently
of each other), or 0.2401. This is also the probability of getting a score of 4.

There are four different ways to get a score of 3: FFFC, FFCF, FCFF, CFFF.
The probability of each of these ways is $0.7^3 \times 0.3 = 0.1029$.
So the probability of getting a score of 3 is $4 \times 0.1029 = 0.4116$.

A2 Find the probability of getting a score of   **(a)** 2   **(b)** 1   **(c)** 5
    (Reminder: 5 is scored when no stick lands flat side up.)

The score is an example of a **discrete random variable**. This means a variable that can take individual values (usually integers), each with a given probability.

Let S stand for the score. (Capital letters are used for random variables.)
$P(S = 3)$ means 'the probability that $S = 3$'.
We have already found that $P(S = 3) = 0.4116$.

The complete set of probabilities (the **probability distribution** of S) is shown in this table.

s	1	2	3	4	5
$P(S = s)$	0.0756	0.2646	0.4116	0.2401	0.0081

Notice that the small letter s is used for individual values of the random variable S.

$P(S = s)$ is also called the **probability function** of S.

A3 What is the sum of all the probabilities in the table?

The probability distribution can also be shown in a 'stick graph'. The total of the heights of the sticks is 1.

The probability distribution would be useful to someone wanting to design a computer version of Senet. The scoring device would need to have this distribution if it were to behave like the sticks.

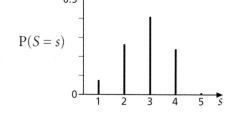

The simplest type of probability distribution is one where all the probabilities are equal (as, for example, with the score on a fair dice).
Such a distribution is called **uniform**.

The random variable X shown here has a uniform distribution.

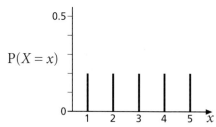

Exercise A (answers p 164)

1 A company that makes games has the idea of using a dice in the shape of a cuboctahedron. This has two kinds of face, squares and triangles.

The company makes a prototype dice and rolls it 500 times. It lands with square uppermost 300 times and triangle uppermost 200 times.

(a) Write down the estimates of the probabilities of 'square' and 'triangle'.

In the planned game, two of the dice are rolled. If both land triangle uppermost the player scores 3. If both land square uppermost the player scores 2. Otherwise the player scores 1.

(b) Let S be the score. Using a tree diagram or otherwise, find $P(S = 1)$, $P(S = 2)$ and $P(S = 3)$.
Make a table and a stick graph showing the probability distribution of S.

2 A pack contains four cards: Ace, King, Queen, Jack. In a game played with this pack, the scoring system is as follows.

Pick a card at random: if it is the Ace, score 3; if it isn't, pick again without replacing the first card. If the card picked this time is the Ace, score 2; otherwise pick again without replacing. If you get the Ace this time, score 1. Otherwise score 0.

(a) With the help of a tree diagram, make a table showing the probability distribution of the score S. Sketch a stick graph of the distribution.

(b) What type of distribution is it?

3 Two children play a game where they roll two ordinary dice. The score D is the difference between the numbers on the dice. (The difference is always positive.)

(a) Copy and complete the table on the right which shows the value of D for every possible outcome.

		1st dice					
		1	2	3	4	5	6
2nd dice	1	0	1	2	3		
	2	1	0	1			
	3	2	1	0			
	4						
	5						
	6						

(b) Copy and complete this table to show the probability distribution of D.

d	0	1	2	3	4	5
$P(D = d)$	$\frac{6}{36}$					

(c) Sketch a stick graph of the distribution.

(d) One child suggests a simple dice game:
'I win if the difference is less than 3; you win if the difference is 3 or more.'
Is this a fair game? If not, suggest a different, but fair, rule for winning, still based on differences.

4 A game is played with a single ordinary dice. The scoring system is as follows.

Roll a six first time: score 3; otherwise roll again.
Roll a six second time: score 2; otherwise roll again.
Roll a six third time: score 1, otherwise score 0.

Make a table showing the probability distribution of the score, S.

5 The probability function of a discrete random variable X is defined by
$P(X = x) = \frac{1}{10}x$, $x = 1, 2, 3, 4$.

For example, $P(X = 4) = \frac{1}{10} \times 4 = 0.4$

Find $P(X = 1)$, $P(X = 2)$, $P(X = 3)$ and $P(X = 4)$ and show that they add up to 1.

*6 X is a discrete random variable.
The probability function $P(X = x)$ is defined by $P(X = x) = kx^2$, $x = 1, 2, 3, 4$.

(a) Write down, in terms of k, the values of $P(X = 1)$, $P(X = 2)$, $P(X = 3)$ and $P(X = 4)$.

(b) Explain why the value of k must be $\frac{1}{30}$.

B Mean, variance and standard deviation (answers p 164)

Here again is the probability distribution of the score S when throwing the Senet sticks.

s	1	2	3	4	5
$P(S = s)$	0.0756	0.2646	0.4116	0.2401	0.0081

Imagine throwing the sticks 10 000 times.
The number of times you would expect to get a score of 1 is $10\,000 \times 0.0756 = 756$.
Similarly, a score of 2 would be expected 2646 times, and so on.

These frequencies can be used to calculate a mean score:

$$\text{Mean score} = \frac{(1 \times 756) + (2 \times 2646) + (3 \times 4116) + (4 \times 2401) + (5 \times 81)}{10\,000} = 2.84 \quad \text{(to 2 d.p.)}$$

It was unnecessary to multiply all the probabilities by 10 000 and then divide by 10 000 at the end. The mean score can be calculated using the probabilities themselves:

$$\begin{aligned}\text{Mean score} &= (1 \times 0.0756) + (2 \times 0.2646) + (3 \times 0.4116) + (4 \times 0.2401) + (5 \times 0.0081) \\ &= 2.84 \text{ (to 2 d.p.)}\end{aligned}$$

2.84 is the mean of the random variable S.

To calculate it, each possible value of the random variable is multiplied by its probability, and the products are added together.

$$\text{Mean of } S = \sum s \times P(S = s)$$

B1 Find the mean of the random variable X whose probability distribution is shown in this table.

x	0	1	2	3
$P(X = x)$	0.35	0.3	0.2	0.15

B2 The probability distributions for the scores X and Y in two different games are given below.

Game A

x	0	1	2	3	4
$P(X = x)$	0.15	0.25	0.25	0.25	0.10

Game B

y	0	1	2	3	4
$P(Y = y)$	0.05	0.25	0.50	0.15	0.05

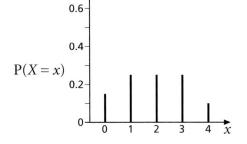

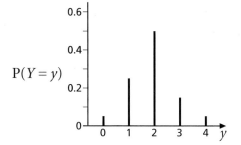

(a) Calculate the mean score for each game.

(b) The distributions are alike as far as the mean score is concerned. What is different about them?

The **variance** of a random variable is defined in a similar way to the variance of a frequency distribution. The score X in game A in question B2 will be used here as an example.

The mean of a random variable is usually denoted by the Greek letter μ ('mu'). In this case, $\mu = 1.9$.

The deviation of each possible value from the mean is found. This is $x - \mu$.

Each deviation is squared: $(x - \mu)^2$.

Each squared deviation is multiplied by the corresponding probability $P(X = x)$.

The total, 1.49, is the variance.

x	$x - \mu$	$(x - \mu)^2$	$P(X = x)$	$(x - \mu)^2 \times P(X = x)$
0	−1.9	3.61	0.15	0.5415
1	−0.9	0.81	0.25	0.2025
2	0.1	0.01	0.25	0.0025
3	1.1	1.21	0.25	0.3025
4	2.1	4.41	0.10	0.4410

Variance = 1.49

K
The **standard deviation** of a random variable is denoted by σ (the small Greek letter 'sigma'). This is the square root of the variance, so the variance is denoted by σ^2.

In the example above, $\sigma^2 = 1.49$, so $\sigma = \sqrt{1.49} = 1.22$ (to 3 s.f.).

K
The definitions of the mean and variance are:

$\mu = \Sigma x \times P(X = x)$

$\sigma^2 = \Sigma(x - \mu)^2 \times P(X = x)$

As in the case of a frequency distribution, an equivalent expression for the variance is easier to use in practice:

$\sigma^2 = \Sigma x^2 \times P(X = x) - \mu^2$

B3 Calculate the variance and standard deviation of the score in game B in question B2. Which of the two games has the wider variation in scores? How could you also tell this from the graphs?

Exercise B (answers p 164)

1 The probability distribution of the score S on an ordinary dice is shown here. Calculate

s	1	2	3	4	5	6
$P(S = s)$	$\frac{1}{6}$	$\frac{1}{6}$	$\frac{1}{6}$	$\frac{1}{6}$	$\frac{1}{6}$	$\frac{1}{6}$

(a) the mean of S (b) the variance of S (c) the standard deviation of S

2 Two ordinary dice are rolled.
The score D is the difference between the two numbers (as in exercise A, question 3).

Here is the probability distribution of D.

d	0	1	2	3	4	5
$P(D = d)$	$\frac{6}{36}$	$\frac{10}{36}$	$\frac{8}{36}$	$\frac{6}{36}$	$\frac{4}{36}$	$\frac{2}{36}$

Calculate

(a) the mean of D (b) the variance of D (c) the standard deviation of D

Key points

- A discrete random variable takes individual values (usually integers), each with a given probability. The probability distribution can be shown in a table or a graph. (p 53)

- The mean, μ, of a discrete random variable is defined by $\mu = \sum x \times P(X = x)$. (p 55)

- The variance, σ^2, is defined by $\sigma^2 = \sum (x - \mu)^2 \times P(X = x)$.
  An equivalent form of this equation is $\sigma^2 = \sum x^2 \times P(X = x) - \mu^2$. (p 56)

- Standard deviation $= \sqrt{\text{variance}}$. (p 56)

Test yourself (answers p 165)

1 The diagram shows a fair spinner.
Let X be the score when the spinner is spun.
The table shows part of the probability distribution of X.

x	1	2	3
$P(X = x)$	$\frac{1}{2}$		

(a) Copy and complete the table.

(b) Calculate the mean of X.

(c) Calculate the variance of X.

2 (a) The probability distribution of the litter size S in a species of animal is given in this table.

s	1	2	3	4
$P(S = s)$	0.3	0.2	0.3	0.2

  (i) Find $P(S \geq 3)$.

  (ii) Calculate the mean of S.

  (iii) Calculate the variance of S.

(b) The probability distribution of the litter size T in a second species is as follows.

t	1	2	3	4
$P(T = t)$	0.05	0.4	0.5	0.05

  (i) Calculate the mean of T.

  (ii) Calculate the variance of T.

(c) (i) In which species is litter size larger, on average?

  (ii) In which species is there wider variation in litter size?

5 Binomial distribution

In this chapter you will learn
- what the binomial distribution is
- how to recognise situations where the binomial model applies
- how to find probabilities for a given binomial distribution, by calculation and from tables
- how to find the mean, variance and standard deviation of a binomial distribution

A Pascal's triangle (answers p 165)

The picture on the right shows a binostat. It is like a pinball machine; balls are fed in at the top, fall through a triangular grid and collect in a series of slots. Each time a ball hits a pin, it is equally likely to fall to the left or the right.

The picture shows the distribution in the slots after a number of balls have passed through the grid.

If you do not have access to a binostat, you can use the grid shown here.

Use pennies for the balls.
To decide whether a ball falls
to left or right, spin a coin or
roll a dice (even left, odd right).

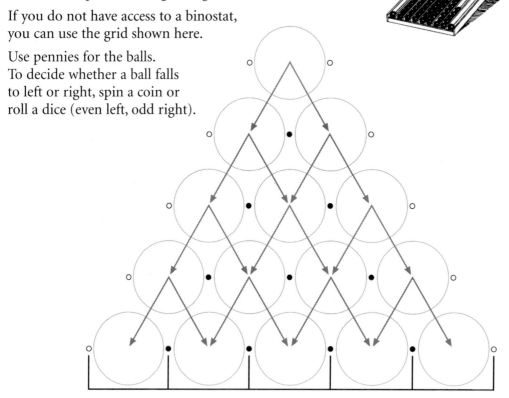

A1 Put 20 balls through the grid and see how many end up in each of the slots at the base. Collect together the results for the whole class. Does any pattern emerge?

A2 Can you explain why a ball is more likely to end up in one of the middle slots than in one of the end slots?

To see in more detail what is going on, consider this simple binostat. The rows and slots have been labelled for reference. You will see later why it is helpful to label the slots starting with 0 rather than 1.

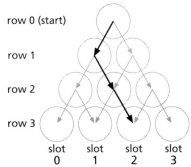

Each time a ball falls from one row to the next, the probabilities of falling left or right are each $\frac{1}{2}$.

The heavy arrows show one possible route for a ball that ends up in slot 2.

A3 (a) How many different routes are there from the start to slot 2?

(b) What is the probability of each of these routes?

(c) So what is the probability that a ball ends in slot 2?

A4 The number of the slot that a ball ends in is a discrete random variable. Call it S. In the previous question you found $P(S = 2)$.
Find $P(S = 0)$, $P(S = 1)$ and $P(S = 3)$, and hence write down the probability distribution of S in the form of a table.

s	0	1	2	3
$P(S = s)$				

In question A3, you found the probability of ending in slot 2 like this:

Find the number of routes to slot 2.
Find the probability of each route.
Multiply the number of routes by the probability of each route.

For a larger binostat the method is the same. The probability of each route is $\left(\frac{1}{2}\right)^n$, where n is the last row's number. But you also need to find the number of routes to a particular slot. The next questions are about this.

A5 This binostat has an extra row.
Think about the routes that lead to slot 3.
They will have to go through either position A or position B.

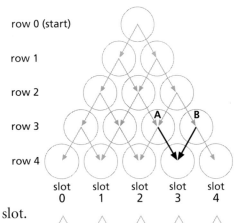

In question A3 (a), you found that there are 3 routes to position A.
How many are there to position B?
So how many are there to slot 3?

A6 (a) Find the number of routes to each of the other slots in this binostat.

(b) Find the probability of ending up in each slot.

A7 Suppose the binostat has another row added.

(a) Use a similar argument to find the number of routes to each slot.

(b) Find the probability of ending up in each slot.

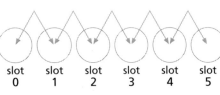

The number of routes to each position in the binostat grid is shown in this table, called **Pascal's triangle**, after the French mathematician and philosopher Blaise Pascal (1623–63).

Each number is the sum of the two numbers immediately to left and right in the previous row.

The heavy lines show one of the 15 routes leading to row 6, slot 2.

Let L stand for a fall to the left and R for a fall to the right. The route shown is LLRLRL.

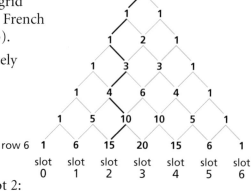

A8 Check that each of these routes leads to row 6 slot 2:

LRRLLL   RLLRLL   LLLLRR   RLLLLR

The routes to slot 2 consist of all the different ways of arranging two Rs and four Ls.

The numbers in Pascal's triangle have another important use.
Suppose you have 6 objects A, B, C, D, E, F and you want to know how many ways there are of picking 2 of them.

Each possible way corresponds to saying 'yes' (Y) to 2 objects and 'no' (N) to the other 4.
There are 15 ways, each corresponding to one of the ways of arranging two Ys and four Ns:

A B C D E F	A B C D E F	A B C D E F	A B C D E F	A B C D E F
Y Y N N N N	Y N Y N N N	Y N N Y N N	Y N N N Y N	Y N N N N Y

A B C D E F	A B C D E F	A B C D E F	A B C D E F	A B C D E F
N Y Y N N N	N Y N Y N N	N Y N N Y N	N Y N N N Y	N N Y Y N N

A B C D E F	A B C D E F	A B C D E F	A B C D E F	A B C D E F
N N Y N Y N	N N Y N N Y	N N N Y Y N	N N N Y N Y	N N N N Y Y

The number of ways of selecting 2 objects out of 6 is denoted by $\binom{6}{2}$.

From Pascal's triangle, $\binom{6}{2} = 15$.

The number of ways of selecting r objects from n is denoted by $\binom{n}{r}$.

A9 (a) Write down rows 7 and 8 of Pascal's triangle.

(b) Hence write down the value of

(i) $\binom{7}{3}$ (ii) $\binom{7}{5}$ (iii) $\binom{8}{4}$

A10 (a) Explain why $\binom{10}{3} = \binom{10}{7}$

(b) Explain why $\binom{n}{n-r} = \binom{n}{r}$

Another notation for $\binom{n}{r}$ is $_nC_r$ (or ^nC_r). (The C stands for 'combinations', another word for selections.) Your calculator should have have an $_nC_r$ key.

To find, say, $\binom{9}{3}$, enter 9, press $_nC_r$, enter 3, then press $=$.

The next example shows how values of $\binom{n}{r}$ are used to work out probabilities.

Example 1

A coin is tossed 7 times. Find the probability of getting exactly 3 heads.

Solution

One way of getting 3 heads is HHHTTTT. The probability of this is $\left(\frac{1}{2}\right)^7$.

Other ways are HTHHTTT, HHTHTTT, and so on. Each has the probability $\left(\frac{1}{2}\right)^7$.

There are $\binom{7}{3}$ ways altogether.

So P(3 heads) $= \binom{7}{3} \times \left(\frac{1}{2}\right)^7 = 35 \times \frac{1}{128} = \frac{35}{128}$.

Exercise A (answers p 165)

1 A coin is tossed six times.

   (a) How many ways are there of getting exactly four heads?

   (b) What is the probability of each of these ways (for example HTHTHH)?

   (c) What is the probability of getting exactly four heads?

2 An ordinary pack of 52 playing cards is cut at random seven times.
The outcome can be 'red' (diamonds or hearts) or 'black' (clubs or spades).
Find the probability that the outcome is red on exactly four occasions.

3 Assume that boy and girl births are equally likely and that the sex of a child is independent of the sex of previous children.
Find the probability that in a family of five children

   (a) none is a boy   **(b)** one is a boy   **(c)** two are boys

   (d) three are boys   **(e)** four are boys   **(f)** there are more girls than boys

4 A coin is tossed six times.

   (a) Find, as a fraction, the probability of getting

      (i) no heads   **(ii)** one head   **(iii)** two heads

   (b) The number of heads, H, is a discrete random variable which can take the values 0, 1, 2, 3, 4, 5, 6.
Copy and complete this table to show the probability distribution of H.

h	0	1	2	3	4	5	6
$P(H = h)$							

B Unequal probabilities

In every case looked at so far, there have been two possible outcomes (left or right, yes or no, and so on) each with probability $\frac{1}{2}$.

In this section we look at cases where there are still two possible outcomes, but with unequal probabilities. For example, if an ordinary dice is rolled, we can consider the possible outcomes as either a six, with probability $\frac{1}{6}$, or not a six, with probability $\frac{5}{6}$.

Example 2

An ordinary dice is rolled 5 times. Find the probability that it shows six exactly 3 times.

Solution

Let S stand for 'six' and N for 'not a six'. One way of getting 3 sixes is SSSNN.

The probability of this particular outcome is $\left(\frac{1}{6}\right)^3 \times \left(\frac{5}{6}\right)^2$.

The probability of each other outcome with 3 sixes and and 2 non-sixes is also $\left(\frac{1}{6}\right)^3 \times \left(\frac{5}{6}\right)^2$.

There are $\binom{5}{3}$ different ways of getting 3 sixes and 2 non-sixes.

So P(3 sixes in 5 rolls) $= \binom{5}{3} \times \left(\frac{1}{6}\right)^3 \times \left(\frac{5}{6}\right)^2 = 0.0322$ (to 3 s.f.)

Exercise B (answers p 166)

1 An ordinary dice is rolled three times. Find the probability of getting

(a) a six on the first two rolls but not on the third

(b) a six on any two rolls and a non-six on the other

2 A fair tetrahedral dice has four faces. One is red and the other three are black. The dice is rolled five times. Find the probability that the dice shows red

(a) three times   (b) four times   (c) at least three times

3 A box contains two red counters and three white counters. A counter is picked at random from the box and then replaced. This is done six times. Find the probability that a red counter is picked

(a) three times   (b) four times   (c) five times

4 An ordinary pack of 52 playing cards is cut at random eight times.

(a) Find the probability of cutting diamonds

(i) never   (ii) once   (iii) twice   (iv) three times

(b) Hence find the probability of cutting diamonds more than three times.

5 An ordinary dice is rolled five times. The number of sixes, S, is a discrete random variable. Copy and complete this table for the probability distribution of S.

s	0	1	2	3	4	5
$P(S = s)$						

C Using the binomial distribution (answers p 166)

The cases we have looked at so far can be described as follows.

A given number of 'trials' are carried out (for example, rolling a dice five times).

There are two possible outcomes of each trial: call them 'success' and 'failure' (for example, 'success' could mean 'getting a six').

The trials are independent of each other and the probability of success is the same in every trial.

Suppose the number of trials is n and the probability of success in each trial is p. When you know the values of n and p, you can work out the probability of getting a given number of successes.

Example 3

Given that the number n of independent trials is 5, and the probability p of success in each trial is 0.4, find the probability of getting 3 successes.

Solution

The probability of failure $= 1 - p = 0.6$.

One way to get 3 successes is SSSFF (S = success and F = failure).
The probability of this particular outcome is $(0.4)^3 \times (0.6)^2$.

The probability of each other outcome with 3 successes and 2 failures is also $(0.4)^3 \times (0.6)^2$.

There are $\binom{5}{3}$ different ways of getting 3 successes and 2 failures.

So P(3 successes) $= \binom{5}{3} \times (0.4)^3 \times (0.6)^2 = 0.230$ (to 3 s.f.)

C1 The number of successes in the example above is a discrete random variable, X, which can take the values 0, 1, 2, 3, 4, 5.
You have already seen that $P(X = 3) = 0.230$ (to 3 s.f.).
Find the other values of $P(X = x)$ and show the probability distribution of X in a table.

x	0	1	2	3	4	5
$P(X = x)$				0.230		

(The probabilities may not add up to 1 exactly because of rounding errors.)

C2 Change the values of n and p to $n = 4$ and $p = 0.8$.
Let X denote the number of successes.
Calculate the values of $P(X = x)$ for $x = 0, 1, 2, 3$ and 4 and show the probability distribution of X in a table.

x	0	1	2	3	4
$P(X = x)$					

D

C3 What is the general formula for the probability of getting x successes in n trials when the probability of success in each trial is p?

K The set-up we have been working with is called the **binomial probability model**.
It is defined as follows.

- A given number, n, of independent trials are carried out.
- Each trial has two possible outcomes: success (probability p) or failure (probability $1 - p$).

The number of successes, X, is a discrete random variable whose probability distribution
is given by the formula

$$P(X = x) = \binom{n}{x} p^x (1 - p)^{n - x}.$$

This distribution is called the **binomial distribution with parameters n and p**.

'Parameters' are values which need to be given in order to define the distribution completely.

The words in bold are abbreviated as B(n, p).
'X follows the binomial distribution with $n = 7$ and $p = 0.2$' is written '$X \sim$ B(7, 0.2)'.

Here are two examples of binomial distributions shown graphically.

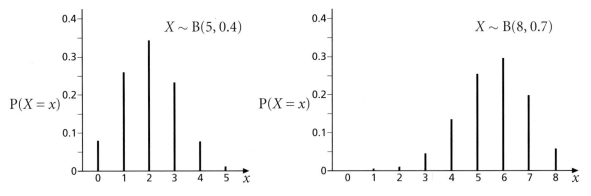

Example 4

The probability that a Glo-brite light bulb is still working after 1000 hours of use is 0.3.
Six new Glo-brite bulbs are installed. Find the probability that exactly four of them are
working after 1000 hours of use. (Assume that the bulbs behave independently.)

Solution

Each of the six bulbs is a 'trial', so $n = 6$.
'Success' means 'still working after 1000 hours', so $p = 0.3$.

Let X be the number of bulbs working after 1000 hours. Then X is B(6, 0.3).

So $\quad P(X = x) = \binom{6}{x} \times (0.3)^x \times (0.7)^{6 - x}$

$\quad\quad P(X = 4) = \binom{6}{4} \times (0.3)^4 \times (0.7)^2 = 0.0595$ (to 3 s.f.)

Example 5

In a large population of animals it is known that the proportion of males is 45%.
A random sample of 10 animals is selected.
Calculate the probability that the sample contains exactly 3 males.

Solution

The population is described as 'large'. This means you can assume that the
proportion of males is altered so little when a few animals are taken out that
you can treat it as constant. So the probability of picking a male is always 0.45.

The number of males in the sample is B(10, 0.45).

So P(3 males) = $\binom{10}{3}(0.45)^3(0.55)^7 = 0.166$ (to 3 s.f.)

Exercise C (answers p 166)

1 A six-sided dice is loaded (biased) so that the probability of getting a six is 0.1.
The dice is rolled 5 times.
Calculate the probability of getting three sixes.

2 In a large population of animals of a certain type, it is known that 35% have
black fur and the rest brown fur.
Four of the animals are caught at random.
Find the probability that two have black fur and two brown fur.
(You may assume that the population is so large that the percentage with
black fur is not changed when a few animals are taken out.)

3 A test has eight questions, with yes or no answers.
James takes the test but spins a coin to decide each of his answers, so the
probability of a correct answer to each question is $\frac{1}{2}$.
Calculate the probability that he gets exactly four correct answers.

4 Records show that on the island of Notascorcha it rains on 70% of days.
Why might it be inappropriate to use the binomial model to find the
probability that it rains on five out of the seven days in a week?

*5 In a large population of animals, males and females are in the ratio $3:2$.
30% of the animals are susceptible to a certain disease.
This susceptibility is independent of the animal's sex.

(a) What is the probability that an animal chosen at random is a male
that is susceptible to the disease?

(b) A sample of ten animals is selected at random from the population.
Calculate the probability that three of these animals are males susceptible
to the disease.

D Using tables of the binomial distribution (answers p 166)

Often in problems it is necessary to find the sum of a number of individual probabilities. For example, suppose you want to find the probability of getting 3 or fewer successes in 6 trials where the probability of success is 0.3.

Here is the binomial distribution for $n = 6$ and $p = 0.3$.

$n = 6$	x	0	1	2	3	4	5	6
$p = 0.3$	$P(X = x)$	0.1176	0.3026	0.3241	0.1852	0.0596	0.0102	0.0007

The probability of getting 3 or fewer successes is found by adding:
$$P(X = 0) + P(X = 1) + P(X = 2) + P(X = 3) = 0.1176 + 0.3026 + 0.3241 + 0.1852 = 0.9295$$
This is a **cumulative** probability. It is the probability that $X \leq 3$ or, in symbols, $P(X \leq 3)$.

Here is the complete table of cumulative probabilities.

$n = 6$	x	0	1	2	3	4	5	6
$p = 0.3$	$P(X \leq x)$	0.1176	0.4202	0.7443	0.9295	0.9891	0.9993	1.0000

p	0.01	0.25	0.30	0.35	0.40	0.45	0.50	p
x	$n = 6$							x
0	0.9415	0.1780	0.1176	0.0754	0.0467	0.0277	0.0156	0
1	0.9985	0.5339	0.4202	0.3191	0.2333	0.1636	0.1094	1
2	0.100	0.8306	0.7443	0.6471	0.5443	0.4415	0.3438	2
3		0.9624	0.9295	0.8826	0.8208	0.7447	0.6563	3
		0.9954	0.9891	0.9777	0.9590	0.9308	0.8906	4
		0.9998	0.9993	0.9982	0.9959	0.9917	0.9844	5
		1.0000	1.0000	1.0000	1.0000	1.0000	1.0000	6

Tables of cumulative binomial probabilities are provided in a booklet for AS/A2 exams and are on pages 148–153 of this book. There is a separate table for each value of n. Values of p are printed across the page and the cumulative probabilities down the page.

You can use these tables to find $P(X = x)$ for individual values of x, or probabilities like $P(2 \leq X \leq 4)$, as the next example shows.

Example 6

Use the table of cumulative probabilities for $n = 6$, $p = 0.3$ to find
(a) $P(X = 3)$ (b) $P(2 \leq X \leq 4)$ (c) $P(X \geq 4)$

Solution

(a) *The table tells you that* $P(X = 0, 1, 2 \text{ or } 3) = 0.9295$ *and that* $P(X = 0, 1 \text{ or } 2) = 0.7443$. $P(X = 3)$ *is the difference between these.*
$$P(X = 3) = P(X \leq 3) - P(X \leq 2) = 0.9295 - 0.7443 = 0.1852$$

(b) *The inequality* $2 \leq X \leq 4$ *means the values* 2, 3, 4. *The table tells you that* $P(X = 0, 1, 2, 3 \text{ or } 4) = 0.9891$ *and that* $P(X = 0 \text{ or } 1) = 0.4202$. $P(2 \leq X \leq 4)$ *is the difference between these.*
$$P(2 \leq X \leq 4) = P(X \leq 4) - P(X \leq 1) = 0.9891 - 0.4202 = 0.5689$$

(c) *The inequality* $X \geq 4$ *means the values* 4, 5, 6. *The table tells you that* $P(X = 0, 1, 2, 3, 4, 5 \text{ or } 6) = 1$ *(which is obvious!) and that* $P(X = 0, 1, 2 \text{ or } 3) = 0.9295$.
$$P(X \geq 4) = 1 - P(X \leq 3) = 1 - 0.9295 = 0.0705.$$

D1 Use the table for $n = 6$ and $p = 0.35$ on the opposite page to find

    (a) $P(X = 2)$ **(b)** $P(1 \leq X \leq 4)$ **(c)** $P(X \geq 3)$ **(d)** $P(X < 3)$

In the tables, the values of p go up to 0.5. If p is greater than this, then you need to find the probability of a failure $(1 - p)$ and think about the number of failures.

For example, suppose there are 6 trials and the probability of a success in each trial is 0.8. If X is the number of successes, then the number of failures is $6 - X$. Call this Y. Y has the binomial distribution with $n = 6$ and $p = 1 - 0.8 = 0.2$, so is in the tables.

Then, for example, $P(X = 2) = P(Y = 4)$.

Similarly, $P(2 \leq X \leq 5) = P(1 \leq Y \leq 4)$, as this diagram shows.

X	0	1	2	3	4	5	6
Y	6	5	4	3	2	1	0

Example 7

A fair octahedral dice has eight faces. Six faces are red and the other two are white. The dice is rolled 10 times. Find the probability that it shows red at least 4 times.

Solution

The probability of red in each trial is $\frac{6}{8} = 0.75$. As this is greater than 0.5, use $p = 0.25$ and the number W of whites, so $W \sim B(10, 0.25)$ (*Binomial, with $n = 10, p = 0.25$*).

'At least 4 reds' is equivalent to '$W \leq 6$'.
P(at least 4 reds) $= P(W \leq 6) = 0.9965$ (from tables).

red	0	1	2	3	4	5	6	7	8	9	10
white	10	9	8	7	6	5	4	3	2	1	0

Exercise D (answers p 166)

Where possible, use the statistical tables on pages 148–153 to help answer these questions.

  1 A coin is spun 12 times. Find the probability of getting fewer than 3 heads.

  2 The probability that a person, picked at random, is left-handed is about 0.1. Find the probability that in a group of 8 people picked at random the number of left-handed people is   **(a)** 4 or more   **(b)** 2 or 3   **(c)** less than 2

  3 A manufacturer of balloons produces 40 per cent that are oval and 60 per cent that are round. Packets of 20 balloons may be assumed to contain random samples of balloons. Determine the probability that such a packet contains

    (a) an equal number of oval balloons and round balloons

    (b) fewer oval balloons than round balloons

    A customer selects packets of 20 balloons at random from a large consignment until she finds a packet with exactly 12 round balloons.

    (c) Give a reason why a binomial distribution is **not** an appropriate model for the number of packets selected.   AQA 2002

  4 70% of a large population of animals are infected with a disease. A random sample of 20 animals is selected. Find the probability that the sample contains

    (a) more than 15 infected animals   **(b)** fewer than 10 infected animals

5 Dwight, a clerical worker, is employed by a benefits agency to calculate the weekly payments due to unemployed adults claiming benefit. These payments vary according to personal circumstances. During the first week of his employment, the probability that he calculates a payment incorrectly is 0.25 for each payment.

  (a) Given that Dwight calculates 40 payments during his first week of employment, find the probability that

   (i) five or fewer are incorrect   (ii) more than 30 are **correct**

  (b) A random sample of 40 payments is taken from those calculated by Dwight during his first **year** of employment. Give a reason why a binomial distribution may not provide a suitable model for the number of incorrect payments in the sample.

AQA 2001

6 The proportions of people with blood groups O, A, B and AB in a particular population are in the ratio 48:35:12:5 respectively.
Determine the probability that a random sample of 20 people from the population contains

  (a) exactly 10 with blood group O   (b) at most 2 with blood group AB

  (c) at least 8 with blood group A

AQA 2003

E Mean, variance, standard deviation (answers p 166)

Suppose a dice is loaded so that the probability of getting a six is 0.3.
The number of sixes, X, in 5 rolls of the dice follows B(5, 0.3).
The probability distribution of X is shown in the following table and graph.

$X \sim B(5, 0.3)$

x	0	1	2	3	4	5
$P(X = x)$	0.1681	0.3601	0.3087	0.1323	0.0284	0.0024

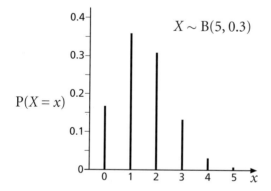

The mean of a discrete random variable was defined in the previous chapter (page 56).
The mean, μ, of the distribution above is given by

$$\mu = \Sigma x \times P(X = x)$$

$$= 0 \times 0.1681 \ + \ 1 \times 0.3601 \ + \ 2 \times 0.3087 \ + \ ... \ + \ 5 \times 0.0024$$

E1 Complete the calculation of μ.
For this distribution, $n = 5$ and $p = 0.3$. You should find that $\mu = np$.

6 Normal distribution

In this chapter you will
- learn about the properties of a normal distribution
- solve problems using tables of the normal distribution function
- meet some other examples of continuous probability distributions

A Proportions (answers p 167)

One advantage of using quartiles as a measure of spread is that we know that 25% of the population lies between the median and each of the upper and lower quartiles.

In the following investigation the proportions of data that lie in ranges defined by the mean and standard deviation will be considered.

A1 The set of data below shows the weights of 100 2p coins, in grams. This stem-and-leaf diagram displays the values of the second decimal place in two rows to show the distribution more clearly.

```
6.8 | 0
    | 6
6.9 | 2 4
    | 5 6 7 8 8 9
7.0 | 0 0 0 1 1 1 3 4 4 4
    | 5 5 5 5 5 6 6 7 7 7 8 8 8 8 9 9 9 9 9
7.1 | 0 0 0 0 1 1 1 1 1 1 1 1 2 2 2 2 2 3 3 3 4 4 4
    | 5 5 5 6 6 6 7 7 7 7 7 8 8 8 8 8 9 9 9 9
7.2 | 0 0 1 2 2 2 3 4 4
    | 5 6 6 7 9 9
7.3 | 1 4
    | 
7.4 | 0
```

Key	
7.3 | 4	stands for 7.34

(Mean = 7.117 g; standard deviation = 0.099 g)

(a) In this case one standard deviation above the mean is $7.117 + 0.099 = 7.216$. Verify that 34% of this distribution is between the mean and one standard deviation above the mean. What percentage lies between the mean and one standard deviation below the mean?

(b) What percentage of the data lies between 1 and 2 standard deviations above the mean? What percentage lies between 1 and 2 standard deviations below the mean?

(c) Find the percentages that lie between 2 and 3 standard deviations above and below the mean.

(d) What percentage lies more than 3 standard deviations from the mean in each direction?

A2 Use your results from A1 to complete the following table.

Standard deviations from the mean							
< –3	–3 to –2	–2 to –1	–1 to 0	0 to 1	1 to 2	2 to 3	> 3
				34%			

Comment on the results.

A3 This set of data shows the IQ scores of 120 students at a school.

```
 6 | 3

 7 | 1 2
   | 5
 8 | 1 2 4 4
   | 5 6 6 8 8
 9 | 0 0 0 1 1 1 2 3 4 4 4
   | 5 5 5 6 6 6 7 8 8 8 9 9
10 | 0 0 0 1 1 2 2 2 3 4 4 4 4 4
   | 5 5 5 5 6 6 7 7 7 7 8 8 8 9 9 9
11 | 0 0 0 1 1 1 2 2 2 3 4 4 4 4
   | 5 5 6 6 7 7 7 8 8 8 9 9 9
12 | 0 0 0 1 1 2 3 3 4 4
   | 5 5 5 6 8 8 9 9 9
13 | 0 1 1 1 3
   | 5 7
14 | 3
```

14 | 3   means an IQ of 143

(Mean = 107.4; standard deviation = 15.2)

(a) Complete a table like the one in A2 for this set of data.

(b) Compare the values in this table with the ones in A2.

A4 This data shows the time in minutes that 80 cars stayed in a bay with a one-hour parking limit during one day.

```
0 | 2 2 3 3 4 4 6 6 7 7 8
1 | 0 0 0 0 1 1 1 2 2 3 4 4 5 6 7
2 | 0 3 3 4 4 4 5 5 5 5 8 8 8
3 | 0 0 0 0 2 2 2 4 4 5 6 7 9
4 | 0 2 4 4 5 5 6 6 6 7 8 8 9 9
5 | 1 2 2 2 3 3 4 6 6 6 7 7 8 9
```

5 | 1   means 51 minutes

(Mean = 30.0; standard deviation = 17.6)

(a) Complete a table like the one in A2 for this set of data.

(b) Compare the values in this table with the ones for the two previous sets of data.

Here is part of the standard normal table.

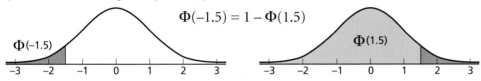

z	0.00	0.01	0.02	0.03	0.04	0.05	0.06
0.0	0.50000	0.50399	0.50798	0.51197	0.51595	0.51994	0.5239
0.1	0.53983	0.54380	0.54776	0.55172	0.55567	0.55962	0.5635
0.2	0.57926	0.58317	0.58706	0.59095	0.59483	0.59871	0.60257
0.3	0.61791	0.62172	0.62552	0.62930	0.63307	0.63683	0.6405

$\Phi(0.24)$

Values of $\Phi(z)$ are not given for negative values of z, because they can be found by subtraction using the symmetry of the curve.

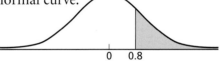

$$\Phi(-1.5) = 1 - \Phi(1.5)$$

$\Phi(-1.5)$ $\Phi(1.5)$

Example 2

Use the table to find the area shaded under this standard normal curve.

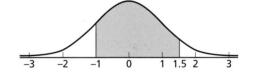

Solution

From the table, $\Phi(0.8) = 0.788\,14$

Area $= 1 - 0.788\,14 = 0.211\,86$

Example 3

Use the table to find the area shaded here.

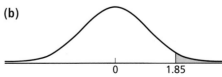

Solution

From the table, $\Phi(1.50) = 0.933\,19$

$\Phi(-1.00) = 1 - \Phi(1.00) = 1 - 0.841\,34 = 0.158\,66$

Shaded area $= \Phi(1.50) - \Phi(-1.00) = 0.933\,19 - 0.158\,66 = 0.774\,53$

Exercise B (answers p 168)

1 Use the table to find the areas shaded under these standard normal curves.

(a)

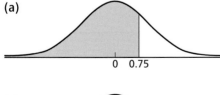

0   0.75

(b)

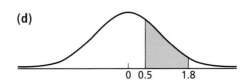

0   1.85

(c)

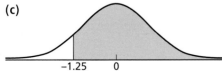

−1.25   0

(d)

0   0.5   1.8

2 Draw sketches showing the probability that Z lies in each of these ranges. Use the table to find each probability.

   (a) $0 < Z < 1.8$ **(b)** $1.25 < Z < 3.5$ **(c)** $-1.5 < Z < 0.85$ **(d)** $-2.43 < Z < -1.06$

3 Use the table to find, to two decimal places, the value of z for which

   (a) $\Phi(z) = 0.95$ **(b)** $\Phi(z) = 0.9$ **(c)** $\Phi(z) = 0.99$ **(d)** $\Phi(z) = 0.75$

4 Use the table to find, as accurately as you can, the value of z in these diagrams.

(a)

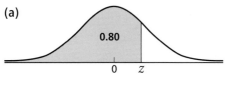

(b)

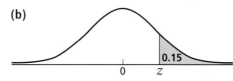

(c)

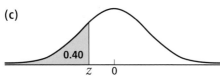

(d)

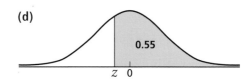

C Solving problems

The word 'normal' is a technical term, not a judgement, when it refers to a distribution. It does not imply that other distributions are 'abnormal'.

Once we know, or can assume, that a normal distribution is an appropriate model for a set of data, and we know the mean and standard deviation, the proportion or probability for any given interval can be found.

Coin-operated machines rely on coins being a certain weight. The weights of 2p coins are known to be normally distributed with mean 7 g and standard deviation 0.1 g.

If W is the weight of a 2p coin, the distribution of W is shown here.

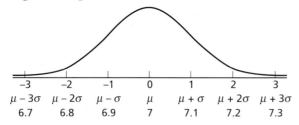

A particular machine rejects coins if they weigh less than 6.85 g.
If we want to know the probability of a randomly chosen coin being rejected then we need to find $P(W < 6.85)$.

To relate the value 6.85 g to the standard normal distribution we need to know how many standard deviations below the mean this is. This is found by calculating
$$\frac{6.85 - 7}{0.1} = -1.5,$$ so 6.85 is 1.5 standard deviations below the mean.

The diagram above confirms this.

K The variable $\dfrac{W - \mu}{\sigma}$ is the **standard normal variable** corresponding to

the random variable W. A standard normal variable is always denoted by Z.

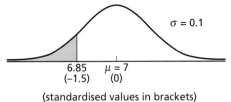

σ = 0.1

6.85 $\mu = 7$
(−1.5)   (0)

(standardised values in brackets)

Finding $P(W < 6.85)$ is the same as finding $P(Z < -1.5)$.

$\Phi(1.5) = 0.933\,19$ (from tables)

$P(Z < -1.5) = \Phi(-1.5)$
$\qquad\qquad = 1 - \Phi(1.5)$
$\qquad\qquad = 1 - 0.933\,19 = 0.066\,81$

That is, roughly 7% of 2p coins will be rejected.

K A normal distribution is completely specified when two **parameters**, the mean (μ) and the standard deviation (σ), are known.

If a variable X has a distribution which is modelled by a normal probability distribution, and has mean μ and standard deviation σ, then this is denoted by

$$X \sim N(\mu, \sigma^2)$$

(Note that the variance is given, not the standard deviation).

The distribution of the weights in grams of the 2p coins can be denoted by $W \sim N(7, 0.01)$.

Example 4

The length of life, in months, of a type of hair-dryer is approximately normally distributed with mean 90 months and standard deviation 15 months.
Each dryer is sold with a 5 year guarantee.
What proportion of dryers fail before their guarantee expires?

Solution

If T is the life of a dryer in months, then $T \sim N(90, 15^2)$.

5 years is 60 months, so we require $P(T < 60)$.

The standardised value for 60 is

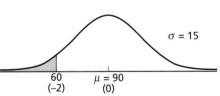

σ = 15

60   $\mu = 90$
(−2)   (0)

$\dfrac{60 - 90}{15} = -2$ s.d.s from the mean

From tables $\Phi(2.0) = 0.977\,25$.
The probability needed here is shown by the shaded area.

$P(T < 60) = P(Z < -2) = 1 - 0.977\,25 = 0.022\,75$

So we would expect 2.3% of dryers to fail before their guarantee expires.

Note that when finding probabilities it does not matter whether you find
$P(X < n)$ or $P(X \le n)$ since the probability of getting an exact value is 0.

Exercise C (answers p 168)

In each of the following questions, assume that the variable is normally distributed.

1 The lifetime of a type of battery has a mean of 10 hours with standard deviation 2 hours. What proportion of batteries have a lifetime

(a) greater than 15 hours

(b) between 8 and 12 hours

2 A machine turns out bolts of mean diameter 1.5 cm and standard deviation 0.01 cm. If bolts measuring over 1.52 cm are rejected as oversize, what proportion are rejected in this way?

3 IQ tests for young people are designed so that nationally they have a mean of 100 and a standard deviation of 15.
What percentage of children have an IQ of 132 or more?

4 A machine produces bags of sugar which have mean weight 1.5 kg and standard deviation 0.01 kg. What is the probability of producing a bag of sugar which weighs less than 1.475 kg?

5 The mean lifespan for a species of locust is 28 days with standard deviation 5 days. What is the probability of a locust surviving

(a) for longer than 31 days

(b) for longer than 24 days

6 Simply More Pure margarine is sold in tubs with a mean weight of 500 g and standard deviation 4 g.
What proportion of tubs weigh between 498.5 g and 500.5 g?

7 The heights of girls in a particular year group have mean 154.2 cm and standard deviation 5.1 cm.
What percentage of the girls are between 150 cm and 155 cm tall?

8 At the end of a course, students are given a mark based on their assignments during the course. The marks are found to have a mean of 82 and a standard deviation of 12. The students are awarded a certificate according to these rules:

Distinction	above 110
Credit	over 90 and up to 110
Pass	over 60 and up to 90
Fail	60 or less

(a) Find the probability of a student being awarded each type of certificate.

(b) If there are 90 students on the course, how many certificates of each type are awarded?

D Further problems (answers p 168)

Sometimes a problem requires the normal distribution to be used 'in reverse': the probability or proportion is given and the corresponding value is required.

For example, a manufacturer fills cans with beans. The weight of beans in a can is normally distributed with mean 250 g and standard deviation 10 g. The manufacturer is required to quote a weight on the cans such that 90% of all cans contain that weight or more.

We require z such that $\Phi(z) = 0.90$. The table for $\Phi(z)$ could be scanned to find the nearest probability to 0.90. However, since reverse use is common, a table is also produced of **percentage points** of the standard normal distribution for frequently used percentages.

The percentage points table shows for a given probability p, the value of z such that $P(Z < z) = p$.

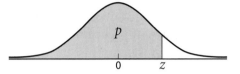

This is part of the table supplied for the exam and printed on page 155 of this book.

p	0.00	0.01	0.02	0.03
0.5	0.0000	0.0251	0.0502	0.0
0.6	0.2533	0.2793	0.3055	0.33
0.7	0.5244	0.5534	0.5828	0.612
0.8	0.8416	0.8779	0.9154	0.95
0.9	1.2816	1.3408	1.4051	1.4

This says that the probability of being less than 1.2816 s.d.s above the mean is 0.90.

In the beans example, to ensure that 90% of all cans contain more than the given amount, the stated weight must be 1.28 standard deviations below the mean.

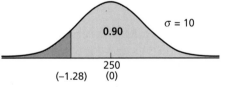

The stated weight must therefore be
$250 - (1.28 \times 10) = 237.2\,\text{g}$.

D1 The sales achieved by a group of insurance workers were found to be normally distributed with mean £35 000 and standard deviation £1500. Those in the top 5% of sales are to be given a bonus. What sales must someone have achieved to get the bonus?

D2 The heights of a group of boys are known to be normally distributed with mean 174 cm and standard deviation 8 cm. Give an interval, symmetrical about the mean, within which 90% of the heights of these boys lie.

In any problem involving the normal distribution, there are always four quantities:

- the mean of the distribution
- the standard deviation or the variance of the distribution
- a given value or values of the variable
- a probability or proportion

In any problem you will be given some of these quantities and asked to find others. The following examples show some of the variations.

Example 5

A machine produces packages with standard deviation 8 g. The mean can be adjusted to any given value. The company requires the machine to be set so that only 2.5% of packets weigh less than the weight stated on the packet, 250 g. To what mean weight must the machine be set?

Solution

The larger area is $1 - 0.025 = 0.975$.
From the percentage points table, for $p = 0.975$, $z = 1.96$.

To have only 2.5% of packets below 250 g requires this value to be 1.96 standard deviations below the mean.

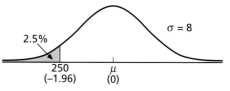

So $\mu = 250 + (1.96 \times 8) = 265.68$.
So the machine must be set to give a mean weight of 265.68 g.

Example 6

A salmon farm has a large population of fish whose weights are known to be normally distributed. However, the mean and standard deviation of the weights are not known. A large number of fish were netted and it was found that 4% of these weighed less than 3 kg, and 2.3% weighed more than 6 kg. Use this information to estimate the mean and standard deviation of the salmon.

Solution

Sketch the details.

At the lower tail the percentage points table gives, for $p = 0.96$, $z = 1.75(07)$.

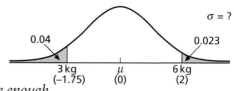

At the upper tail the percentage points table is not accurate enough.
However, you can search in the body of the standard normal tables. $\Phi(2.0) = 0.977(25)$

So 3 kg is 1.75 s.d.s below the mean, giving $\quad \mu - 1.75\sigma = 3 \qquad (1)$
And 6 kg is 2 s.d.s above the mean, giving $\quad \mu + 2\sigma = 6 \qquad (2)$

Subtract equation (1) from (2). $\qquad 3.75\sigma = 3 \Rightarrow \sigma = 3 \div 3.75 = 0.8$
Use equation (2). $\qquad \mu + 1.6 = 6 \Rightarrow \mu = 4.4$

So the fish have an approximate mean weight 4.4 kg and standard deviation 0.8 kg.

The packers' rules

The normal distribution is important to manufacturers, who must meet quality control regulations.

When you buy items with a given weight or volume you may have noticed an 'e' symbol in front of the amount. This means that the amount is an 'average quantity' and companies are bound by law to follow the 'packers' rules' for this average. These state that:

- The actual contents of packages must on average be the stated amount.

- No more than 2.5% may be 'non-standard', that is less than the given amount minus the tolerable negative error (TNE). The TNE depends on the size of the packet.

- No package may be 'inadequate', that is more than two TNEs less than the stated amount.

The TNE for a packet labelled 'e125 g' is $4\frac{1}{2}$% so a manufacturer would need to make sure that only 2.5% of packets weighed less than 119.375 g (125 less 4.5%).

Weights and volumes in containers, weights of mass-produced items and other measures in manufacturing often follow a normal distribution.

Exercise D (answers p 169)

In each of the following questions, assume that the variable is normally distributed.

1 The marks in an examination have mean 47 and standard deviation 12. The top 15% are to be awarded an A grade. What mark must be achieved in order to gain an A grade?

2 A machine packing bags of sugar fills them with a weight whose standard deviation is 0.0025 kg. To what value should the mean weight be set so that 90% of all bags are over 1 kg in weight?

3 The mean lifetime of a light bulb is 1500 hours with standard deviation 200 hours. The packaging must quote a guaranteed minimum lifetime. What value should be quoted so that 1% of all bulbs have a lifetime less than this minimum?

4 A machine fills bottles of oil with mean volume 265 ml and standard deviation 10 ml.
   (a) What proportion of bottles are filled with less than 250 ml?
   (b) An engineer claims he can reduce the standard deviation of the amount the bottles are filled with. What must the standard deviation be changed to so that 1 in 200 bottles have a volume less than 250 ml?

5 The time taken to fit a new exhaust on a car at Speedy's Exhausts was found to have mean 20 minutes and a standard deviation of 3 minutes.
   (a) What is the probability of it taking less than 15 minutes to fit an exhaust?
   (b) What is the fitting time that will only be exceeded on 10% of occasions?
   (c) At Superfast the standard deviation of fitting times is 4 minutes. The probability of it taking more than 10 minutes to fit an exhaust at Superfast is 0.9332. What is the mean fitting time at Superfast?

6 The mean length of a species of snake is 80 cm with standard deviation 7 cm. Give an interval which is symmetrical about the mean within which 95% of the lengths of these snakes lie.

7 In an examination, 10% of candidates scored more than 70 marks and 15% scored fewer than 35 marks. Find the mean and standard deviation.

8 A production process making bars of chocolate rejects any bars which weigh more than 165 g as too heavy and any weighing less than 140 g as too light. In a large batch of bars 5.5% were rejected as too heavy and 11.5% as too light. Find the mean and standard deviation of the weight of the chocolate bars.

*9 A machine produces ball bearings whose mean diameter is 224 mm with standard deviation 4 mm. The machine has a filter which removes ball bearings over a certain diameter.

    (a) If the largest 16% of ball bearings have been removed, what diameter has been specified?

    (b) Given that the largest 16% are removed, find the median diameter of the remaining ball bearings.

E Other continuous distributions

A random variable whose distribution is normal is an example of a **continuous random variable**.

The probability that the random variable takes a value within a given interval is shown by the area under a graph. In the case of a normally distributed variable, the graph has the shape shown here.

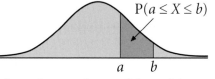

$P(a \leq X \leq b)$

Other types of continuous distribution with different shaped graphs are also useful models. To be a probability distribution the total area under the graph must be 1. The graph must also not drop below zero as this would give negative probabilities.

The diagram here shows the **uniform** or **rectangular** distribution over the interval $2 \leq x \leq 7$. The probability that the random variable lies in an interval of a given width is the same wherever the interval is chosen. For example $P(3 < X < 4) = P(5.5 < X < 6.5)$

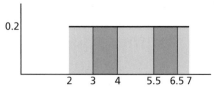

The height of the rectangle must be 0.2 to make the total area 1.

The distribution shown here is a **triangular** distribution.

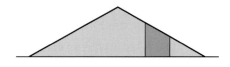

Key points

- The probability distribution of a continuous random variable is represented by a curve. The area under the curve in a given interval gives the probability of a value lying in that interval.   (p 77)

- If a variable X follows a normal probability distribution, with mean μ and standard deviation σ, we write $X \sim N(\mu, \sigma^2)$.   (p 81)

- The variable $Z = \dfrac{X - \mu}{\sigma}$ is called the standard normal variable corresponding to X. (p 81)

- If Z is a continuous random variable such that $Z \sim N(0, 1)$ then $\Phi(z) = P(Z < z)$. (p 78)

- The percentage points table shows, for a probability p, the value of z such that $P(Z < z) = p$.   (p 83)

Mixed questions (answers p 169)

1 The weight of pistachios put into bags by a machine is normally distributed with mean 265 g and standard deviation 7 g.
  What minimum weight should be quoted on the packets so that only 1 in 1000 packets weigh less than this value?

2 The volume of honey that a machine pours into a jar can be modelled by a normal distribution with mean 275 ml and standard deviation 15 ml.
  (a) What is the probability that the machine pours between 260 ml and 290 ml of honey into a jar?
  (b) The jars have a capacity of 300 ml. What is the probability that a jar is filled with more than 300 ml of honey and so overflows?
  (c) Ten filled jars of honey are randomly chosen from this machine. What is the probability that more than two of these have overflowed? (Hint: A binomial distribution is helpful here.)

3 (a) The diameter of a toad's blood corpuscles are thought to follow a normal distribution with mean 0.0158 mm and standard deviation 0.002 mm. What is the probability of a toad blood corpuscle having a diameter of less than 0.0155 mm?
  (b) The standard deviation of a frog's blood corpuscles is also 0.002 mm. In an experiment it was found that 26% of blood corpuscles from a frog were larger than 0.0155 mm. Find the mean diameter of a frog's blood corpuscle.

4 A soft drinks vending machine pours the chosen drink into a cup at the press of a button. The volume of drink poured follows a normal distribution with mean 475 ml and standard deviation 20 ml.

(a) Find the probability that the volume of drink delivered will be

(i) less than 480 ml

(ii) between 460 ml and 490 ml

(b) The cups that the drinks are poured into have a capacity of 500 ml. Find the probability that the amount of drink poured into a cup is greater than the capacity of the cup and so overflows.

(c) To reduce the problem of overflowing cups, an engineer can adjust the mean value that is poured. To what should the mean value be adjusted so that the probability of a cup overflowing is 0.001?

Test yourself (answers p 170)

1 The lengths of components produced by a particular machine may be modelled by a normal distribution with mean 901.0 mm and standard deviation 2.0 mm. Find the probability that the length of a randomly selected component will be less than 902.5 mm.
AQA 2002

2 The weights of bags of red gravel may be modelled by a normal distribution with mean 25.8 kg and standard deviation 0.5 kg.

(a) Determine the probability that a randomly selected bag of red gravel will weigh

(i) less than 25 kg

(ii) between 25.5 kg and 26.5 kg

(b) Determine, to two decimal places, the weight exceeded by 75% of bags.
AQA 2003

3 The number of miles that Anita's motorbike will travel on one gallon of petrol may be modelled by a normal distribution with mean 135 and standard deviation 12.

(a) Given that Anita starts a journey with one gallon of petrol in her motorbike's tank, find the probability that, without refuelling, she can travel

(i) more than 111 miles

(ii) between 141 and 150 miles

(b) Find the longest journey that Anita can undertake, if she is to have a probability of at least 0.9 of completing it on one gallon of petrol.
AQA 2002

4 The contents, in milligrams, of vitamin C in a litre carton of cranberry juice can be modelled by a normal distribution with a mean of 32 and a standard deviation of 2.

(a) Determine the probability that, for a carton chosen at random, the vitamin C content is less than 30 mg.

(b) Find, to the nearest milligram, the value of the mean required to ensure that the percentage of cartons with a vitamin C content of less than 30 mg is 2.5. AQA 2002

5 Kevin uses his mobile phone for X minutes each day.
X is a random variable which may be modelled by a normal distribution with mean 28 minutes and standard deviation 8 minutes.

  (a) Find the probability that on a particular day Kevin uses his mobile phone for

    (i) less than 30 minutes

    (ii) between 10 and 20 minutes

  (b) Calculate an interval, symmetrical about 28 minutes, within which X will lie on 80% of days.　　　　　　　　　　　　　　　　　　　AQA 2003

6 A steel rolling mill has two machines, A and B, for cutting steel bars.
For each machine the length of a cut bar can be modelled by a normal distribution.

  (a) Bars cut by machine A have a mean length of 1212 mm and a standard deviation of 5 mm.

    (i) Determine the probability that the length of a bar is greater than 1205 mm.

    (ii) Calculate the length exceeded, on average, by one bar in five hundred.

Bars with lengths less than 1200 mm are rejected as too short, and bars with lengths greater than 1225 mm are rejected as too long.

  (b) Of the bars cut by machine B, 1.5 per cent are rejected as too short and 1.9 per cent are rejected as too long.
Calculate, to one decimal place, the mean and standard deviation of the lengths of the bars cut by this machine.　　　　　　　　AQA 2002

7 (a) The time, X minutes, taken by Fred Fast to install a satellite dish may be assumed to be a normal random variable with mean 134 and standard deviation 16.

    (i) Determine $P(X < 150)$.

    (ii) Determine, to one decimal place, the time exceeded by 10 per cent of installations.

  (b) The time, Y minutes, taken by Sid Slow to install a satellite dish may be also be assumed to be a normal random variable, but with

$$P(Y < 170) = 0.14 \text{ and } P(Y > 200) = 0.03$$

Determine, to the nearest minute, values for the mean and standard deviation of Y.　　　　　　　　　　　　　　　　　　　AQA 2003

7 Estimation

In this chapter you will learn
- how population parameters are estimated from sample statistics
- about the sampling distribution of the mean of a sample from a normal distribution
- how and when to apply the central limit theorem
- how to find an unbiased estimator for the population variance

A The sampling distribution of the mean (answers p 171)

In most real-life applications of statistics there is a large **population** which we want to know something about. However, in most cases it is impossible to collect data for every individual in the population. A **sample** has to be taken from which inferences are made about the population.

If inferences are to be made about a population from a sample, it is vital that the sample is representative of the population. In this chapter a **simple random sample** will be assumed in every case. This involves using a method, such as random numbers, to choose the sample so that every individual has an equal chance of being selected. The use of random numbers is described on pages 7–8.

The heights of 150 male sixth-formers are shown below. The numbers on the rows and columns are to help you choose individuals from this population.

Heights of 150 male sixth-formers (cm)

	0	1	2	3	4	5	6	7	8	9
0	170.1	172.2	179.3	176.4	168.9	178.1	181.1	180.4	178.3	179.6
10	176.6	175.0	170.5	181.2	168.5	178.8	172.4	163.6	167.0	176.3
20	173.3	179.4	177.9	165.2	172.5	175.3	186.1	176.6	169.6	174.1
30	165.9	162.7	166.2	168.7	163.7	171.4	170.0	181.5	181.0	176.6
40	184.3	175.1	188.0	181.4	171.7	175.9	173.0	173.0	175.0	178.1
50	175.0	162.8	178.4	163.7	163.7	169.0	163.6	167.9	164.9	181.9
60	167.1	174.1	172.0	180.1	176.7	159.9	160.2	173.7	173.7	169.4
70	168.5	170.0	176.3	166.2	163.4	167.8	171.0	179.9	177.2	183.8
80	179.7	167.4	172.7	175.8	168.7	179.0	177.6	160.8	186.7	182.3
90	171.3	162.2	173.3	170.0	184.9	165.2	173.1	180.2	175.1	168.8
100	178.2	171.8	175.2	178.0	173.9	163.7	189.1	175.1	171.0	171.1
110	182.6	173.7	168.8	183.3	170.3	167.9	179.4	171.2	170.6	175.5
120	171.0	174.8	176.1	172.9	170.5	174.8	178.4	180.9	177.2	163.3
130	170.6	185.9	173.2	179.5	179.7	175.6	172.2	178.9	164.9	172.0
140	178.8	182.0	160.5	183.6	163.6	172.3	169.6	182.9	168.2	159.9

Student number 123

This bar chart shows that the distribution of students' heights appears to be approximately normal.

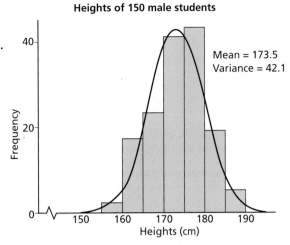

Heights of 150 male students

Mean = 173.5
Variance = 42.1

In this case, unlike in many statistical investigations, we have values for the whole population. The mean μ and variance σ^2 of the population can, therefore, be calculated exactly. In this case, $\mu = 173.5$ and $\sigma^2 = 42.1$.

In the investigations which follow we shall imagine that we do not have the whole population and will have to estimate the parameters μ and σ^2 from a sample. We will investigate how reliable such estimates from samples are.

The obvious way to estimate μ is to use the mean of a random sample.

A1 (a) Using random numbers from tables, a calculator or a spreadsheet, select a random sample of size 5 from the population of sixth-formers.

(b) Calculate the mean height of your sample.

(c) Collect at least 30 separate samples of size 5 by pooling together the results of your class and record the mean of each of the samples.

(d) Put the results in a grouped frequency table, using an interval of 5 cm, and use this to draw a bar chart.

(Keep a record of the five values in each sample. You will need them later in this chapter.)

You should have a set of results looking something like this.

Mean height	Frequency
$160 \leq x < 165$	1
$165 \leq x < 170$	5
$170 \leq x < 175$	13
$175 \leq x < 180$	10
$180 \leq x < 185$	1
Total	30

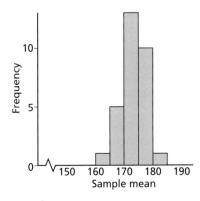

The frequency table and bar chart show the **distribution of the sample means** for random samples of size 5. The distribution is called the **sampling distribution** of sample means.

A2 What type of distribution do the sample means appear to follow?

A3 Calculate the mean and variance of your 30 or so sample means. Compare this mean with the population mean.

Your results from A1 to A3 should show that:

- The distribution of sample means is approximately normal.
- The mean of the distribution of the sample means is approximately equal to the population mean of 173.5.

This second point is very important. It says that on average using the sample mean as an estimator for the population mean will give an estimate close to the true value. So using the sample mean to estimate the population mean is a sensible thing to do.

> **K** A **statistic** is a quantity calculated from the values in a sample.
> A statistic can be used as an **estimator** of a parameter.
>
> If X is a random variable (in our example, X is the height of a student), then the mean of a sample of size n is also a random variable, denoted by $\overline{X}$.
>
> $\overline{X}$ is an **unbiased estimator** of the population mean μ because the mean of the distribution of $\overline{X}$ is μ, the parameter it is an estimator for.

A4 (a) Repeat A1 to A3 but using a sample of size 10.

(b) Does using a sample size of 10 still give an unbiased estimate of the population mean?

(c) In what way is the distribution of sample means using a sample of size 10 different from that with samples of size 5?

(Keep a record of the 10 values in each sample. You will need them later in this chapter.)

Whatever the size of the sample, the sample mean, $\overline{X}$, is always an unbiased estimator of the population mean, μ.

Exercise A (answers p 171)

1 A random sample of 12 students at a sixth-form college have their systolic blood pressure, in millimetres of mercury, measured with the following results.

111 120 125 115 108 114 124 133 128 124 98 107

Calculate an unbiased estimate for the mean blood pressure of all students in this college.

2 An entomologist wants to estimate the mean length of the population of a new species of beetle she has discovered. She captures a random sample of 15 beetles and measures their lengths, in millimetres, as

43 38 49 57 34 46 19 37 48 51 40 38 45 42 41

(a) Calculate an unbiased estimate for the mean length of this population of beetles.

(b) The following week she catches another sample with 40 beetles in it. She calculates the mean of the sample as 43.5 mm. Which of the two estimates would you say was the more reliable?

B Reliability of estimates (answers p 171)

Thirty random samples of size 20 were taken from the population of students' heights given in section A. These are the means of those samples.

177.0	174.6	174.1	172.2	172.3	175.0	175.1	173.8	176.4	171.4
173.1	173.9	172.8	171.2	171.5	174.7	174.6	172.8	172.6	172.3
171.4	173.7	174.1	173.8	174.4	173.7	173.2	173.2	172.5	170.9

(You could have generated samples and found their means yourself.)

B1 (a) Calculate the mean of these sample means.

(b) Calculate the variance of these sample means.

(c) Do you think that estimates of the mean using a sample of size 20 are more reliable than estimates using a sample of size 5 or 10? Give a reason.

The larger the sample used, then the more reliable $\overline{X}$ will be as an estimator of the population mean. This is because, as bigger samples are taken, the variance of the distribution of sample means becomes smaller.

B2 (a) Complete this table showing the variance of the distribution of sample means for each different size sample used so far.

Sample size	5	10	20
Variance of $\overline{X}$			

(b) The variance of the population in this case is 42.1. What appears to be the connection between this and the variance of the distribution of sample means, $\overline{X}$, for different sample sizes?

(c) If samples of size 40 were taken, what would you expect the variance of the distribution of sample means to be?

It can be shown that the variance of the distribution of sample means is equal to the population variance divided by the sample size.

When the mean of a sample of size n is used as an estimator of the mean of a population with known variance σ^2, then the variance of the distribution of sample means is $\dfrac{\sigma^2}{n}$.

The square root of this value, $\dfrac{\sigma}{\sqrt{n}}$, is usually referred to as the **standard error of the sample mean**. It is useful in comparing the reliability of estimates from different size samples.

In the example above the standard error for a sample of size 8 is $\sqrt{42.1 \div 8} = 2.29$.

The standard error for a sample of size 25 is $\sqrt{42.1 \div 25} = 1.30$.

An estimate based on a sample of size 25 has a smaller standard error than one based on a sample of size 8.

Example 1

An entomologist wants to know the mean wingspan, in mm, of a large population of moths of the species *Arctia caja* in a chalk pit. The wingspan of this species is known to have a variance of 8.4 in the population. She measures a sample of 12 moths and finds they have these wingspans, in mm.

43   47   41   39   38   50   44   45   49   40   41   42

(a) Estimate the mean wingspan of the population.

(b) Calculate the standard error of an estimate from a sample of size 12.

Solution

(a) From the data $\bar{x} = 43.25$ mm. This is an estimate of the population mean.

(b) The standard error for a sample of size 12 is $\dfrac{\sigma}{\sqrt{n}} = \dfrac{\sqrt{8.4}}{\sqrt{12}} = 0.837$ mm.

Exercise B (answers p 171)

1 A trout fishery knows that the fish it produces have weights, in grams, which are normally distributed with variance 14 400. In order to estimate the mean weight of a batch of fish, 12 trout are caught and weighed, in grams, as follows.

838 1123 1043 1141 1066 1123 1037 1042 873 928 1235 963

(a) Calculate an unbiased estimate of the mean of all the fish in this batch.

(b) Find the standard error of an estimate with this sample size.

2 A chicken farmer breeds two types of chicken. He wants to compare the mean weights of the large populations of each type that he has.

(a) He knows that the chickens of breed A have weights which are normally distributed with standard deviation 0.25 kg. He takes a random sample of 10 chickens and finds their weights, in kilograms, are

2.06 1.97 2.53 1.63 1.86 1.88 1.93 2.06 2.00 1.92

   (i) Calculate an unbiased estimate of the mean of this breed.

   (ii) Find the standard error of an estimate with this sample size.

(b) Chickens of breed B have weights which are normally distributed with standard deviation 0.32 kg. The farmer takes a random sample of 15 chickens. Their weights in kilograms are

2.33 2.36 2.38 3.04 2.61 2.30 2.52 2.20 2.71 2.63
1.76 2.39 2.52 2.54 1.85

   (i) Calculate an unbiased estimate of the mean of this breed.

   (ii) Find the standard error of this sampling process.

(c) Which of the two estimates of the population means is the more reliable? Give your reasons.

C Further problems

Summary of results

The investigations so far in this chapter suggest three facts about taking a random sample from a normal population and calculating the sample mean in order to estimate the population mean.

- The mean of the distribution of the sample means is equal to the mean of the population.
- The distribution of the sample means is approximately normal.
- The variance of the distribution of the sample means is equal to the population variance divided by the sample size.

These results are important in making inferences about sample means. They can be written more formally as:

K If random samples of size n are taken from a population which can be modelled by a normal distribution $N(\mu, \sigma^2)$ then we can assume three facts about the sampling distribution of the sample mean $\overline{X}$.

- The mean of the sampling distribution of $\overline{X}$ is μ.
- The variance of the sampling distribution of $\overline{X}$ is $\dfrac{\sigma^2}{n}$.
- The sampling distribution of $\overline{X}$ is a normal distribution.

These can be summarised as: if $X \sim N(\mu, \sigma^2)$ then $\overline{X} \sim N\left(\mu, \dfrac{\sigma^2}{n}\right)$.

The standard deviation is used when probabilities are found from a normal distribution. In the case of the sampling distribution the standard deviation is the standard error, $\dfrac{\sigma}{\sqrt{n}}$.

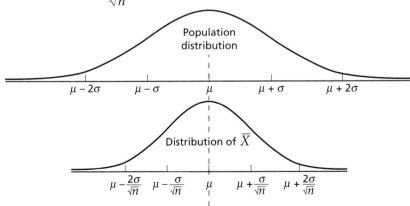

Problems involving sample means can be solved using the standard normal distribution and the tables published for it.

Example 2

The heights, in centimetres, of 150 sixth-form girls are normally distributed with mean 161.4 and variance 42.2. Random samples of size 10 are taken from this population. What percentage of samples of size 10 would have a mean greater than 165 cm?

Solution

Write down the distribution of the sample mean $\bar{X}$ and the standard error.

$\bar{X} \sim N\left(161.4, \frac{42.2}{10}\right)$

so the standard error of $\bar{X}$ is $\sqrt{4.22} = 2.05$ cm

Sketch the distribution.

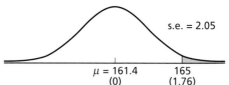

s.e. = 2.05

$\mu = 161.4$ 165
(0)   (1.76)

Standardise the height of 165 cm.

$z = \dfrac{165 - 161.4}{2.05} = \dfrac{3.6}{2.05}$

$= 1.76$ standard errors above the mean

Use tables to find the area to the left of 1.76.

$\Phi(1.76) = 0.960\,80$

Find $1 - \Phi(1.76)$ as the area >165 is required. Answer the question as posed.

$P(Z > 165) = 1 - 0.960\,80 = 0.039\,20$

So 4% (to the nearest 1%) of samples would have a mean greater than 165 cm.

Example 3

A food manufacturer produces packets of crisps whose weights are normally distributed with mean 30 g and standard deviation 2.8 g. To check that the weight of the 100 bags of crisps in each batch is correct, an inspector weighs 15 bags chosen randomly and finds their mean weight. He will reject the batch if the mean of the sample is below a certain minimum level.

What should the minimum level be set at so that only 5% of batches are rejected?

Solution

Write down the distribution of the sample mean $\bar{X}$.

$\bar{X} \sim N\left(30, \frac{2.8^2}{15}\right)$

so the standard error of $\bar{X}$ is $\dfrac{2.8}{\sqrt{15}} = 0.723$

Sketch the distribution

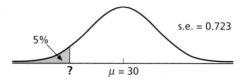

s.e. = 0.723

5%

? $\mu = 30$

Use the table of percentage points of the normal distribution to find the z-value for 5%.

$\Phi^{-1}(0.05) = 1.6449$

Convert this value to a weight in grams.

The minimum level is 1.645 s.e. below the mean
$= 30 - 1.645 \times 0.723 = 28.8$ g (to 3 s.f.)

1 A machine that measures the blood alcohol content of an individual gives a reading that is known to be normally distributed about the individual's true value with standard deviation 5 mg/l.

    (a) Six syringes of blood are taken from one individual and the alcohol content measured in mg/l as

        125   118   129   124   132   128

      (i) Find an estimate for the true blood alcohol content of this individual.

      (ii) What is the standard error of a sample mean from six syringes?

    (b) What is the probability that an individual with a blood alcohol content of 75 mg/l produces a sample mean from six syringes that is greater than 80 mg/l?

2 The length of a particular species of worm is normally distributed with mean 5.6 cm and standard deviation 0.4 cm. What is the probability that the mean length of a random sample of 12 worms is greater than 5.7 cm?

3 Trout in a fish farm are known to have weights, W grams, for which $W \sim N(980, 100^2)$. What is the probability that a catch of 10 fish will have a mean weight of more than 1 kg?

4 A machine, when set correctly, makes bars of chocolate with mean weight 100 g. The distribution of the weights is known to be normal with standard deviation 3.5 g. Random samples of 10 bars are taken at regular intervals and the mean weight of the sample is measured.

    Find the probability that, when the machine is set correctly,

    (a) a sample of 10 bars has a mean weight less than 98 g

    (b) a sample of 10 bars has a mean weight between 99 g and 100 g

5 The bolts produced in a factory are known to be normally distributed with mean length 7.3 cm and standard deviation 0.078 cm.
What size sample should be taken to ensure that less than 5% of sample means exceed 7.33 mm?

6 The heights of a large population of 17-year-old girls are known to be normally distributed with mean 165 cm and standard deviation 6 cm. A random sample of 10 girls is to be taken from this population.

    Calculate an interval, symmetrical about the mean, within which 90% of the sample means should lie.

D The central limit theorem (answers p 172)

In all the examples looked at so far, the population was known, or assumed, to be normally distributed. In many real-life cases we cannot necessarily make that assumption. The following investigation is about what happens with other types of population distribution.

200 patients at a hospital clinic were observed. The time between when they arrived and when they were seen by a doctor was recorded.
These are the recorded times in minutes.

	0	1	2	3	4	5	6	7	8	9
0	3	10	30	3	11	50	65	76	5	18
10	41	28	36	33	4	8	8	15	15	52
20	37	15	24	40	11	7	38	8	25	20
30	24	17	23	41	44	5	3	7	21	7
40	29	17	60	36	29	21	61	8	48	5
50	3	15	47	38	42	58	8	5	47	9
60	38	14	9	6	42	54	6	1	26	23
70	39	13	7	30	4	50	6	5	15	28
80	38	12	4	55	8	3	8	7	16	29
90	38	11	30	5	10	55	30	0	3	20
100	5	17	35	16	5	6	66	16	12	8
110	48	27	27	10	15	24	22	18	15	36
120	44	23	32	39	23	8	8	16	14	18
130	2	6	7	14	23	9	9	16	14	15
140	6	5	9	12	46	7	25	28	64	26
150	37	8	27	12	17	8	29	25	3	30
160	45	28	29	12	12	24	1	7	5	35
170	9	14	35	51	46	8	45	18	10	5
180	19	17	17	4	18	27	25	8	14	23
190	19	16	19	6	6	28	14	6	8	15

This bar chart shows the results.

The mean of this population is 21.26 minutes and the standard deviation is 15.99 minutes, so the variance is $15.99^2 = 255.65$.

In this case the population does not follow a normal distribution. (This type of distribution is called an exponential distribution.)

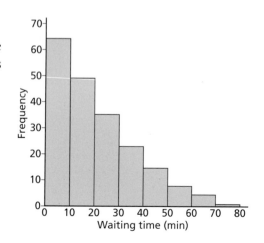

D1 (a) Take at least 30 random samples of size 5 from this population and calculate the mean of each of your samples. Find the mean and variance of these sample means and show the distribution of the sample means as a bar chart.

(b) Compare the mean, the variance, and the shape of the sampling distribution with those of the population.

D2 A spreadsheet can generate random numbers for a uniform distribution. In Excel RANDBETWEEN(1, 100)* gives a random integer between 1 and 100 inclusive. This distribution has a mean of 50.5 and a variance of 833.25.

Generate 50 samples of size 10 from this distribution by copying and pasting this command over 50 rows and 10 columns. Find the mean (AVERAGE in Excel) of each of the 50 samples. Look at the distribution of these sample means and the mean and variance (VARP) of the distribution. Compare these with the population distribution.

D3 Repeat D2 using a sample size of 20.

What the examples above reveal is that even if the population distribution is not a normal distribution, the distribution of $\overline{X}$ is still approximately normal with the same mean, μ, as the population distribution and with variance $\dfrac{\sigma^2}{n}$. The larger the sample size the better the approximation is. This result is summarised in the central limit theorem.

> **K** The **central limit theorem (CLT)** says that if a random sample of size n is taken from any distribution with mean μ and variance σ^2 then, provided n is large enough
>
> $$\overline{X} \sim N\left(\mu, \frac{\sigma^2}{n}\right) \text{ approximately}$$

The central limit theorem is a very important result. In many real-life situations we do not know the distribution of the population. However, if we take a sample, inferences can be made from the sample mean using the normal distribution.

Some textbooks give a rule of thumb that, for the distribution of sample means to be a good approximation to the normal distribution, n must be greater than 30, or 25. However, you have seen in this section that the theorem holds good even for quite small samples. How large a sample size is needed depends on how different the population distribution is from a normal distribution and how good we require the approximation to be.

Problems involving sample means from any population distribution can be solved using the normal distribution, as before.

---

* RANDBETWEEN may need to be installed. Under *Tools*, click *Add-ins* and tick *Analysis*.

Example 4

A packaging machine produces packs of butter with a mean weight of 250 g and standard deviation 5 g. Random samples of ten packs are taken regularly from the production line and the mean weight of the sample found.
Use the central limit theorem to find the approximate proportion of samples that should have a mean weight greater than 253 g.

Solution

The distribution of the population is not known, but the question implies that n is large enough to use the central limit theorem.

From the CLT, $\bar{X} \sim N\left(250, \dfrac{5^2}{10}\right)$ so the sample means follow a normal

distribution with mean 250 and standard error $\sqrt{\dfrac{25}{10}} = \sqrt{2.5} = 1.58$.

$z = \dfrac{253 - 250}{1.58} = 1.90$ s.e. above the mean.

From tables, $\Phi(1.90) = 0.9713$

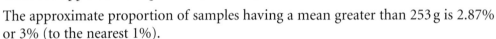

$\mu = 250 \qquad 253$

Since the upper tail is required, $P(\bar{X} > 253) = 1 - 0.9713 = 0.0287$

The approximate proportion of samples having a mean greater than 253 g is 2.87% or 3% (to the nearest 1%).

Exercise D (answers p 172)

In each question, assume that the sample size is sufficiently large to use the CLT.

1 A large survey showed that the mean height of a 16- to 19-year-old male is 174.6 cm with standard deviation 6.75 cm. What is the probability that a group of 15 males in this age group, picked at random, have a mean height greater than 180 cm?

2 At a call centre, over a long period of time, the mean length of a customer call is 4.3 minutes with standard deviation 3.2 minutes. One morning the centre records the length of 25 calls.

(a) What is the probability that the mean length of these 25 calls exceeds 5 minutes?

(b) Why is it impossible for the population distribution to be normal in this case?

3 An insurance company knows that the mean amount claimed on one of its policies is £3450 with standard deviation £840. A random sample of 20 claims on this policy are examined. What is the probability that the mean of this sample

(a) is less than £3000   (b) is in the range £3500 to £3800

4 The weight, in grams, of beans put into cans by a machine has variance 30. The mean μ is easily adjustable. Samples of 15 tins are taken from the machine and weighed, and the mean weight of each sample is calculated.

It is required that only 5% of all mean weights of the sample are less than 250 g. What should the mean μ of the machine be set at for this to be true?

5 The length of a particular species of worm is normally distributed with mean 5.6 cm and standard deviation 0.4 cm.

 (a) What is the probability that a worm chosen at random is longer than 5.7 cm?

 (b) Find the probability that the mean length of a random sample of 12 worms is greater than 5.7 cm.

6 Packets of crisps are filled by a machine.
The mean amount can be varied but the standard deviation is always 3 g.

 (a) If the machine is set to deliver a mean weight of 35 g, what is the probability of a bag weighing under 30 g?

 (b) What must the mean weight be set to so that 2.5% of all bags weigh less than 30 g?

 (c) The mean weight is set to the value required in part (b).
 Samples of size 10 are taken from the machine at random.
 What is the probability that a sample has a mean weight less than 34 g?

 (d) Regulations require that less than 1% of sample means, using a sample of size 10, weigh less than 34 g.
 To what must the population mean of the machine be set to achieve this?

E Estimating the variance (answers p 173)

So far in this chapter we have been looking at estimating the mean. In all the situations met so far the standard deviation or variance of the population was known. In most real-life situations, however, if we do not know the population mean then it is unlikely that we know the population variance either.

If we have taken a sample, it may seem that the variance of this sample could be used as an estimator of the population variance, just as the sample mean is used as an estimator of the population mean. This section will consider whether this sample variance (s_x^2) can be used as an estimator of the unknown population variance (σ^2).

E1 In A1 you selected 30 samples of size 5 from a normal distribution X such that $X \sim N(173.5, 42.1)$.

 (a) For each of these 30 samples, calculate the sample variance.

 (b) Calculate the mean of the sample variances.

 (c) Compare the value in (b) with the population variance. What do you find?

We have already seen that the mean value of $\overline{X}$, the sample mean, is equal to the population mean μ. This showed that $\overline{X}$ is an **unbiased estimator** of μ.

What the investigation above shows is that $s_x^2 = \dfrac{\Sigma(x-\bar{x})^2}{n}$ is **not** an unbiased estimator of the population variance because the mean of the sample variances is **not** equal to the population variance.

Therefore the variance of a sample, $s_x^2 = \dfrac{\Sigma(x-\bar{x})^2}{n}$, cannot be used as an estimator of the population variance σ^2.

E2 In A4 you selected 30 samples of size 10.

(a) Find the sample variance for each of these samples.

(b) Calculate the mean of these 30 sample variances.

(c) Compare this mean of the sample variances with the population variance (42.1). Does taking a sample of size 10 give an estimate closer to the true value?

E3 At the start of section B, the means of 30 samples of size 20 were given. These are the sample variances of those same 30 samples.

33.9 75.2 19.4 67.2 70.9 26.9 52.7 23.9 14.9 41.6 28.9 40.6 32.6 34.9 39.1
35.6 24.5 19.5 40.1 50.7 52.5 58.1 82.0 50.3 32.9 42.8 44.3 29.4 51.4 25.4

(a) Calculate the mean of these sample variances from samples of size 20.

(b) Complete this table showing the mean of the sample variances for different sample sizes.

Sample size	5	10	20
Mean of sample variance			

(c) Roughly what would you expect the mean of the sample variances to be if the sample size were 100?

What your investigations should show is that as the sample size increases the mean of the sample variances gets closer to the population variance σ^2.

This is because the mean of the sample variances is not σ^2 but $\sigma^2 - \dfrac{\sigma^2}{n}$.

This explains why in the investigation in E1, instead of having a mean of 42.1, the sample variances had a mean of approximately $42.1 - \dfrac{42.1}{5} = 33.68$.

The expression $\sigma^2 - \dfrac{\sigma^2}{n}$ can be written as $\dfrac{n\sigma^2 - \sigma^2}{n}$ by using a common denominator.

So the mean of the sample variances is $\dfrac{n\sigma^2 - \sigma^2}{n} = \dfrac{(n-1)\sigma^2}{n}$

Therefore, to get an unbiased estimator of σ^2, the sample variance s_x^2 must be multiplied by $\dfrac{n}{n-1}$.

So the unbiased estimator of σ^2 is $\left(\dfrac{n}{n-1}\right)\dfrac{\Sigma(x_i - \bar{x})^2}{n} = \dfrac{\Sigma(x_i - \bar{x})^2}{n-1}$

This statistic is denoted by S^2.

> **K** The unbiased estimator (S^2) of the population variance (σ^2) from a sample of size n is given by
> $$S^2 = \dfrac{\Sigma(x_i - \bar{x})^2}{n-1}$$

As before, other equivalent calculating forms are often used in practice.
For example:

$$S^2 = \frac{\sum x_i^2 - n\bar{x}^2}{n-1} = \frac{\sum x_i^2 - \frac{(\sum x_i)^2}{n}}{n-1}$$

Example 5

The speeds in kilometres per hour of ten cars entering a village were

    45   40   49   53   48   57   50   60   47   56

Calculate unbiased estimates for the mean μ and variance σ^2 of the
speeds of cars entering this village.

Solution

The unbiased estimate of μ is given by $\bar{X}$.

$\sum x = 505$ and $n = 10$ so $\bar{x} = 50.5$

The unbiased estimator of the variance is given by $S^2 = \dfrac{\sum x_i^2 - \frac{(\sum x_i)^2}{n}}{n-1}$

$\sum x_i^2 = 25\,833$

So $S^2 = \dfrac{25\,833 - \frac{505^2}{10}}{9} = 36.7$

Calculators and spreadsheets usually give the option of using n or $n-1$ in
the calculation of a standard deviation. The keys on a calculator are distinguished
by 'n' or '$n-1$' in the notation.

Similarly, in Excel VARP and VAR are used for the n and $n-1$ formulas for
the variance.

> **E4** Find out how your calculator distinguishes between the sample standard
> deviation and the estimator for the population standard deviation.

Many people get confused about when they should use n and when they
should use $n-1$ as the denominator of the variance or standard deviation.
The rule is:

- If the data entered is for the whole population, then use n as the denominator.
- If the data entered is from a sample of the population and you want to estimate
  the variance of the whole population, then use $n-1$ as the denominator.

If you are given the variance of a sample, this must be multiplied by $\dfrac{n}{n-1}$ to
give an unbiased estimate of the population variance.

1 Calculate unbiased estimates of the mean and variance of the populations from which these random samples are drawn.

(a) A large number of members of a running club compete in a race. The finishing times, in minutes, of 13 members, selected at random, are

32   29   38   29   25   33   34   36   31   44   32   30   26

(b) A nursery grows pine trees for sale as Christmas trees. They measure the growth in one year of 10 randomly chosen trees they have planted. The growths, in cm, are

10   20   15   17   24   17   25   9   15   18

(c) The working lives, in days, of a sample of batteries taken from a large batch were

874   1185   835   754   1209   597   935   817   695   1263   1058   967

(d) Ten separate readings are taken of the wavelength of the radiation from a certain source. The wavelengths in micrometres are:

1.254 1.268 1.262 1.265 1.277 1.283 1.265 1.257 1.267 1.254

2 The contents of a random sample of 50 jars of instant coffee are weighed. The 50 jars have mean weight 153.4 g and standard deviation 27.4 g.

Give unbiased estimates of the population mean and population variance of the weight of coffee in the jars.

3 A random sample of 30 bolts were taken from a production line and the diameters, d mm, of the bolts are accurately measured. It was found that:

$$\Sigma d = 60.85 \qquad\qquad \Sigma d^2 = 123.5$$

Calculate unbiased estimates for the mean and variance of the diameters of all of the bolts produced by this machine.

F Using estimated variances

In the early sections of this chapter you saw that if X is normally distributed then $\bar{X}$ is also normally distributed with mean μ and variance $\dfrac{\sigma^2}{n}$.

The central limit theorem says that, for a sufficiently large sample, this is still approximately true even if the population is not normally distributed. In all of these cases the population variance was known.

The last section showed that, when the population variance σ^2 is unknown, it can be estimated using the unbiased estimator S^2. It may seem that to solve problems involving sample means, the value of S^2 can be substituted for σ^2 and the normal distribution used as before. However, if the sample is small (less than about 30) replacing the expression $\dfrac{\bar{x}-\mu}{\frac{\sigma}{\sqrt{n}}}$ by $\dfrac{\bar{x}-\mu}{\frac{S}{\sqrt{n}}}$ results in a distribution which does not approximate well to the normal distribution.

So if the population variance has been estimated using the unbiased estimator of the variance from a sample of size less than 30, normal probability tables cannot be used to solve problems.

However, for random samples of size 30 or more, the sample mean $\overline{X}$ follows the normal distribution whose parameters are μ and the value of $\dfrac{S^2}{n}$, where S^2 is the unbiased estimator of σ^2. Where the population is not known to be normal, the central limit theorem can still be used.

This means that, when an unbiased estimate of the population variance has been calculated from a sample of size ≥ 30, tables of the normal distribution can be used to solve problems as if the population variance were equal to its estimated value.

Example 6

A bird sanctuary records the weights, w grams, of 40 adult barn owls as follows.

214 222 209 202 210 204 200 187 199 200 200 212 207 211 213 196
202 214 201 221 199 200 220 193 212 210 198 197 180 218 205 222
202 214 223 204 208 219 218 209

(a) Given that $\Sigma w^2 = 1\,715\,707$, $\Sigma w = 8275$, calculate an unbiased estimate for the population variance of the weights of these owls.

(b) The sample mean of the weight these owls is 207 g. An expert claims that the population mean weight of barn owls is 210 g. What is the probability of getting a mean of 207 g or less from a sample of 40, given that the population mean is 210 g?

Solution

(a) Given that $\Sigma w^2 = 1\,715\,707$, $\Sigma w = 8275$ and $n = 40$

$$S^2 = \dfrac{1\,715\,707 - \dfrac{8275^2}{40}}{39} = 97.9$$

(b) Irrespective of the population distribution, $\overline{X} \sim N\left(\mu, \dfrac{\sigma^2}{n}\right)$ and, since $n \geq 30$, the unbiased estimate of the population variance, S^2, can be substituted for σ^2.

Hence $\overline{X} \sim N\left(210, \dfrac{97.9}{40}\right)$

To find $P(\overline{X} \leq 207)$ *first standardise the normal distribution.*

$$z = \dfrac{207 - 210}{\sqrt{\dfrac{97.9}{40}}} = -1.92 \text{ s.e. from the mean}$$

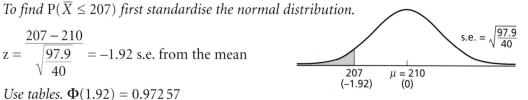

Use tables. $\Phi(1.92) = 0.972\,57$

$P(Z < 1.92) = 1 - 0.972\,57 = 0.027\,43$

Exercise F (answers p 173)

1 A machine produces metal bolts. A random sample of 50 bolts is taken and their diameter, d mm, is measured. It is found that $\Sigma d = 1396$ and $\Sigma d^2 = 39\,920$.

   (a) Calculate an unbiased estimate of the variance of the diameters of the bolts.

   (b) The mean diameter of the bolts is set to be 28 mm. What is the probability that a random sample of 50 bolts has a mean diameter greater than 28.3 mm?

2 Bottles of ketchup are filled by a machine for which the mean amount can be changed. Thirty bottles filled by the machine are taken at random and the volume of ketchup in each one is measured accurately in millilitres, with the following results.

   433 428 409 447 435 418 448 445 431 423 420 441 414 444 447

   431 417 423 436 432 424 457 433 450 410 433 418 424 432 418

   (a) Calculate an unbiased estimate of the variance of the amount of ketchup in bottles filled by this machine.

   (b) The bottles are marked 'Contents 425 ml'. The company requires that 95% of all samples of size 30 have a mean greater than this figure. To what value should the mean be set?

Key points

- If X is a random variable, then the mean of a sample of size n is also a random variable, denoted by $\overline{X}$. $\overline{X}$ is an unbiased estimator of the population mean μ. (p 92)

- If X can be modelled by a normal distribution $N(\mu, \sigma^2)$ then $\overline{X}$ is also normally distributed such that $\overline{X} \sim N\left(\mu, \dfrac{\sigma^2}{n}\right)$. (p 95)

- The value $\dfrac{\sigma}{\sqrt{n}}$ is usually referred to as the standard error of the sample mean. It is useful in comparing the reliability of estimates from different size samples. (p 93)

- The central limit theorem states that if a sufficiently large sample of size n is taken from a population with mean μ and variance σ^2, then, irrespective of the population distribution, the sample mean $\overline{X}$ approximately follows a normal distribution with mean μ and variance $\dfrac{\sigma^2}{n}$. The larger the sample size, the closer this approximation is. (p 99)

- When estimating the population variance from a sample of size n, the statistic $S^2 = \dfrac{\Sigma(x_i - \bar{x})^2}{n-1}$ is an unbiased estimator of σ^2. (p 102)

- If a sample of size n, where $n \geq 30$, is taken from any distribution where the population variance is unknown then the sample mean $\overline{X}$ is normally distributed with mean μ and variance $\dfrac{\sigma^2}{n}$, where σ^2 can be estimated by the unbiased estimator S^2. (pp 104–105)

Mixed questions (answers p 173)

1 Explain the difference between a parameter and a statistic.   AQA 2003

2 Cans of a brand drink are labelled as containing 330 ml. The machine that fills the cans delivers an amount in each can which is normally distributed with mean 334 ml and standard deviation 5 ml.

  (a) What is the probability that someone who buys a can of drink filled by this machine finds that it contains less than 330 ml?

  (b) An inspector takes a random sample of 10 cans from this machine and measures the content of each one. What is the probability that the mean content of these cans is less than 330 ml?

  (c) The mean content that the machine delivers can be adjusted. What is the lowest value that the mean could be set to so that only 5% of samples of size 10 have a mean content less than 330 ml?

3 The amount of time in minutes, T, taken to apply a plaster to a broken limb at a hospital has a mean of 22 and variance 15.

  (a) What is the probability that for 30 randomly chosen patients the mean time taken to apply the plaster is less than 20 minutes?

  (b) Why was it not necessary to assume anything about the distribution of times in order to answer part (a)?

A new type of plaster bandage is introduced which is thought will speed up the process. The new bandage is used on a sample of 30 patients and the times, t minutes, taken to apply it are recorded. These give $\Sigma t = 560$ and $\Sigma t^2 = 10\,546$.

  (c) Calculate, for the time taken to apply the new bandage, an unbiased estimate of

    (i) the population mean   (ii) the population variance

4 The percentage of impurity in cans of a chemical made by a new process is investigated by taking a random sample of 30 cans and measuring the percentage of impurity in each can. The results are:

    3.45 3.42 3.62 3.56 3.31 2.72 3.24 3.71 3.59 3.55 3.78 3.56 3.40 3.50 3.62

    2.95 3.42 2.84 3.33 3.41 3.36 3.45 3.77 3.00 3.53 3.59 3.64 3.29 3.36 3.43

  (a) Calculate, for the population of cans, an unbiased estimate of

    (i) the mean percentage impurity

    (ii) the variance of the percentage impurity

  (b) The chemical is sent out to factories in large consignments of cans. To ensure the quality of a consignment, a random sample of 10 cans is taken from it and the percentage impurity in each can is measured. If the mean percentage impurity of the sample is greater than 3.6, the consignment is rejected.

    Given that the mean percentage impurity in a particular consignment is 3.4 and the variance is the value as estimated in (a) (ii), what is the probability that this consignment will be rejected?

Test yourself (answers p 174)

1 A study showed the time, T minutes, spent by a customer between entering and leaving Fely's department store has a mean of 20 with a standard deviation of 6.

Assume that T may be modelled by a normal distribution.

(a) Find the value of T exceeded by 20% of customers.

(b) (i) Write down the standard deviation of the mean time spent in Fely's store by a random sample of 90 customers.

(ii) Find the probability that this mean time will exceed 21 minutes. AQA 2003

2 A machine fills bags of frozen peas whose weights have a standard deviation of 50 g. The mean weight μ of the bags filled can be set to different values on the machine. The bags are then randomly packed into boxes of 36 bags.

(a) What is the standard error of the mean weight of a bag of frozen peas in a box?

(b) If the mean weight of a bag is set at 500 g, what is the probability of finding a box where the mean weight of a bag is less than 490 g?

(c) At what mean weight should the machine be set so that 95% of all boxes have a mean bag weight greater than 475 g?

(d) Explain why the use of the central limit theorem in this case is justified.

3 A greengrocer has a large number of oranges in stock. The weights of the oranges may be modelled by a normal distribution with a mean of 210 grams and a standard deviation of 22 grams. A customer decides to buy 10 oranges and asks the greengrocer to select them. On reaching home, the customer weighs the oranges individually and obtains the following weights in grams.

205 194 196 264 198 207 199 203 196 188

(a) Calculate the mean and standard deviation of this sample.

(b) Use the distribution of the greengrocer's oranges described above to calculate the probability that a random sample of 10 oranges will have a mean weight less than 205 grams.

(c) Calculate the probability that a random sample of 10 oranges will contain fewer than two oranges with a weight greater than 210 grams.

(d) Discuss whether or not your calculations in parts (a), (b) and (c) cast doubt on a suggestion that the greengrocer did not select the 10 oranges at random.

(e) The greengrocer now has 240 oranges left in stock. Describe how random numbers could be used to select a random sample of 10 of the greengrocer's oranges.

(f) The greengrocer decides that, in future, customers will be asked to select their own oranges. Give three advantages or disadvantages to the greengrocer of this method of selection compared to either random sampling or selection by the greengrocer. AQA 2001

4 Sunroofs for a particular car are required to have a minimum thickness of 10 mm. The current manufacturing process is known to produce sunroofs whose thickness, T mm, is normally distributed with mean 10.5 mm and standard deviation 1 mm.

   (a) What proportion of sunroofs from this process have a thickness less than 10 mm?

   (b) What is the probability that a random sample of 5 sunroofs has mean thickness less than 10 mm?

   (c) The mean thickness can be altered without changing the standard deviation. To what value should the mean be set so that 5% of all sunroofs have a thickness less than 10 mm?

A new process is introduced to produce sunroofs. In order to check the accuracy of the new process, a sample of 30 sunroofs is checked for thickness. The results give $\sum t = 317$ and $\sum t^2 = 3359$.

   (d) Calculate an unbiased estimate of the population variance of the thickness under the new process.

   (e) To what value should the mean thickness be set in the new process so that only 5% of sunroofs have a thickness less than 10 mm?

   (f) Explain the advantages of the new process to a manager who is keen to make savings at the factory.

5 A gas supplier maintains a team of engineers who are available to deal with leaks reported by customers. Most reported leaks can be dealt with quickly but some require a long time. The time (excluding travelling time) taken to deal with reported leaks is found to have a mean of 65 minutes and a standard deviation of 60 minutes.

   (a) Assuming that the times may be modelled by a normal distribution, estimate the probability that

      (i) it will take more than 185 minutes to deal with a reported leak

      (ii) it will take between 50 minutes and 125 minutes to deal with a reported leak

      (iii) the mean time to deal with a random sample of 90 reported leaks is less than 70 minutes

   (b) A statistician consulted by the gas supplier stated that as the times had a mean of 65 minutes and a standard deviation of 60 minutes, the normal distribution would not prove an adequate model.

      (i) Explain the reason for the statistician's statement.

      (ii) Give a reason why, despite the statistician's statement, your answer to part (a) (iii) is still valid.   AQA 2002

8 Confidence intervals

In this chapter you will learn how to
- find a confidence interval for the population mean using a sample from a normal distribution with known variance
- find a confidence interval for the population mean using a sample from any distribution with known or unknown variance
- make inferences from confidence intervals

A Estimating with confidence (answers p 175)

Regular checks are made of water supplies to ensure that the water in our taps is safe to drink. One measure of pollution is the degree of acidity of the water; this is measured by the pH value. A pH value of 7 indicates that a liquid is neutral, a value less than 7 acidic, and higher than 7 alkaline. EU recommendations specify that safe drinking water should have a pH value between 6.5 and 8.5.

In order to check the water quality, several measurements are made at the same site. The mean, $\bar{x}$, of this sample of measurements is then used to estimate the population mean of all the water at that site.

A water authority has been making regular checks at two sites for some time. A different sampling procedure is used at each of the two sites.

River site The water authority knows that the pH of the water in the river follows a normal distribution with standard deviation 1.2. Measurements of the pH value are made at 10 random points at the river site.

Reservoir The authority knows that the pH of the water in the reservoir follows a normal distribution with standard deviation 0.5. Measurements are made at 15 random points around the reservoir.

A sample of measurements is taken one morning from each site and the pH readings are as follows:

River site   7.1 5.6 6.0 6.2 5.1 7.4 8.0 6.7 5.5 3.7

Reservoir   7.8 7.3 9.1 8.2 7.8 7.9 6.5 7.9 7.9 8.3 7.7 7.8 7.1 7.2 7.8

A1 Calculate an unbiased estimate for the mean pH value at each of the sites using $\bar{x}$, the sample mean.

D **A2** Which of the two estimates do you have more confidence in as a good estimate of the true population value for the site?

How confident we are about an estimate depends on two factors:
- the size of the sample – the larger the size of the sample, the closer the estimate is likely to be to the true population mean
- the variance of the population – if readings are generally more varied the estimate will be less reliable

We know from the last chapter that the standard error of the sample mean of a random sample of size n is $\frac{\sigma}{\sqrt{n}}$, where σ is the population standard deviation.

One way to indicate the reliability of an estimate is to quote the estimate, called a **point estimate**, together with the standard error of the estimator.

For the water samples at the two sites we would quote

River site: mean $= 6.13$, s.e. $= \frac{1.2}{\sqrt{10}} = 0.379$

Reservoir: mean $= 7.75$, s.e. $= \frac{0.5}{\sqrt{15}} = 0.129$

Since the standard error is smaller in the case of the reservoir, we can be more confident that an estimate from this site is closer to the true population value at that site.

Exercise A (answers p 175)

1 A poultry farmer keeps large flocks of two varieties of turkey. The weights of type A are known to be normally distributed with standard deviation 0.4 kg. Type B turkeys vary with standard deviation 0.6 kg. A random sample of each type of turkey was taken and weighed. These are the weights in kilograms.

    Type A   3.1 3.8 3.0 2.8 3.8 3.4 3.1 2.5 3.1

    Type B   4.3 3.4 3.6 4.1 3.7 2.9 3.6 3.0 4.1 3.2 3.5 3.3

(a) Find an unbiased estimate of the mean weight of the turkeys in each flock. Give the standard error of the estimator in each case.

(b) Which of the two estimates do you think is more likely to be closer to the population mean for that type of turkey?

2 The pH of rainfall in an area is known to vary with standard deviation 0.8. 10 measurements were taken on one day and the sample mean was found to be 4.9.

(a) Find the standard error of the sampling means for a sample of size 10.

(b) It is said that rain falling through clean air has an average pH of 5.7. Does the sample mean suggest this is a likely value for the population mean in that area?

3 The wingspans of a species of butterfly are known to be normally distributed with mean 48 mm and standard deviation 5 mm. An entomologist captures a sample of 10 butterflies which she thinks are of this species and finds they have a mean wingspan of 45 mm.

(a) How many standard errors from the population mean is the sample mean?

(b) Do you think it is reasonable to say that the sample came from the population of the species?

B Confidence intervals (answers p 175)

Quoting a point estimate on its own is of limited use. Giving the standard error of a sample mean is only really useful when comparing two estimates of the same or a similar parameter, as with the water samples.

It is often more useful to give a range of values within which we are reasonably confident that the true population value lies. This is called an **interval estimate**.

In the case of the water at the river site, we knew that the pH was normally distributed with standard deviation 1.2, so that the standard error of the sample mean was $\dfrac{1.2}{\sqrt{10}} = 0.379$. We also know, from the previous chapter, that the sample means are normally distributed.

The chapter on the normal distribution showed that roughly 96% of the distribution lies in an interval given by ±2 standard deviations from the mean. In fact, 95% of a normal distribution lies within ±1.96 s.d. from the mean.

Since the sample means follow a normal distribution with standard error $\dfrac{\sigma}{\sqrt{n}}$ there is a 95% chance of a sample mean falling within ±1.96 standard errors of the population mean. For the samples at the river site, 95% of sample means are within $1.96 \times 0.379 = 0.743$ above and below the unknown population mean.

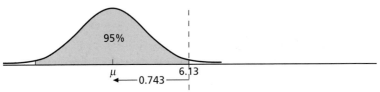

Using this 95% restriction, if we obtained a sample mean of 6.13, then the lowest possible population mean that could produce a sample mean of 6.13 would be 1.96 standard errors below it.

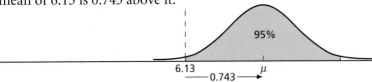

Similarly, the highest possible population mean that could produce a sample mean of 6.13 is 0.743 above it.

Using the 95% restriction, we can say that if the sample mean is 6.13 we can be reasonably confident that the population mean μ will lie in the interval 6.13 ± 0.743, that is, $5.387 \le \mu \le 6.873$.

 This interval is known as a **95% confidence interval**. This is because we can be 95% sure that this interval contains the population mean. There is only a 5% chance that the true population mean lies outside this interval.

The notation $(5.387, 6.873)$ can be used to describe the interval we have just found.

B1 The pH value of the water at the reservoir is known to be normally distributed with standard deviation 0.5. The mean of the sample of 15 measurements was calculated to be 7.75. Use these results to find a 95% confidence interval for the population mean at the reservoir.

B2 (a) EU regulations state that safe drinking water should not have a pH higher than 8.5. Is it likely that the mean pH of the reservoir is higher than 8.5?

(b) Is it likely that the mean pH at the two sites is actually the same?

Investigating with a spreadsheet

It is possible in Excel to generate random numbers to fit a particular distribution.

In *Tools → Data Analysis*, choose *Random Number Generation*.
(Check that the add-in Data Analysis Tool is installed.)

In the pop-up box, set up the spreadsheet to create 100 samples of size 5 from a normal distribution with mean 7.3 and standard deviation 0.5.

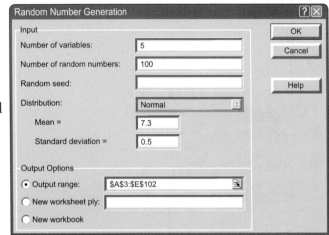

Now use the spreadsheet to do this.

- Find the mean (AVERAGE(range of cells) in Excel) of each sample of 5.

- Calculate the upper and lower values of a 95% confidence interval.

- Use a logical statement such as IF(AND(I3<7.3,J3>7.3),"√","X") to identify which sets of limits actually contain the population mean value.

The resulting spreadsheet should look something like this.

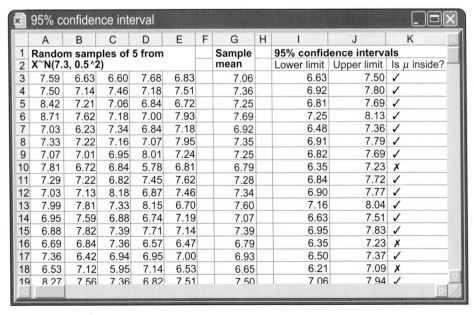

95% confidence interval

	A	B	C	D	E	F	G	H	I	J	K
1	Random samples of 5 from						Sample		95% confidence intervals		
2	X~N(7.3, 0.5^2)						mean		Lower limit	Upper limit	Is μ inside?
3	7.59	6.63	6.60	7.68	6.83		7.06		6.63	7.50	✓
4	7.50	7.14	7.46	7.18	7.51		7.36		6.92	7.80	✓
5	8.42	7.21	7.06	6.84	6.72		7.25		6.81	7.69	✓
6	8.71	7.62	7.18	7.00	7.93		7.69		7.25	8.13	✓
7	7.03	6.23	7.34	6.84	7.18		6.92		6.48	7.36	✓
8	7.33	7.22	7.16	7.07	7.95		7.35		6.91	7.79	✓
9	7.07	7.01	6.95	8.01	7.24		7.25		6.82	7.69	✓
10	7.81	6.72	6.84	5.78	6.81		6.79		6.35	7.23	X
11	7.29	7.22	6.82	7.45	7.62		7.28		6.84	7.72	✓
12	7.03	7.13	8.18	6.87	7.46		7.34		6.90	7.77	✓
13	7.99	7.81	7.33	8.15	6.70		7.60		7.16	8.04	✓
14	6.95	7.59	6.88	6.74	7.19		7.07		6.63	7.51	✓
15	6.88	7.82	7.39	7.71	7.14		7.39		6.95	7.83	✓
16	6.69	6.84	7.36	6.57	6.47		6.79		6.35	7.23	X
17	7.36	6.42	6.94	6.95	7.00		6.93		6.50	7.37	✓
18	6.53	7.12	5.95	7.14	6.53		6.65		6.21	7.09	X
19	8.27	7.56	7.36	6.82	7.51		7.50		7.06	7.94	✓

The following diagram was produced from a spreadsheet and shows the confidence intervals created by 100 samples where $X \sim \text{N}(7.3, 0.5^2)$. Each vertical line represents a confidence interval and the horizontal line represents the population mean.

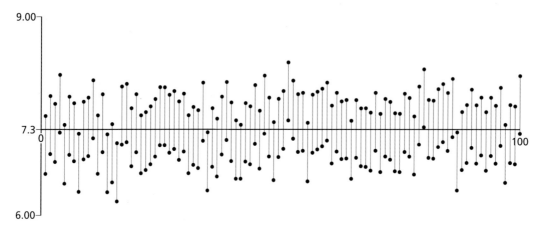

For this set of results, 93 out of the 100 confidence intervals created include the population mean and 7% do not. This is close to the 95% of intervals that we would expect to contain the true population value.

By resetting the random number generator, this experiment can be repeated several times quickly, or a larger number of trials can be used. By making small changes other variations can be investigated.

- By altering the parameters of the randomly generated population, that is using different values of μ and σ, find confidence intervals for other normal distributions.
- Investigate what happens if different size samples are used with the same population.

Confidence intervals for other percentages

Confidence intervals using other percentages are also possible. The higher the percentage, the greater the chance there is that the confidence interval contains the population value. However, higher percentages will also mean the interval is wider and thus less precise. Percentages of 90% and above are commonly used.

To create a 90% confidence interval requires the percentage point of the normal distribution that leaves 5% out at each end.

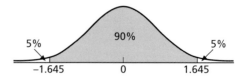

From the percentage points table, $p = 0.95$ gives 1.6449.

So a 90% confidence interval is given by

$$\bar{x} \pm 1.645 \frac{\sigma}{\sqrt{n}}$$

K If a random sample of size n is taken from a normal population and the sample mean $\bar{x}$ is found, then the 95% confidence interval for the population mean

is given by $\left(\bar{x} - 1.96\dfrac{\sigma}{\sqrt{n}}, \bar{x} + 1.96\dfrac{\sigma}{\sqrt{n}}\right)$,

where σ is the standard deviation of the population.

There is a probability of 0.95 that the interval contains the true population mean. Confidence intervals for other percentage levels can be found using the appropriate percentage points of the normal distribution.

B3 How many standard errors either side of the mean would you use for a 99% confidence interval for a population mean?

B4 Find 99% confidence intervals for the population mean pH at the river site and at the reservoir using the data at the start of this chapter.

Example 1

The systolic blood pressure of a particular age group of women is known to be normally distributed with standard deviation 9.5. The systolic blood pressures of 10 randomly chosen women in this age group were measured as

120 134 128 116 120 132 85 98 125 113

(a) Construct a 90% confidence interval for the mean systolic blood pressure of all women in this age group.

(b) It is claimed that the mean systolic blood pressure of the population from which this group was sampled is in fact 120. Does the confidence interval support this claim?

Solution

(a) *Find the sample mean.*
Find the required percentage points.

$\bar{x} = 117.1$
A 90% interval requires 5% of the distribution to be left out at each end. The percentage point when $p = 0.95$ is 1.645. A 90% confidence interval is given by

$$\mu \pm 1.645\frac{\sigma}{\sqrt{n}}.$$

Calculate the interval.

The interval is given by $117.1 \pm 1.645 \times \dfrac{9.5}{\sqrt{10}}$

which gives the interval $(112.16, 122.04)$.

(b) Since 120 is within the confidence interval, this supports the claim that 120 is the population mean.

Exercise B (answers p 176)

1 An electronics company makes resistors whose resistance, in ohms, is known to be normally distributed with standard deviation 35 ohms. A random sample of 9 resistors was taken from a large batch and their resistances were measured. The results were

   2385   2363   2362   2334   2404   2375   2316   2458   2396

   Calculate a 95% confidence interval for the mean resistance of the batch.

2 The weight, in grams, of Italian grated cheese in cartons may be assumed to be normally distributed with mean μ and standard deviation 1.6.

   From a random sample of 64 such cartons, the mean weight of grated cheese per carton is found to be 80.8 grams.

   Construct a 95% confidence interval for μ. AQA 2003

3 Steel girders used in construction are tested by applying a load until they break. The breaking load of a type of girder is known to be normally distributed with standard deviation 2.4 kN. Ten girders were chosen at random from a new delivery from a factory and the breaking loads, in kN, were measured. The results were

   23.3   26.8   24.3   19.3   23.8   22.8   18.7   23.6   24.8   22.4

   Calculate a 99% confidence interval for the mean breaking load of the girders.

4 A factory produces jars of jam whose weight W is normally distributed with standard deviation 8.2 g. To estimate the mean weight of the jars from a particular machine, 12 jars are taken at random and their total weight found.

   For a particular sample of 12 jars it was found that $\Sigma w = 5330.4$ g.

   (a) Calculate a 95% confidence interval for the mean weight of the jars from this machine.

   (b) The factory requires that the mean weight of the jars filled by any machine must be greater than 450 g. Based on this sample would you say that this is likely to be true for this particular machine?

5 The tree sparrow and house sparrow are very similar in appearance but vary in weight. Tree sparrows are known to have a mean weight of 23 g and house sparrows a mean weight of 31 g. The weights of both species are thought to be normally distributed with standard deviation 3 g.

   A small flock of sparrows of the same family is captured and each sparrow is weighed. The weights, in grams, are

   25.8   31.7   33.1   27.2   30.2   26.3   31.2   28.5   34.2   22.3
   33.8   29.5   33.3   27.7   30.1

   (a) Calculate a 95% confidence interval for the mean weight of the population from which this flock came.

   (b) State, with reasons, which of the two species of sparrow this flock is most likely to belong to.

C Other population distributions

In all the examples in the previous section, the population was normally distributed. However, the central limit theorem states that, provided the sample size is large enough, the mean of a random sample from any distribution is approximately normally distributed with standard error $\frac{\sigma}{\sqrt{n}}$.

So we can find an approximate confidence interval for a population mean, even if we cannot assume that the population is normally distributed, provided that the sample size is sufficiently large.

Example 2

A machine fills jars with olives. The weight of the olives has a standard deviation 15 g. A sample of 25 jars is randomly selected and the contents of each jar are weighed. The weights, in grams, are

232.3 267.9 258.0 270.1 260.7 267.9 257.2 257.7 236.6 243.5 281.9 247.9
241.1 241.3 263.0 274.2 268.4 274.8 255.6 261.8 255.1 290.8 253.4 205.6 272.2

Find a 90% confidence interval for the mean weight in jars filled by this machine.

Solution

Sample mean = 257.6 g

The 90% confidence interval is given by $257.6 \pm 1.645 \times \dfrac{15}{\sqrt{25}}$.
So the confidence interval is (252.7, 262.5).

If a random sample of size n, where n is sufficiently large, is taken from any distribution with standard deviation σ, then an approximate 95% confidence interval for the population mean is given by

$$\left(\bar{x} - 1.96 \frac{\sigma}{\sqrt{n}}, \ \bar{x} + 1.96 \frac{\sigma}{\sqrt{n}} \right)$$

Other intervals can be found using percentage points of the normal distribution.

Example 3

The standard deviation of waiting times at a doctor's surgery is known to be 6 minutes. A random sample of 50 patients is observed and these are found to have a mean waiting time of 26 minutes.

Calculate an approximate 95% confidence interval for the mean waiting time.

The practice manager claims that the average waiting time is less than 20 minutes. Does this sample support this claim?

Solution

The approximate 95% confidence interval is given by $26 \pm 1.96 \times \dfrac{6}{\sqrt{50}} = 26 \pm 1.663$.

The 95% interval is therefore (24.34, 27.66).
Since 20 minutes is not in this interval, it is unlikely that the mean is 20 minutes or less.

Exercise C (answers p 176)

1 The breaking strains of rope are measured in newtons by a machine. The readings on the machine are known to have standard deviation 1.6 newtons. Fifteen samples are taken at random from a large coil of rope and tested. The breaking strains are given as

42.9 43.7 42.2 41.1 41.0 41.4 42.4 42.4 43.0 42.8 44.5 40.4 39.3 44.9 43.8

Calculate a 95% confidence interval for the mean breaking strain of the rope.

2 The weights of kilogram bags of rice filled by a machine are known to have standard deviation 0.03 kg. A random sample of 10 bags was weighed and the total weight was 9.974 kg.
Calculate a 90% confidence interval for the mean weight of the bags produced by this machine.

3 Tyres are tested on a machine which simulates driving conditions. The tyres are tested until they are worn below the legal limit. The distance 'travelled', in thousands of kilometres, is recorded. Past experience suggest that the distances vary with standard deviation 6 thousand kilometres. In a test on 18 tyres, chosen at random from a particular batch, these results were obtained.

39 41 38 44 37 45 38 32 51 34 39 42 36 44 32 41 39 32

(a) Calculate a 95% confidence interval for the mean distance tyres in this batch should travel.

(b) The manufacturer claims that the mean distance that its tyres travel is 40 000 km. Does this trial support the manufacturer's claim?

4 The number of eggs carried by female shrimps is known to have standard deviation 4. A biologist collects 20 female shrimps at random from a particular site and counts the number of eggs on each, with these results.

15 14 14 14 13 13 16 12 13 18 20 14 10 15 13 19 14 17 18 10

(a) Calculate a 95% confidence interval for the mean number of eggs on female shrimps in the population at this site.

(b) The previous year a large survey was carried out and the mean number of eggs was found to be 17. Does this sample support the claim that the mean number of eggs is still 17?

5 The body temperature of a human, in °F, is known to have a standard deviation of 0.73. A doctor measures the body temperature of a random sample of 16 healthy people. Their body temperatures, in °F, are

97.1 97.4 97.8 98.0 98.2 98.5 99.5 97.7 98.0 98.2 98.4 98.6 98.8 98.9 98.8 99.2

(a) Calculate a 95% confidence interval for the mean body temperature of the population.

(b) The normal body temperature of a human is thought to be 98.6 °F. Does your answer to (a) agree with this view?

3 (a) Machine A produces plastic balls which have diameters that are normally distributed with a mean of 10.3 cm and a standard deviation of 0.16 cm.

    (i) Determine the proportion of balls which have diameters less than 10.5 cm.

    (ii) Calculate the diameter exceeded by 75 per cent of balls.

(b) Machine B produces beach balls which have diameters that are normally distributed with a mean of μ cm and a standard deviation of 0.24 cm.

    The diameter, d cm, of each ball in a random sample of 144 beach balls was measured. This gave

$$\Sigma d = 3585.6$$

    (i) Calculate an unbiased estimate of μ.

    (ii) Calculate the standard error of your estimate.

    (iii) Construct a 95% confidence interval for μ, giving its limits to two decimal places.

    (iv) Hence state, with a reason, whether you agree with a claim that $\mu = 25$.   AQA 2002

4 The contents of each of a random sample of 100 cans of a soft drink are measured. The results have a mean of 331.28 ml and a standard deviation of 2.97 ml.

  (a) Show that an unbiased estimate of the population variance is 8.91 ml^2.

  (b) Construct a 99% confidence interval for the population mean, giving the limits to two decimal places.

  (c) Explain why, in answering part (b), an assumption regarding the distribution of the contents of cans was not necessary.   AQA 2003

5 A company has three machines, I, II and III, each producing chocolate bar ice creams of a particular variety.

  (a) Machine I produces bars whose weights are normally distributed with a mean of 48.1 grams and a standard deviation of 0.25 grams. Determine the probability that the weight of a randomly selected bar is less than 47.5 grams.

  (b) Machine II produces bars whose weights are normally distributed with a standard deviation of 0.32 grams. Given also that 85 per cent of bars have weights below 50.0 grams, determine the mean weight of bars.

  (c) From a random sample of 36 bars, selected at random from those produced on machine III, calculations gave a mean weight of 52.46 grams and an unbiased estimate of the population variance of 0.1764 grams^2.

    (i) Construct a 95% confidence interval for the mean weight of bars produced by machine III, giving the limits to two decimal places.

    (ii) Name the theorem that you have used and explain why it was applicable in this case.   AQA 2001

9 Linear regression

In this chapter you will learn
- how to calculate a least squares regression line and use it to make predictions
- how to use residuals
- how a regression equation is affected by a linear transformation of either of the variables

A The least squares regression line (answers p 177)

In an experiment, some students let a toy car run down a ramp and measured the distance it travelled along the floor from the bottom of the ramp.
The ramp was raised to different heights above the ground and the distance travelled was measured for each height.

These are the results that they obtained.

Height (cm)	5	10	15	20	25	30	35	40	45
Distance (cm)	40	44	106	91	175	138	169	175	187

A1 Draw a scatter diagram of this data on graph paper with height on the x-axis and distance on the y-axis.
What does this suggest about the relationship between the two variables?

The relationship of interest is how the height of the ramp affects the distance the car travels along the floor. In this case the height is the **explanatory variable** as it is the height of the ramp that affects the distance travelled. The explanatory variable is usually plotted as x. In this case height is also a **controlled** variable, that is it goes up in regular steps decided by the experimenter.

The distance travelled depends on the height, so distance is the **response variable**. The response variable is usually plotted as y.

If the ramp height is fixed, at say 20 cm, and the car is released several times, it would travel a different distance each time. The distance travelled is a random variable. The height, being decided by the experimenter, is not a random variable.

A2 Until now, you have probably drawn lines of best fit 'by eye'.
   (a) Draw a line of best fit 'by eye' on your scatter diagram.
   (b) Find the equation of your line in the form $y = a + bx$.
   (c) Find the mean of the x-values, $\bar{x}$, and the mean of the y-values, $\bar{y}$.

This scatter diagram shows all the points from the ramp experiment. The point $(\bar{x}, \bar{y})$ has also been plotted.

Since this point can be thought of as the 'centre' of the data, it seems reasonable that any line of best fit should pass through $(\bar{x}, \bar{y})$. In fact it can be mathematically proved that this is the case, although the proof is beyond the scope of this course.

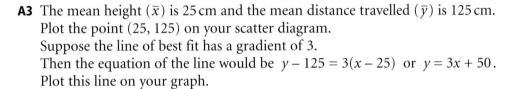

Once we know that the line passes through this point, we need to find the gradient (b) of the line that best fits the data.

The equation of the straight line will then be given by

$$(y - \bar{y}) = b(x - \bar{x})$$

or $\qquad y = bx + (\bar{y} - b\bar{x})$ where $(\bar{y} - b\bar{x})$ is the intercept.

We can now investigate different values of b to see which gives the best fit.

A3 The mean height ($\bar{x}$) is 25 cm and the mean distance travelled ($\bar{y}$) is 125 cm.
Plot the point (25, 125) on your scatter diagram.
Suppose the line of best fit has a gradient of 3.
Then the equation of the line would be $y - 125 = 3(x - 25)$ or $y = 3x + 50$.
Plot this line on your graph.

In order to decide on the 'best' gradient, a method of comparison is needed. The vertical distance, d_i, can be measured from each actual point to the corresponding point predicted by the line. A line which passes closer to the points will generally have smaller values of d_i.

One method of finding the best straight line through these points is to find the gradient which minimises these deviations.

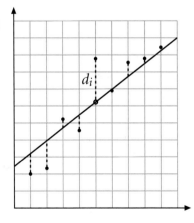

D **A4** Using a spreadsheet on a computer or graphic calculator, calculate a predicted value of y on the line $y = 3x + 50$ for each value of x in the original data set.
Hence calculate each vertical deviation d_i as actual y – predicted y.
Calculate $\sum d_i$ for the line with gradient 3. What do you find?

A5 For each of the points in A4 calculate d_i^2 and find $\sum d_i^2$ for the line with gradient $b = 3$.

A6 Now re-calculate $\sum d_i^2$ for $b = 2.0, 2.5, 3.5, 4.0, 4.5$ and 5.0.
Plot a graph of the values of $\sum d_i^2$ against b for all the values you have recorded.
What does this suggest is the value of b that minimises $\sum d_i^2$?
Use your spreadsheet to try to find a more accurate value for b.
Compare this value with your equation in A2(b).

The line which minimises the sum of the squared vertical deviations of the actual values from the line of best fit is called the **least squares regression line of y on x.** The value of the gradient b which gives the line of best fit is called the **regression coefficient.**

The method of finding the gradient b which gives the line of best fit is given below. The result can be proved, but the proof is beyond the scope of this book.

K The regression coefficient of y on x is $\dfrac{S_{xy}}{S_{xx}}$

where $S_{xy} = \Sigma(x_i - \bar{x})(y_i - \bar{y}) = \Sigma x_i y_i - \dfrac{(\Sigma x_i)(\Sigma y_i)}{n} = \Sigma x_i y_i - n\bar{x}\,\bar{y}$

and $S_{xx} = \Sigma(x_i - \bar{x})^2 = \Sigma x_i^2 - \dfrac{(\Sigma x_i)^2}{n} = \Sigma x_i^2 - n\bar{x}^2$, with n being the number of data pairs.

The least squares regression line of y on x is $y = a + bx$, where $a = \bar{y} - b\bar{x}$.

Example 1

Calculate the equation of the least squares regression line for the car and ramp data at the start of this chapter and add the line to the scatter diagram.

Solution

Using a calculator, $\bar{x} = 25$, $\bar{y} = 125$, $\Sigma x_i y_i = 33\,895$, $\Sigma x_i^2 = 7125$

$$b = \frac{33895 - 9 \times 25 \times 125}{7125 - 9 \times 25^2} = 3.85 \text{ (to 2 d.p.)}$$

$a = \bar{y} - b\bar{x} = 125 - 3.85 \times 25 = 28.83$

so the least squares regression line is given by $y = 28.83 + 3.85x$.

To plot this on the diagram: When $x = 5$, $y = 3.85 \times 5 + 28.83 = 48.1$
When $x = 45$, $y = 3.85 \times 45 + 28.83 = 202.1$

Often the reason for calculating a regression equation is to use it to predict values for which we have no reading. In the ramp experiment the distance the car might be expected to travel if the ramp was raised to different heights can be predicted using the regression equation.

A7 Use the regression equation to predict how far the car might be expected to travel if the ramp was raised to

(a) 17 cm (b) 3 cm (c) 60 cm

In A7 (a), the value of x is within the range of the observed values of x. Predicting a value within the range of the given data is called **interpolation.** If a straight line is an appropriate model then predictions by interpolation are usually reliable.

In A7 (b) and (c), however, the values of x are outside the range of the original data. Predicting in these cases is called **extrapolation**. Values predicted by extrapolation must be treated with caution. In the car and ramp experiment if the ramp is lowered beyond a certain height the car will not overcome friction and will fail to move. Similarly, as the ramp is raised higher the car may reach a maximum speed and not go beyond a certain distance.

In making predictions by extrapolation the assumption that the linear relationship continues to hold outside the observed range must be checked.

Fitting a straight line to a set of data is called fitting a **linear regression model**. Before doing this, check (for example, with a scatter diagram) that the data appears to follow a linear relationship.

Exercise A (answers p 178)

1 A horticulturist applies different amounts of fertiliser to 10 plots of tomatoes and records the average growth of the plants over a two-week period. These are the results.

Fertiliser (mg/l)	0	5	10	15	20	25	30	35	40	45
Growth (cm)		13.4	15.1	21.2	22.9	25.6	26.3	28.1	30.9	31.7	30.2

(a) Draw a scatter diagram of this data.
Is a linear regression model appropriate in this case?

(b) Calculate the least squares regression line of growth (y) on amount of fertiliser (x) in the form $y = a + bx$.

(c) Plot your regression line on the graph.

(d) Use your regression equation to predict the growth of plants to which the following amounts of fertiliser were applied.

(i) 22 mg/l   (ii) 3 mg/l   (iii) 50 mg/l

(e) Say, with reasons, how reliable you think each of your estimates in (d) is.

2 An elastic band is hung from a hook and different weights are attached to it. The length of the elastic band is measured for each weight.

Weight (grams)	0	25	50	75	100	125	150	175	200
Length (cm)		10.5	18.8	26.2	40.1	46.2	53.8	65.3	70.1	89.2

(a) Draw a scatter diagram of this data.
Is it appropriate to fit a straight line to this data?

(b) Calculate the least squares regression line of length (l) on weight (w).

(c) Plot your regression line on the graph.

(d) Use your regression equation to predict the length of the elastic band if the weights attached were

(i) 60 g   (ii) 300 g

(e) Why might the answer to (d) (ii) be unreliable?

B Explanatory variables

In the examples in section A, the explanatory variable was controlled by the experimenter. In many cases it may not be possible to control the explanatory variable. For example, someone looking at how the temperature affects the sales of ice cream cannot choose the temperature at a given time but must work with the values that happen to occur.

This data shows the temperature (°C) at midday in a seaside resort on various days one summer and the number of ice creams sold at a seafront kiosk.

Temperature (°C)	25	26	16	23	24	18	21	18	19	28
Ice cream sales	305	373	77	162	316	132	184	148	178	402

In this case, it is clearly the temperature which affects the ice cream sales, not the other way round. Temperature is therefore the explanatory variable. Ice cream sales is the response variable.

As shown in the previous section, a regression line is often used to predict a value for the response variable when the value of the explanatory variable is known. The choice of explanatory and response variables will depend on which of the variables the experimenter wants to predict.

For example, it sometimes happens in criminal or archaeological investigations that a single human bone, say a thigh bone, is found. Police and archaeologists may want to predict a person's height from the length of the bone.

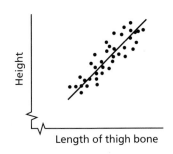

In this case, bone length is taken as the explanatory variable and height as the response variable, since it is the height that is being predicted. Extensive data on heights and bone lengths has been collected. The regression line of height on bone length from this data is used to estimate height for a given bone length.

Interpreting the intercept and gradient

In an equation of the form $y = a + bx$, a represents the **intercept** on the y-axis, that is, the value of y when $x = 0$.

The example on the right comes from an experiment in which the pressure of a gas was measured at various temperatures. The intercept a represents the value given by the regression line for the pressure at $0\,°C$.
The gradient, b, gives the increase in pressure resulting from each $1\,°C$ rise in temperature.

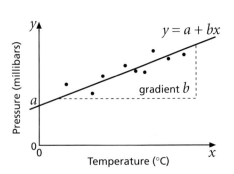

Using a calculator

Many scientific calculators have a regression function which will calculate the values b and a for the regression equation $y = a + bx$. After you have obtained these values it is a good idea to check by keying in the data a second time in a different order.

Exercise B (answers p 178)

1 (a) Use a calculator to find the equation of the regression line for the ice cream data opposite.

  (b) Use the equation to predict the sales when the midday temperature is 20 °C.

  (c) What is the significance of the gradient, b, in this case?

2 A travelling salesman wants to be able to predict his journey time to clients from the distance. He records the distances he travels to 11 clients and his journey times.

Distance (miles)	65	137	257	84	105	346	124	157	201	98	132
Time (hours)	2	2.5	6	2.25	3	7.75	3.25	3.75	4.5	2.75	3.5

  (a) Which variable, distance or time, is the explanatory variable and which the response variable in this case?

  (b) Plot this data on a scatter diagram and check that a linear model is suitable.

  (c) Calculate the least squares regression line of time on distance and plot this on the scatter diagram.

  (d) What is the significance of the value of the intercept, a, in this case? What is the significance of the gradient, b?

  (e) Use the regression equation to predict the time taken for a journey of

    (i) 180 miles   (ii) 50 miles   (iii) 420 miles

  (f) Which of these predictions are likely to be reliable? Explain why the other prediction(s) may not be reliable.

3 A y on x regression equation is to be calculated for two variables x and y. Given that $n = 9$, $\Sigma xy = 2501$, $\Sigma x = 32$, $\Sigma y = 289$ and $\Sigma x^2 = 636$, calculate the least squares regression line of y on x.

4 Atmospheric pressure is often a good indicator of weather conditions to come.

A meteorologist is interested in the possibility of predicting the maximum wind speed in an approaching tropical storm from the lowest atmospheric pressure before the storm is expected to start.

Here is data collected from seven recent storms in an area.

Lowest atmospheric pressure (millibars)	1003	976	990	935	985	931	954
Maximum wind speed (km/h)	66	160	105	230	128	242	210

  (a) Plot this data on a scatter diagram and check that a linear model is suitable.

  (b) Calculate the least squares regression line for predicting wind speed given lowest atmospheric pressure.

  (c) What does the value of the gradient, b, tell you in this case?

  (d) Use the regression equation to predict the maximum wind speed in an approaching storm when the lowest atmospheric pressure beforehand is

    (i) 900 millibars   (ii) 1200 millibars   (iii) 950 millibars

  (e) Which of these predictions do you think is most reliable? Explain why the other predictions may not be so reliable.

C Scaling

This is the data on midday temperature and ice cream sales used in section B.

Temperature (°C) x	25	26	16	23	24	18	21	18	19	28
Ice cream sales y	305	373	77	162	316	132	184	148	178	402

The least squares regression equation in this case was given by $y = 26.2x - 344$.

If the ice cream vendor wanted to predict the daily sales from the forecast midday temperature she could use this equation. However, if she only had temperatures given in Fahrenheit the values would need converting or the equation rewriting in terms of Fahrenheit.

The temperature in Fahrenheit (t) can be found from the temperature in Celsius (x) using the linear scaling

$$t = \tfrac{9}{5}x + 32$$

So $\quad x = \tfrac{5}{9}(t - 32)$

Substituting this into the regression equation gives

$$y = 26.2\left(\tfrac{5}{9}(t - 32)\right) - 344$$

which simplifies to

$$y = 14.6t - 809.8$$

So if the temperature was $80\,°F$ on a particular day, the predicted sales would be

$$14.6 \times 80 - 809.8 = 358$$

K Any regression equation where either variable has been transformed using a linear scaling can be dealt with by substituting the transformation into the regression equation.

Exercise C (answers p 179)

1 This table gives the heights in inches and weights in pounds of a group of school pupils in the USA. A researcher is interested in estimating a person's weight from their height.

Height (inches) x	64	58	55	76	68	65	61	68	64	62
Weight (pounds) y	132	100	82	154	148	130	84	126	108	95

(a) Given that a linear model is suitable in this case, find the least squares regression equation for weight (y) on height (x).

(b) The researcher wants a regression equation which connects heights in centimetres (h) and weights in kilograms (w). Given that 1 inch = 2.54 cm and 1 pound = 0.454 kg, find the regression equation of w on h.

D Residuals (answers p 179)

This table gives the engine size and top speed of a range of saloon cars.

Car	A	B	C	D	E	F	G	H	I	J	K	L	M	N	O
Engine (litres)	3.6	3.25	3.5	3.0	2.5	2.0	2.0	1.8	1.6	1.4	1.3	1.5	1.3	1.1	1.0
Speed (m.p.h.)	181	159	134	149	124	137	106	121	117	118	102	101	96	101	90

Taking the engine size as the explanatory variable x and top speed as the response variable y gives the least squares regression equation $y = 25.5x + 70$.

D1 Use this regression equation to find the predicted value of y for each value of x in the table above.

Calculate the difference d_i between each actual top speed and its predicted value.

> **K** The differences between the observed values of y and those predicted by the regression equation are called the **residuals**.

D2 (a) Which car has the largest positive residual?
What can you say about the top speed of this car relative to its engine size?

(b) Which car has the largest negative residual?
What can you say about the top speed of this car relative to its engine size?

Residuals can be useful in different ways.

- They can identify individual items which underperform or exceed expectations.
- They can be used to identify unusual or extreme items of data called **outliers**.
- They can be used to judge whether a straight line is a good model for the data.

D3 A teacher gives his students a revision test just before an exam. He marks the test out of 20. He claims that this mark is a good predictor of the final exam mark. These are the test marks and final exam marks for the ten students in his group.

Test mark (x)	17	12	15	8	11	18	12	7	5	14
Exam (%) (y)	73	45	58	39	41	68	53	61	30	55

(a) For this data the regression equation is $y = 2.41x + 23.6$.
Plot a scatter diagram of this data and draw the regression line on your graph.

(b) Use the regression equation to calculate predicted exam marks for each of the test scores in the original data. (A spreadsheet is useful here.)
Calculate the residuals for each data pair.

(c) Judging from the residuals, how good do you think the regression line is at predicting the final exam mark?

D4 (a) Identify the data pair in D3 that gives the highest residual.

   (b) Eliminate this pair of results from the data and recalculate the regression equation. Plot this new regression line on the graph.

   (c) Calculate the residuals for the new regression line.

   (d) Which of the two lines you have drawn fits its data better?

   (e) Why might it be reasonable to eliminate the outlier in this case?

Outliers can have a dramatic effect on the regression equation and eliminating them may make the regression line a more effective tool for prediction.

Exercise D (answers p 180)

1 This is the data for the ice cream sales and midday temperature used earlier.

Temperature (°C) x	25	26	16	23	24	18	21	18	19	28
Ice cream sales y	305	373	77	162	316	132	184	148	178	402

The least squares regression equation in this case is given by $y = 26.2x - 344$.

   (a) Calculate the predicted value of y for each of the temperatures in the data and hence the residuals of each daily ice cream sales from the predicted value.

   (b) The ice cream vendor was ill on one of the recorded days and went home early. Which data pair do you think was for this day?

2 Bleep tests are used to measure people's fitness. A higher score means a higher level of fitness. Twelve people had their pulse rate measured and then took part in a bleep test. This table gives the results:

Person		A	B	C	D	E	F	G	H	I	J	K	L
Pulse rate	x	60	54	69	59	65	68	90	79	88	80	96	83
Bleep score	y	10.5	11.2	8.8	4.3	10.0	9.4	5.8	5.8	5.3	7.0	3.6	5.3

   (a) Given that $\Sigma xy = 6177$, $\Sigma x^2 = 68\,197$, $\Sigma x = 891$, $\Sigma y = 87$ and $n = 12$ find the least squares regression equation of y on x.

   (b) Draw a scatter diagram of the data and plot the least squares regression line on it.

   (c) Find the residual for person

   (i) B   (ii) H   (iii) D

   (d) It came to light that one person tripped and fell during the test and finished with a much lower bleep score than expected. Which person do you think this was?

   (e) Remove the person in (d) from the data and recalculate the least squares regression line. Add this line to your scatter diagram.

   (f) Which of the two regression equations you have calculated do you think is better to use when predicting bleep scores from a pulse rate? Use this equation to predict the bleep score of someone with a pulse rate of 100.

Mixed questions (answers p 180)

1 The heights of twelve girls were measured at the age of 8 and again at age 18. This table shows the results.

Height aged 8 (cm)	123	148	132	145	141	138	131	138	123	131	144	129
Height aged 18 (cm)	155	169	165	169	166	169	165	165	157	159	174	161

(a) Plot this data on a scatter diagram and check that a linear model is suitable for this data.

(b) Taking the height at age 8 as the explanatory variable, calculate the least squares regression equation for height at age 18 on height at age 8.
Plot the regression line on your graph.

(c) Use your equation to estimate the height that a girl who is 150 cm tall at age 8 will be at age 18. How reliable do you think your estimate is?

2 The engine capacity of 13 cars with different sized petrol engines was recorded together with their fuel economy in miles per gallon.

Car	A	B	C	D	E	F	G	H	I	J	K	L	M
Engine size (litres)	3.6	3.25	3.5	3.0	2.5	3.0	2.0	1.8	1.6	1.5	1.3	1.1	1.0
Fuel economy (m.p.g.)	18	19	23	32	40	25	33	42	39	40	44	46	47

(a) Explain why engine size is the explanatory variable in this case.

(b) Find the least squares regression equation of fuel economy on engine size.

(c) Calculate the residual for each car.

(d) Cars D, E and H are all made by the same manufacturer.
In the light of the residuals what can you say about the fuel efficiency of the cars from this manufacturer?

Test yourself (answers p 181)

1 Andrew (A), Charles (C) and Edward (E) are employed at the Palace Hotel. Each is responsible for one floor of the building and their duties include cleaning the bedrooms.

The number of bedrooms occupied on each floor varies from day to day.

The following table shows 10 observations of the number, x, of bedrooms to be cleaned and the time taken, y minutes, to carry out the cleaning. The employee carrying out the cleaning is also indicated.

Employee	A	C	E	E	C	A	A	E	C	C
x	8	22	12	24	19	14	22	16	10	21
y	110	211	132	257	184	165	248	171	97	196

(a) Plot a scatter diagram of the data. Identify the employee by labelling each point.

(b) Calculate the equation of the regression line of y on x. Draw the line on your scatter diagram.

(c) Use your regression equation to estimate the time it would take to clean 18 bedrooms.

(d) Calculate the residuals for the three observations when Andrew did the cleaning.

(e) Modify your estimate in part (c) given that the 18 bedrooms are to be cleaned by Andrew.   AQA 2003

2 A pop group undertakes a countrywide tour. It is accompanied by two roadies who pack up the equipment and load it into a removal van after each performance. They also hire local people at each venue to assist with this task. In order to estimate the best number of local people to hire they experiment by varying the number, x, hired and recording the time, y minutes, taken to load the van. The results are tabulated below.

Performance	1	2	3	4	5	6	7	8	9
x	2	3	4	6	6	7	9	9	10
y	384	359	347	322	315	312	299	294	283

(a) Plot a scatter diagram of the data.

(b) Calculate the equation of the regression line of y on x and draw the line on your scatter diagram.

(c) If the line is of the form $y = a + bx$ give an interpretation to each of a and b in the context of this question.

(d) Give two reasons why it would be unwise to use the regression equation to estimate the time taken if 50 people were hired.

(e) The data above for the first nine performances shows that at each performance the number of local people hired was either greater than or equal to the number of people hired at the previous performance. Why does this fact make it more difficult to interpret the result?   AQA 2002

3 As part of an investigation into how accurately witnesses are able to describe incidents, Paulo observed a number of staged incidents. Afterwards he was asked to estimate the ages of some of the participants. Paulo's estimates, y years, together with the actual ages, x years, are shown in the table below.

Participant	A	B	C	D	E	F	G	H	I	J	K
x	86	55	28	69	45	7	17	11	37	2	78
y	74	51	22	59	38	8	15	9	38	2	66

(a) Draw a scatter diagram of Paulo's estimate, y, and the actual age, x.

(b) Calculate the equation of the regression line of y on x and draw it on your diagram.

(c) Calculate the residuals for participants D and I.

(d) Discuss whether a small residual indicates a good estimate of age. Illustrate your answer by making reference to the residuals you have calculated in part (c). *AQA 2002*

4 To investigate a process which is carried out repeatedly in a chemical works, the amount, x kg, of a chemical added to a mixture is varied and the concentration, y%, of the final product is noted.

x	1.0	1.5	2.0	2.5	3.0	3.5	4.0	4.5	5.0
y	2.7	3.0	3.1	3.6	3.5	3.8	4.3	4.4	4.7

(a) Draw a scatter diagram of the data.

(b) Calculate the equation of the regression line of y on x, and draw it on your scatter diagram.

(c) Evaluate the residuals for the points where $x = 3.0$ and $x = 3.5$.

The desirable value for the concentration of the final product is 4.0. The works manager wishes to ensure that it is consistently in the range 3.9 to 4.1.

(d) State, with a reason, whether varying the amount of chemical added is an effective way of controlling the final concentration.

It is decided that in future, 3.65 kg of chemical will be added.

(e) Making reference to your answers in part (c), indicate whether or not the final concentration is likely to be consistently within the required range. *AQA 2001*

10 Correlation

In this chapter you will learn
- how to measure and interpret correlation
- about the effects of scaling data on correlation

A Measuring correlation (answers p 182)

In many areas of interest, statisticians are concerned about whether there is
a connection between two random variables and how strong that connection is.
For example, we might expect a connection between weight and waist size but
not between shoe size and IQ. This chapter is about how we can measure the
strength of any such connections.

Here are four sets of data.

Set 1: snails

This table gives the foot area and mass of 15 snails of the South American species
Biomphalaria glabrate.

Foot area (mm^2)	20	16	35	25	20	7	13	7	3	10	4	1	35	24	38
Mass (g)	0.64	0.21	0.85	0.53	0.18	0.06	0.20	0.07	0.01	0.05	0.02	0.01	0.81	0.38	0.61

Set 2: coins

This table shows the age and mass of ten 2p coins.

Age (years)	7	12	19	16	18	28	12	10	13	19
Mass (g)	7.21	7.34	6.84	7.25	7.24	6.93	7.13	7.33	7.15	7.12

Set 3: reactions

Eleven surgeons injected themselves with a drug to change their heart rate.
They then measured their heart rates and used a computer test to measure
their reaction times. These are the results.

Heart rate (b.p.m.)	134	133	132	123	118	110	98	90	84	80	80
Reaction time (ms)	438	438	467	505	531	557	541	562	591	603	617

Set 4: blood pressure

A group of 20 students weighed themselves and measured their systolic blood pressure (in millimetres of mercury) with an electronic monitor.
This is what they found.

Weight (kg)	60	45	50	37	70	67	55	41	48	38
Blood pressure (mmHg)	141	116	132	114	109	92	95	107	98	97
	59	48	52	38	49	44	43	59	50	40
	98	85	115	104	163	153	86	122	106	97

A1 Draw a scatter diagram for each of the four sets of data. You may find a spreadsheet or a graph plotter useful for this.

What do the graphs tell you about any connection between the two variables in each set of data?

Data that consists of pairs of values of two random variables is called **bivariate data**.

When investigating the connection between two variables we examine whether there tends to be a linear relationship. When there is, the two variables are said to be **correlated**.

To judge how strongly a particular pair of variables is correlated, a suitable numerical measure is necessary. Consider the following scatter diagram, where the plotted points are approximately in a straight line.

Dotted lines for $\bar{x}$ and $\bar{y}$ have been drawn.
They divide the diagram into four 'quadrants' A, B, C, D.

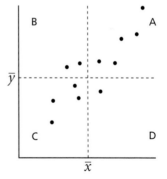

A2 If a point (x, y) is in quadrant A, what is the sign of

(a) $x - \bar{x}$ (the deviation of x from the mean)

(b) $y - \bar{y}$ (the deviation of y from the mean)

(c) $(x - \bar{x})(y - \bar{y})$ (the product of the deviations)

A3 What sign is the product of the deviations for each of the quadrants B, C and D?

A4 If the product of the deviations is found for every point on a scatter diagram and summed to give $\Sigma(x_i - \bar{x})(y_i - \bar{y})$, what can you say about this sum in each of these cases?

(a) When all of the points lie in quadrants A and C and the points approximate to a straight line with a positive gradient

(b) When all of the points lie in quadrants B and D and the points approximate to a straight line with a negative gradient

(c) When the points are spread evenly over all four quadrants

A5 (a) For each of these four sets of bivariate data,

- sketch a scatter diagram
- calculate the sum of the products of the deviations, $\Sigma(x_i - \bar{x})(y_i - \bar{y})$

(i)

x	1	2	3	4	5
y	3	5	2	4	1

(ii)

x	1	2	3	4	5
y	1	2	3	4	5

(iii)

x	1	2	3	4	5
y	5	4	3	2	1

(iv)

x	1	2	3	4	5
y	2	1	3	5	4

(b) How does the sum of the products of the deviations help to describe the correlation in these cases?

As with the variance and standard deviation, in order to make comparisons between sets of data with different numbers of pairs, the sum needs to be averaged out over the number of items of data.

The result is called the **covariance**.

K The covariance is defined as $s_{xy} = \dfrac{\Sigma(x_i - \bar{x})(y_i - \bar{y})}{n}$.

The covariance measures the extent to which the values of x and y are associated, high with high and low with low.

A6 Calculate the covariance for the snails data on page 136.

A7 Calculate the covariance for the coins, reaction times and blood pressure data at the start of this chapter. Looking at your answers to A1, what does the covariance tell you in each case about the correlation between the two variables?

You will already have seen that there are alternative easier ways of calculating the variance. In a similar way the covariance can be calculated using the formula

$$s_{xy} = \frac{\Sigma x_i y_i - n\bar{x}\,\bar{y}}{n} \quad \text{or} \quad \frac{\Sigma x_i y_i - \dfrac{\Sigma x_i \Sigma y_i}{n}}{n}$$

Your results so far should show that, when a set of data roughly fits a straight line with a positive gradient, the covariance is positive. The two variables are then said to be **positively correlated.**

Similarly, when the set of data roughly fits a straight line with a negative gradient, the covariance is negative. The two variables are then said to be **negatively correlated.**

When the data pairs are widely spread and do not approximate to a straight line, there is little or no correlation and the covariance is close to zero.

D **A8** A scientist collected some data on the size in millimetres of some fleas and the heights in metres they were able to jump. She calculated the covariance to be 0.345. Does this tell you anything about how strong the correlation is between the size of a flea and the height it can jump?

The covariance can show whether a correlation is positive or negative but it does not by itself easily measure how closely the data fits a straight line, because its size is dependent on the scales of the data.

A9 The table below shows, for the snails data, the standard deviation of the x values (s_x), the standard deviation of the y values (s_y) and the product of s_x and s_y. The covariance (s_{xy}) is also shown.

	s_x	s_y	$s_x \times s_y$	s_{xy}
Snails	11.850	0.292	3.460	3.194
Coins				

Complete the table, adding results for the other three sets of data.

A10 What does the result of A9 suggest about the product of the two standard deviations in relation to the covariance when there is

(a) strong positive correlation   (b) strong negative correlation

(c) very little correlation

The English statistician Karl Pearson (1857–1936) developed this idea by devising the **product moment correlation coefficient**. This is usually abbreviated to p.m.c.c. and denoted by the letter r.

The p.m.c.c. is given by $r = \dfrac{s_{xy}}{s_x s_y}$.

A11 Find the p.m.c.c. for the snails data on page 136.

Note that when calculating the p.m.c.c. you should use any values from your calculator to the full number of decimal places and avoid rounding until the final result. The final result is usually given to three decimal places.

A12 These values of x and y lie exactly on a straight line with a positive gradient. Show, using surds, that they give a p.m.c.c. of exactly 1.

x	1	2	4	5
y	1	5	13	17

A13 Without calculating, explain why these values would give a p.m.c.c. of −1.

x	1	2	4	5
y	17	13	5	1

A14 Sketch a scatter diagram for these values.
Calculate the p.m.c.c. and explain your result.

x	1	1	3	3
y	1	3	1	3

The p.m.c.c. can be written as $r = \dfrac{\dfrac{1}{n}\sum(x_i - \bar{x})(y_i - \bar{y})}{s_x s_y}$

If the points (x_i, y_i) lie on a straight line with equation $y = px + q$, then $r = 1$ if p, the gradient, is positive and $r = -1$ if p is negative.

This can be shown as follows.

From the work on scaling in chapter 2, we know that

$$\bar{y} = p\bar{x} + q$$

and $s_y^2 = p^2 s_x^2$, so $s_y = |p| s_x$ (where $|p|$ is the absolute value* of p)

So $(y_i - \bar{y}) = (px_i + q) - (p\bar{x} + q) = p(x_i - \bar{x})$

So $r = \dfrac{\dfrac{1}{n}\sum(x_i - \bar{x})(y_i - \bar{y})}{s_x s_y} = \dfrac{\dfrac{1}{n}\sum p(x_i - \bar{x})^2}{|p| s_x^2} = \dfrac{p s_x^2}{|p| s_x^2} = \dfrac{p}{|p|}$

If p is positive, then $\dfrac{p}{|p|} = 1$, so $r = 1$. If p is negative, then $\dfrac{p}{|p|} = -1$, so $r = -1$.

It can also be shown that $s_{xy}^2 \le s_x^2 s_y^2$ and hence $-1 \le r \le 1$.

When investigating the correlation between two variables, it is not necessary to calculate the standard deviations first. An easier calculating form can then be used:

K

$$r = \dfrac{\sum x_i y_i - \dfrac{\sum x_i \sum y_i}{n}}{\sqrt{\left(\sum x_i^2 - \dfrac{(\sum x_i)^2}{n}\right)\left(\sum y_i^2 - \dfrac{(\sum y_i)^2}{n}\right)}}$$

The values needed in this formula can usually be read from a scientific calculator. Most such calculators will even complete the calculation.

K

The p.m.c.c., r, is always in the range $-1 \le r \le 1$, with a value of 1 showing perfect positive correlation and a value of -1 perfect negative correlation. A value of 0 shows that there is no correlation between the two variables.

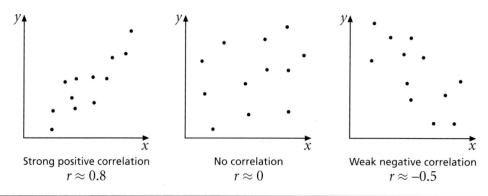

| Strong positive correlation | No correlation | Weak negative correlation |
| $r \approx 0.8$ | $r \approx 0$ | $r \approx -0.5$ |

---

* For example, if $p = 3$, then $|p| = 3$, if $p = -2$ then $|p| = 2$.

A15 Find the product moment correlation coefficient for the data in the coins, reactions and blood pressure data sets at the start of this chapter. Comment on the results.

Exercise A (answers p 183)

1 Twelve cigarettes were sampled from a range of brands and their tar and nicotine content measured. This table shows the results.

Tar (mg)	16	8	4.1	15	8.8	12.4	16.6	14.9	13.7	15.1	11.4	17
Nicotine (mg)	1.06	0.67	0.4	1.04	0.76	0.95	1.12	1.02	1.01	0.9	0.78	1.26

(a) Calculate the p.m.c.c. for this data.

(b) What does this tell you about the amount of tar and nicotine in these cigarettes?

2 A group of students were asked to push a ball through a maze while looking through a mirror. Their time in seconds to complete the course was recorded. Each student completed the experiment first with their dominant hand (the hand they wrote with) and then with their other hand. This table shows the results.

Student	A	B	C	D	E	F	G	H	I	J
Dominant (s)	76	45	32	85	79	105	143	108	56	74
Other hand (s)	113	52	30	78	100	141	181	98	78	105

Draw a scatter diagram of these results and calculate the product moment correlation coefficient between the times taken for the two hands.

3 A family records for a number of days in March the midday temperature outside, in °C, and the number of units of electricity they used that day.

Temperature (°C)	7.4	12.3	9.6	9.0	8.7	14.7	18.2	11.3	10.4	9.3
Units used (kWh)	48	34	42	46	44	36	34	38	48	45

(a) Calculate the p.m.c.c. between the temperature and the units of electricity used.

(b) The family believes that on warmer days they use less electricity. Does the result in (a) support this hypothesis?

4 A doctor records the weights, in kg, and blood pressures, in millimetres of mercury, of the patients who attend his surgery one day. He also notes whether they were male or female. These are the results.

Male/female	M	M	F	M	F	F	M	M	M	F	M	M	F	F
Weight (kg)	60	45	48	50	44	43	48	59	67	41	55	57	38	40
Pressure (mmHg)	143	110	106	129	108	102	101	125	127	97	104	98	102	97

(a) Find the correlation between weight and blood pressure for
  (i) the male patients (ii) the female patients

(b) Which of these two groups shows the stronger correlation between weight and blood pressure, male or female?

B Scaling (answers p 184)

This table shows, for 10 days in the same month, the midday temperature (°C) and the number of units of electricity used by a family that day.

Temperature (°C)	3.4	6.8	5.7	8.9	10.5	8.6	7.3	15.0	12.7	9.2
Units used (kWh)	49	46	58	46	47	48	50	27	36	45

Suppose, however, that the temperature was recorded in degrees Fahrenheit.

To convert temperatures from Celsius (c) to Fahrenheit (f) the following transformation is used:

$$f = \tfrac{9}{5}c + 32$$

B1 Would changing the temperatures to Fahrenheit alter the correlation? Check your answer by calculating the p.m.c.c. for the data using the temperature first in degrees Celsius and then in degrees Fahrenheit. A spreadsheet or graphic calculator is useful.

The graphs below show a set of data, the same set of data with the y-values doubled, and the original data with 5 added to each of the x-values.

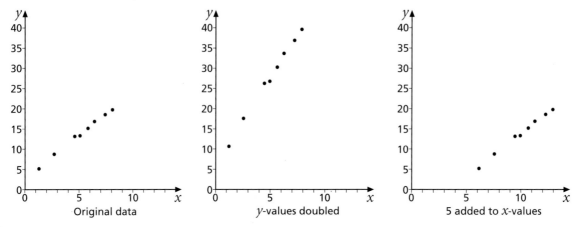

Original data y-values doubled   5 added to x-values

Although the position of the points in relation to the axes is different in each case, the relative positions of the points to one another are unchanged. This is why a linear transformation or scaling of one or both variables does not affect the correlation.

C Interpreting correlation (answers p 184)

You have probably heard the claim 'You can prove anything with statistics'. It is of course untrue: statistics never aims to prove anything but may provide evidence to support a particular theory. However, correlation is often used in inappropriate ways to 'support' claims.

A student carries out a survey of students in her school. To get a representative sample she chooses 5 students from each year group from year 7 to year 13. She records a number of variables for each student.

She draws this scatter diagram of heights and scores in a general knowledge quiz.
The p.m.c.c. for this data is 0.885.

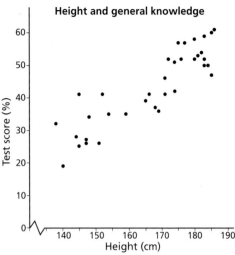

Height and general knowledge

D **C1** Does this suggest that being taller makes you better at general knowledge?

This is a common misuse of correlation. A strong correlation does not mean that one variable is the 'cause' of a second variable. A high positive correlation simply says that high values of one variable occur with high values of the other variable, and low with low. Cases such as this are referred to as **spurious** correlation.

In many cases the apparent link may be the effect of a third variable, as in the example above, where both variables are linked to age, which is likely to be the 'cause' of both variables. Older students are likely to be taller and to have better general knowledge.

There are other circumstances where an apparent correlation is due to something unusual in the data. The next question is about one such case.

C2 This data set shows the heights and weights of a group of year 7 pupils together with their teacher.

Height (cm)	147	154	156	161	150	163	160	158	157	183
Weight (kg)	45	38	59	48	37	60	59	44	45	98

(a) Calculate the p.m.c.c. between height and weight.

(b) The final pair are the height and weight of the teacher. Recalculate the p.m.c.c. without this data pair.

(c) Comment on the differences between the values in (a) and (b).

One or two outliers can have a dramatic effect on a correlation, either to exaggerate a strong correlation or to make an otherwise strong correlation appear weak.

In some cases a correlation may exist within a subgroup of the population but not in the whole population. A student looking for a correlation between leg lengths and running speed collected data from members of her athletics club. She was disappointed to find a very weak correlation in the club members. However, it is still possible that a correlation may exist in the population as a whole.

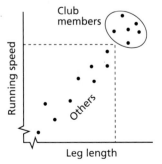

The p.m.c.c. is an appropriate measure only where the
relationship between two random variables is **linear**.

The data in this graph gives a correlation coefficient of –0.1
yet it fits a non-linear relationship closely.

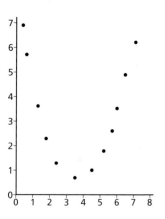

Exercise C (answers p 184)

1 Ten students measured their reaction times, in milliseconds, using their
left hand and then using their right hand. The results were:

Student	A	B	C	D	E	F	G	H	I	J
Left hand (ms)	15.4	18.7	23.4	19.2	22.5	25.4	20.9	16.4	21.1	19.7
Right hand (ms)	19.6	13.2	19.4	15.3	18.6	20.9	17.6	20.3	17.2	14.8

(a) Calculate the p.m.c.c. for these ten students.

(b) Draw a scatter diagram for this data.

(c) Two of the students in this experiment were in fact left-handed.
Which two students do you think these were?

(d) Calculate the p.m.c.c. for the eight students who are right-handed.

(e) Comment on the values you obtained for the p.m.c.c. in (a) and (d).

2 The number of people who visited the cinema the previous week in a sample
of towns in the UK was recorded. A researcher calculated the correlation
between this variable and the numbers of crimes in the towns.
The p.m.c.c. obtained was 0.84.

A campaigner against violent films claimed that this was evidence that going
to the cinema encouraged people to commit crimes.
Say, with reasons, whether the survey supports this point of view.

3 The maximum daily outside temperature and the amount of electricity
used by an office air-conditioning system were recorded as follows:

Temperature (°C)	18.2	8.9	28.2	29.6	16.1	26.7	20.4	21.0	5.4	23.4	12.4	15.5
Units used (kWh)	4.3	13.2	12.7	13.5	7.6	9.6	5.1	6.3	15.8	7.8	11.1	9.1

(a) Calculate the p.m.c.c. between temperature and units of electricity used.
What does this suggest about the link between the temperature and the
amount of electricity used?

(b) Draw a scatter diagram of this data.

(c) Explain why the p.m.c.c. may not be a good measure of the correlation
in this case.

Key points

- The covariance measures the spread of a set of bivariate data.
  It is calculated by the formula

$$s_{xy} = \frac{\sum(x_i - \bar{x})(y_i - \bar{y})}{n} \quad \text{or} \quad s_{xy} = \frac{\sum x_i y_i - n\bar{x}\,\bar{y}}{n}$$

(p 138)

- Correlation is a measure of how well a bivariate set of data follows a linear relationship. Correlation can be measured by the product moment correlation coefficient, which is given by

$$r = \frac{s_{xy}}{s_x s_y} = \frac{\sum x_i y_i - \dfrac{\sum x_i \sum y_i}{n}}{\sqrt{\left(\sum x_i^2 - \dfrac{(\sum x_i)^2}{n}\right)\left(\sum y_i^2 - \dfrac{(\sum y_i)^2}{n}\right)}}$$

The p.m.c.c. always lies in the range $-1 \leq r \leq 1$. (p 140)

- If one or more of the variables is scaled using a linear transformation, then this does not affect the value of r. (p 142)

Test yourself (answers p 185)

1 (a) Estimate the value of the p.m.c.c. in each of these scatter diagrams.

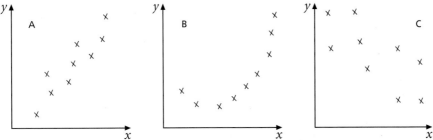

(b) The p.m.c.c. is not an appropriate measure of the connection between the two variables in one of these cases. Say, with reasons, which case this is.

(c) In diagram A, x is the number of ice creams sold in a month and y is the number of car radiators replaced at a garage. Give a possible reason for the apparent connection.

2 A class of statistics students, studying correlation, obtains data by completing a questionnaire and by reference to a register.
They use the data collected to practise their calculations.

A student calculates that the product moment correlation coefficient for the class is

(a) 1.17 between average journey time to school and distance travelled

(b) −0.34 between height and weight

(c) 0.75 between marks in the last test and number of days absent last term

For each calculation, state, giving a reason, whether the result is probably correct, probably incorrect or definitely incorrect.

AQA 2001

3 The table shows a verbal reasoning test score, x, and an English test score, y, for each of a sample of 8 children who took both tests.

Child	A	B	C	D	E	F	G	H
x	112	113	110	113	112	114	109	113
y	69	65	75	70	70	75	68	76

(a) Calculate the value of the product moment correlation coefficient between the scores in verbal reasoning and English.

(b) Comment briefly, in context, on the result obtained in part (a).

AQA 2003

4 The following table shows, for a sample of towns in Great Britain, the number of solicitors, x, and the number of cars stolen last week, y.

x	12	7	11	19	5	21	3	4	17
y	14	3	21	28	6	43	1	12	30

(a) (i) Calculate the value of the product moment correlation coefficient for the data.

(ii) Interpret your result from part (a)(i) in the context of the question.

(b) Comment on the suggestion that most car thieves are solicitors.

AQA 2003

5 Ten golfers are asked to try out a new golf club at a driving range.
They each have two shots, one with the left hand in front and one with the right hand in front.
The distance the ball travels in yards is recorded for each shot.

Golfer	A	B	C	D	E	F	G	H	I	J
Left hand in front	245	190	285	155	215	205	245	230	190	185
Right hand in front	185	150	230	220	175	195	210	195	160	240

(a) Calculate the product moment correlation coefficient between the distance travelled with the left hand in front and the distance travelled with the right hand in front.

(b) Comment on the performances of golfers D and J.

(c) If the product moment correlation coefficient is calculated without golfers D and J it gives the value 0.885, correct to three decimal places. Comment on this value and the value you calculated in (a).

6 An entomologist records the midday temperature in °C and the number of butterflies she finds on a marked square of meadow on several days in August. She calculates the product moment correlation coefficient between these two variables to be 0.57.

She is then told by a colleague that her thermometer was faulty and in fact the temperature readings were all 15% higher than the true temperature. If she adjusts her calculations for this, what effect will this have on the value of the correlation coefficient?

Excel functions

Although current examination requirements make it necessary to practise using statistical tables and the statistical functions of a calculator, spreadsheet functions are valuable for exploring statistical topics or undertaking coursework that involves large data sets.

AVERAGE(range of cells) Calculates the mean of the values in the cells, specified for example as A1:A10.

BINOMDIST($x, n, p,$ TRUE) Works like the cumulative binomial distribution tables (pp 66–67).

COMBIN(n, r) Calculates $\binom{n}{r}$, the number of combinations of r objects from n (pp 60–61).

CORREL(cells for variable 1, cells for variable 2) Calculates the product moment correlation coefficient for bivariate data organised in two corresponding ranges of cells; **PEARSON** does the same (p 139).

COVAR(cells for variable 1, cells for variable 2) Calculates the covariance of bivariate data organised in two corresponding ranges of cells (p 138).

INTERCEPT(cells for response variable, cells for explanatory variable) Calculates the y-intercept of the least squares regression line for the data organised in two corresponding ranges of cells.
SLOPE(cells for response variable, cells for explanatory variable) Calculates the gradient of the least squares regression line (the regression coefficient) (pp 124–128).

MEDIAN(range of cells) Finds the median of the values in the stated cells.

NORMDIST($x,$ mean, standard deviation, TRUE) Works like the normal distribution table, except the variable does not first need to be standardised (pp 80–81).

NORMINV($p,$ mean, standard deviation) Works like the percentage points table but the result is the value of the actual, not the standardised, variable (pp 83–84).

RANDBETWEEN(minimum, maximum) Generates a uniformly distributed random integer in the stated range.

RANDOM Generates samples from a choice of types of distribution with parameters that can be set (see pp 113–114 for how to access the facility and an example of its use in an exploratory way).

STDEV(range of cells) Assumes the values constitute a sample from a population and calculates an unbiased estimate of the population standard deviation (pp 101–103).

STDEVP(range of cells) Finds the population standard deviation where the values in the cells are taken to be the whole population, not a sample (pp 24–27).

VAR(range of cells) Assumes the values constitute a sample from a population and calculates an unbiased estimate of the population variance (pp 101–103).

VARP(range of cells) Finds the population variance where the values in the cells are taken to be the whole population, not a sample (pp 24–27).

Tables

Cumulative binomial distribution function

The tabulated value is $P(X \le x)$, where X has a binomial distribution with parameters n and p.

p	0.01	0.02	0.03	0.04	0.05	0.06	0.07	0.08	0.09	0.10	0.15	0.20	0.25	0.30	0.35	0.40	0.45	0.50	p
x	n = 2																		x
0	0.9801	0.9604	0.9409	0.9216	0.9025	0.8836	0.8649	0.8464	0.8281	0.8100	0.7225	0.6400	0.5625	0.4900	0.4225	0.3600	0.3025	0.2500	0
1	0.9999	0.9996	0.9991	0.9984	0.9975	0.9964	0.9951	0.9936	0.9919	0.9900	0.9775	0.9600	0.9375	0.9100	0.8775	0.8400	0.7975	0.7500	1
2	1.0000	1.0000	1.0000	1.0000	1.0000	1.0000	1.0000	1.0000	1.0000	1.0000	1.0000	1.0000	1.0000	1.0000	1.0000	1.0000	1.0000	1.0000	2
x	n = 3																		x
0	0.9703	0.9412	0.9127	0.8847	0.8574	0.8306	0.8044	0.7787	0.7536	0.7290	0.6141	0.5120	0.4219	0.3430	0.2746	0.2160	0.1664	0.1250	0
1	0.9997	0.9988	0.9974	0.9953	0.9928	0.9896	0.9860	0.9818	0.9772	0.9720	0.9393	0.8960	0.8438	0.7840	0.7183	0.6480	0.5748	0.5000	1
2	1.0000	1.0000	1.0000	0.9999	0.9999	0.9998	0.9997	0.9995	0.9993	0.9990	0.9966	0.9920	0.9844	0.9730	0.9571	0.9360	0.9089	0.8750	2
3				1.0000	1.0000	1.0000	1.0000	1.0000	1.0000	1.0000	1.0000	1.0000	1.0000	1.0000	1.0000	1.0000	1.0000	1.0000	3
x	n = 4																		x
0	0.9606	0.9224	0.8853	0.8493	0.8145	0.7807	0.7481	0.7164	0.6857	0.6561	0.5220	0.4096	0.3164	0.2401	0.1785	0.1296	0.0915	0.0625	0
1	0.9994	0.9977	0.9948	0.9909	0.9860	0.9801	0.9733	0.9656	0.9570	0.9477	0.8905	0.8192	0.7383	0.6517	0.5630	0.4752	0.3910	0.3125	1
2	1.0000	1.0000	0.9999	0.9998	0.9995	0.9992	0.9987	0.9981	0.9973	0.9963	0.9880	0.9728	0.9492	0.9163	0.8735	0.8208	0.7585	0.6875	2
3			1.0000	1.0000	1.0000	1.0000	1.0000	1.0000	0.9999	0.9999	0.9995	0.9984	0.9961	0.9919	0.9850	0.9744	0.9590	0.9375	3
4									1.0000	1.0000	1.0000	1.0000	1.0000	1.0000	1.0000	1.0000	1.0000	1.0000	4
x	n = 5																		x
0	0.9510	0.9039	0.8587	0.8154	0.7738	0.7339	0.6957	0.6591	0.6240	0.5905	0.4437	0.3277	0.2373	0.1681	0.1160	0.0778	0.0503	0.0313	0
1	0.9990	0.9962	0.9915	0.9852	0.9774	0.9681	0.9575	0.9456	0.9326	0.9185	0.8352	0.7373	0.6328	0.5282	0.4284	0.3370	0.2562	0.1875	1
2	1.0000	0.9999	0.9997	0.9994	0.9988	0.9980	0.9969	0.9955	0.9937	0.9914	0.9734	0.9421	0.8965	0.8369	0.7648	0.6826	0.5931	0.5000	2
3		1.0000	1.0000	1.0000	0.9999	0.9999	0.9998	0.9997	0.9995	0.9978	0.9933	0.9844	0.9692	0.9460	0.9130	0.8688	0.8125	3
4					1.0000	1.0000	1.0000	1.0000	1.0000	0.9999	0.9997	0.9990	0.9976	0.9947	0.9898	0.9815	0.9688	4
5											1.0000	1.0000	1.0000	1.0000	1.0000	1.0000	1.0000	1.0000	5
x	n = 6																		x
0	0.9415	0.8858	0.8330	0.7828	0.7351	0.6899	0.6470	0.6064	0.5679	0.5314	0.3771	0.2621	0.1780	0.1176	0.0754	0.0467	0.0277	0.0156	0
1	0.9985	0.9943	0.9875	0.9784	0.9672	0.9541	0.9392	0.9227	0.9048	0.8857	0.7765	0.6554	0.5339	0.4202	0.3191	0.2333	0.1636	0.1094	1
2	1.0000	0.9998	0.9995	0.9988	0.9978	0.9962	0.9942	0.9915	0.9882	0.9842	0.9527	0.9011	0.8306	0.7443	0.6471	0.5443	0.4415	0.3438	2
3		1.0000	1.0000	0.9999	0.9998	0.9997	0.9995	0.9992	0.9987	0.9941	0.9830	0.9624	0.9295	0.8826	0.8208	0.7447	0.6563	3
4					1.0000	1.0000	1.0000	1.0000	1.0000	0.9999	0.9996	0.9984	0.9954	0.9891	0.9777	0.9590	0.9308	0.8906	4
5											1.0000	1.0000	0.9999	0.9998	0.9993	0.9982	0.9959	0.9917	0.9844	5
6												1.0000	1.0000	1.0000	1.0000	1.0000	1.0000	1.0000	6
x	n = 7																		x
0	0.9321	0.8681	0.8080	0.7514	0.6983	0.6485	0.6017	0.5578	0.5168	0.4783	0.3206	0.2097	0.1335	0.0824	0.0490	0.0280	0.0152	0.0078	0
1	0.9980	0.9921	0.9829	0.9706	0.9556	0.9382	0.9187	0.8974	0.8745	0.8503	0.7166	0.5767	0.4449	0.3294	0.2338	0.1586	0.1024	0.0625	1
2	1.0000	0.9997	0.9991	0.9980	0.9962	0.9937	0.9903	0.9860	0.9807	0.9743	0.9262	0.8520	0.7564	0.6471	0.5323	0.4199	0.3164	0.2266	2
3		1.0000	1.0000	0.9999	0.9998	0.9996	0.9993	0.9988	0.9982	0.9973	0.9879	0.9667	0.9294	0.8740	0.8002	0.7102	0.6083	0.5000	3
4				1.0000	1.0000	1.0000	1.0000	0.9999	0.9999	0.9998	0.9988	0.9953	0.9871	0.9712	0.9444	0.9037	0.8471	0.7734	4
5							1.0000	1.0000	1.0000	0.9999	0.9996	0.9987	0.9962	0.9910	0.9812	0.9643	0.9375	5
6											1.0000	1.0000	0.9999	0.9998	0.9994	0.9984	0.9963	0.9922	6
7													1.0000	1.0000	1.0000	1.0000	1.0000	1.0000	7
x	n = 8																		x
0	0.9227	0.8508	0.7837	0.7214	0.6634	0.6096	0.5596	0.5132	0.4703	0.4305	0.2725	0.1678	0.1001	0.0576	0.0319	0.0168	0.0084	0.0039	0
1	0.9973	0.9897	0.9777	0.9619	0.9428	0.9208	0.8965	0.8702	0.8423	0.8131	0.6572	0.5033	0.3671	0.2553	0.1691	0.1064	0.0632	0.0352	1
2	0.9999	0.9996	0.9987	0.9969	0.9942	0.9904	0.9853	0.9789	0.9711	0.9619	0.8948	0.7969	0.6785	0.5518	0.4278	0.3154	0.2201	0.1445	2
3	1.0000	1.0000	0.9999	0.9998	0.9996	0.9993	0.9987	0.9978	0.9966	0.9950	0.9786	0.9437	0.8862	0.8059	0.7064	0.5941	0.4770	0.3633	3
4			1.0000	1.0000	1.0000	1.0000	0.9999	0.9999	0.9997	0.9996	0.9971	0.9896	0.9727	0.9420	0.8939	0.8263	0.7396	0.6367	4
5						1.0000	1.0000	1.0000	1.0000	0.9998	0.9988	0.9958	0.9887	0.9747	0.9502	0.9115	0.8555	5
6											1.0000	0.9999	0.9996	0.9987	0.9964	0.9915	0.9819	0.9648	6
7												1.0000	1.0000	0.9999	0.9998	0.9993	0.9983	0.9961	7
8														1.0000	1.0000	1.0000	1.0000	1.0000	8

p	0.01	0.02	0.03	0.04	0.05	0.06	0.07	0.08	0.09	0.10	0.15	0.20	0.25	0.30	0.35	0.40	0.45	0.50	p
x	**n = 9**																		**x**
0	0.9135	0.8337	0.7602	0.6925	0.6302	0.5730	0.5204	0.4722	0.4279	0.3874	0.2316	0.1342	0.0751	0.0404	0.0207	0.0101	0.0046	0.0020	0
1	0.9966	0.9869	0.9718	0.9522	0.9288	0.9022	0.8729	0.8417	0.8088	0.7748	0.5995	0.4362	0.3003	0.1960	0.1211	0.0705	0.0385	0.0195	1
2	0.9999	0.9994	0.9980	0.9955	0.9916	0.9862	0.9791	0.9702	0.9595	0.9470	0.8591	0.7382	0.6007	0.4628	0.3373	0.2318	0.1495	0.0898	2
3	1.0000	1.0000	0.9999	0.9997	0.9994	0.9987	0.9977	0.9963	0.9943	0.9917	0.9661	0.9144	0.8343	0.7297	0.6089	0.4826	0.3614	0.2539	3
4			1.0000	1.0000	1.0000	0.9999	0.9998	0.9997	0.9995	0.9991	0.9944	0.9804	0.9511	0.9012	0.8283	0.7334	0.6214	0.5000	4
5						1.0000	1.0000	1.0000	1.0000	0.9999	0.9994	0.9969	0.9900	0.9747	0.9464	0.9006	0.8342	0.7461	5
6										1.0000	1.0000	0.9997	0.9987	0.9957	0.9888	0.9750	0.9502	0.9102	6
7												1.0000	0.9999	0.9996	0.9986	0.9962	0.9909	0.9805	7
8													1.0000	1.0000	0.9999	0.9997	0.9992	0.9980	8
9															1.0000	1.0000	1.0000	1.0000	9
x	**n = 10**																		**x**
0	0.9044	0.8171	0.7374	0.6648	0.5987	0.5386	0.4840	0.4344	0.3894	0.3487	0.1969	0.1074	0.0563	0.0282	0.0135	0.0060	0.0025	0.0010	0
1	0.9957	0.9838	0.9655	0.9418	0.9139	0.8824	0.8483	0.8121	0.7746	0.7361	0.5443	0.3758	0.2440	0.1493	0.0860	0.0464	0.0233	0.0107	1
2	0.9999	0.9991	0.9972	0.9938	0.9885	0.9812	0.9717	0.9599	0.9460	0.9298	0.8202	0.6778	0.5256	0.3828	0.2616	0.1673	0.0996	0.0547	2
3	1.0000	1.0000	0.9999	0.9996	0.9990	0.9980	0.9964	0.9942	0.9912	0.9872	0.9500	0.8791	0.7759	0.6496	0.5138	0.3823	0.2660	0.1719	3
4			1.0000	1.0000	0.9999	0.9998	0.9997	0.9994	0.9990	0.9984	0.9901	0.9672	0.9219	0.8497	0.7515	0.6331	0.5044	0.3770	4
5					1.0000	1.0000	1.0000	1.0000	0.9999	0.9999	0.9986	0.9936	0.9803	0.9527	0.9051	0.8338	0.7384	0.6230	5
6									1.0000	1.0000	0.9999	0.9991	0.9965	0.9894	0.9740	0.9452	0.8980	0.8281	6
7											1.0000	0.9999	0.9996	0.9984	0.9952	0.9877	0.9726	0.9453	7
8												1.0000	1.0000	0.9999	0.9995	0.9983	0.9955	0.9893	8
9														1.0000	1.0000	0.9999	0.9997	0.9990	9
10																1.0000	1.0000	1.0000	10
x	**n = 11**																		**x**
0	0.8953	0.8007	0.7153	0.6382	0.5688	0.5063	0.4501	0.3996	0.3544	0.3138	0.1673	0.0859	0.0422	0.0198	0.0088	0.0036	0.0014	0.0005	0
1	0.9948	0.9805	0.9587	0.9308	0.8981	0.8618	0.8228	0.7819	0.7399	0.6974	0.4922	0.3221	0.1971	0.1130	0.0606	0.0302	0.0139	0.0059	1
2	0.9998	0.9988	0.9963	0.9917	0.9848	0.9752	0.9630	0.9481	0.9305	0.9104	0.7788	0.6174	0.4552	0.3127	0.2001	0.1189	0.0652	0.0327	2
3	1.0000	1.0000	0.9998	0.9993	0.9984	0.9970	0.9947	0.9915	0.9871	0.9815	0.9306	0.8389	0.7133	0.5696	0.4256	0.2963	0.1911	0.1133	3
4			1.0000	1.0000	0.9999	0.9997	0.9995	0.9990	0.9983	0.9972	0.9841	0.9496	0.8854	0.7897	0.6683	0.5328	0.3971	0.2744	4
5					1.0000	1.0000	1.0000	0.9999	0.9998	0.9997	0.9973	0.9883	0.9657	0.9218	0.8513	0.7535	0.6331	0.5000	5
6								1.0000	1.0000	1.0000	0.9997	0.9980	0.9924	0.9784	0.9499	0.9006	0.8262	0.7256	6
7											1.0000	0.9998	0.9988	0.9957	0.9878	0.9707	0.9390	0.8867	7
8												1.0000	0.9999	0.9994	0.9980	0.9941	0.9852	0.9673	8
9													1.0000	1.0000	0.9998	0.9993	0.9978	0.9941	9
10															1.0000	1.0000	0.9998	0.9995	10
11																		1.0000	11
x	**n = 12**																		**x**
0	0.8864	0.7847	0.6938	0.6127	0.5404	0.4759	0.4186	0.3677	0.3225	0.2824	0.1422	0.0687	0.0317	0.0138	0.0057	0.0022	0.0008	0.0002	0
1	0.9938	0.9769	0.9514	0.9191	0.8816	0.8405	0.7967	0.7513	0.7052	0.6590	0.4435	0.2749	0.1584	0.0850	0.0424	0.0196	0.0083	0.0032	1
2	0.9998	0.9985	0.9952	0.9893	0.9804	0.9684	0.9532	0.9348	0.9134	0.8891	0.7358	0.5583	0.3907	0.2528	0.1513	0.0834	0.0421	0.0193	2
3	1.0000	0.9999	0.9997	0.9990	0.9978	0.9957	0.9925	0.9880	0.9820	0.9744	0.9078	0.7946	0.6488	0.4925	0.3467	0.2253	0.1345	0.0730	3
4			1.0000	1.0000	0.9999	0.9998	0.9996	0.9991	0.9984	0.9973	0.9957	0.9761	0.9274	0.8424	0.7237	0.5833	0.4382	0.3044	0.1938	4
5					1.0000	1.0000	1.0000	0.9999	0.9998	0.9997	0.9995	0.9954	0.9806	0.9456	0.8822	0.7873	0.6652	0.5269	0.3872	5
6								1.0000	1.0000	1.0000	0.9999	0.9993	0.9961	0.9857	0.9614	0.9154	0.8418	0.7393	0.6128	6
7											1.0000	0.9999	0.9994	0.9972	0.9905	0.9745	0.9427	0.8883	0.8062	7
8												1.0000	0.9999	0.9996	0.9983	0.9944	0.9847	0.9644	0.9270	8
9													1.0000	1.0000	0.9998	0.9992	0.9972	0.9921	0.9807	9
10															1.0000	0.9999	0.9997	0.9989	0.9968	10
11																1.0000	1.0000	0.9999	0.9998	11
12																		1.0000	1.0000	12

p	0.01	0.02	0.03	0.04	0.05	0.06	0.07	0.08	0.09	0.10	0.15	0.20	0.25	0.30	0.35	0.40	0.45	0.50	p
x	**n = 13**																		**x**
0	0.8775	0.7690	0.6730	0.5882	0.5133	0.4474	0.3893	0.3383	0.2935	0.2542	0.1209	0.0550	0.0238	0.0097	0.0037	0.0013	0.0004	0.0001	0
1	0.9928	0.9730	0.9436	0.9068	0.8646	0.8186	0.7702	0.7206	0.6707	0.6213	0.3983	0.2336	0.1267	0.0637	0.0296	0.0126	0.0049	0.0017	1
2	0.9997	0.9980	0.9938	0.9865	0.9755	0.9608	0.9422	0.9201	0.8946	0.8661	0.6920	0.5017	0.3326	0.2025	0.1132	0.0579	0.0269	0.0112	2
3	1.0000	0.9999	0.9995	0.9986	0.9969	0.9940	0.9897	0.9837	0.9758	0.9658	0.8820	0.7473	0.5843	0.4206	0.2783	0.1686	0.0929	0.0461	3
4		1.0000	1.0000	0.9999	0.9997	0.9993	0.9987	0.9976	0.9959	0.9935	0.9658	0.9009	0.7940	0.6543	0.5005	0.3530	0.2279	0.1334	4
5				1.0000	1.0000	0.9999	0.9999	0.9997	0.9995	0.9991	0.9925	0.9700	0.9198	0.8346	0.7159	0.5744	0.4268	0.2905	5
6						1.0000	1.0000	1.0000	0.9999	0.9999	0.9987	0.9930	0.9757	0.9376	0.8705	0.7712	0.6437	0.5000	6
7									1.0000	1.0000	0.9998	0.9988	0.9944	0.9818	0.9538	0.9023	0.8212	0.7095	7
8											1.0000	0.9998	0.9990	0.9960	0.9874	0.9679	0.9302	0.8666	8
9												1.0000	0.9999	0.9993	0.9975	0.9922	0.9797	0.9539	9
10													1.0000	0.9999	0.9997	0.9987	0.9959	0.9888	10
11														1.0000	1.0000	0.9999	0.9995	0.9983	11
12																1.0000	1.0000	0.9999	12
13																		1.0000	13
x	**n = 14**																		**x**
0	0.8687	0.7536	0.6528	0.5647	0.4877	0.4205	0.3620	0.3112	0.2670	0.2288	0.1028	0.0440	0.0178	0.0068	0.0024	0.0008	0.0002	0.0001	0
1	0.9916	0.9690	0.9355	0.8941	0.8470	0.7963	0.7436	0.6900	0.6368	0.5846	0.3567	0.1979	0.1010	0.0475	0.0205	0.0081	0.0029	0.0009	1
2	0.9997	0.9975	0.9923	0.9833	0.9699	0.9522	0.9302	0.9042	0.8745	0.8416	0.6479	0.4481	0.2811	0.1608	0.0839	0.0398	0.0170	0.0065	2
3	1.0000	0.9999	0.9994	0.9981	0.9958	0.9920	0.9864	0.9786	0.9685	0.9559	0.8535	0.6982	0.5213	0.3552	0.2205	0.1243	0.0632	0.0287	3
4		1.0000	1.0000	0.9998	0.9996	0.9990	0.9980	0.9965	0.9941	0.9908	0.9533	0.8702	0.7415	0.5842	0.4227	0.2793	0.1672	0.0898	4
5				1.0000	1.0000	0.9999	0.9998	0.9996	0.9992	0.9985	0.9885	0.9561	0.8883	0.7805	0.6405	0.4859	0.3373	0.2120	5
6						1.0000	1.0000	1.0000	0.9999	0.9998	0.9978	0.9884	0.9617	0.9067	0.8164	0.6925	0.5461	0.3953	6
7									1.0000	1.0000	0.9997	0.9976	0.9897	0.9685	0.9247	0.8499	0.7414	0.6047	7
8											1.0000	0.9996	0.9978	0.9917	0.9757	0.9417	0.8811	0.7880	8
9												1.0000	0.9997	0.9983	0.9940	0.9825	0.9574	0.9102	9
10													1.0000	0.9998	0.9989	0.9961	0.9886	0.9713	10
11														1.0000	0.9999	0.9994	0.9978	0.9935	11
12															1.0000	0.9999	0.9997	0.9991	12
13																1.0000	1.0000	0.9999	13
14																		1.0000	14
x	**n = 15**																		**x**
0	0.8601	0.7386	0.6333	0.5421	0.4633	0.3953	0.3367	0.2863	0.2430	0.2059	0.0874	0.0352	0.0134	0.0047	0.0016	0.0005	0.0001	0.0000	0
1	0.9904	0.9647	0.9270	0.8809	0.8290	0.7738	0.7168	0.6597	0.6035	0.5490	0.3186	0.1671	0.0802	0.0353	0.0142	0.0052	0.0017	0.0005	1
2	0.9996	0.9970	0.9906	0.9797	0.9638	0.9429	0.9171	0.8870	0.8531	0.8159	0.6042	0.3980	0.2361	0.1268	0.0617	0.0271	0.0107	0.0037	2
3	1.0000	0.9998	0.9992	0.9976	0.9945	0.9896	0.9825	0.9727	0.9601	0.9444	0.8227	0.6482	0.4613	0.2969	0.1727	0.0905	0.0424	0.0176	3
4		1.0000	0.9999	0.9998	0.9994	0.9986	0.9972	0.9950	0.9918	0.9873	0.9383	0.8358	0.6865	0.5155	0.3519	0.2173	0.1204	0.0592	4
5			1.0000	1.0000	0.9999	0.9999	0.9997	0.9993	0.9987	0.9978	0.9832	0.9389	0.8516	0.7216	0.5643	0.4032	0.2608	0.1509	5
6					1.0000	1.0000	1.0000	0.9999	0.9998	0.9997	0.9964	0.9819	0.9434	0.8689	0.7548	0.6098	0.4522	0.3036	6
7								1.0000	1.0000	1.0000	0.9994	0.9958	0.9827	0.9500	0.8868	0.7869	0.6535	0.5000	7
8											0.9999	0.9992	0.9958	0.9848	0.9578	0.9050	0.8182	0.6964	8
9											1.0000	0.9999	0.9992	0.9963	0.9876	0.9662	0.9231	0.8491	9
10												1.0000	0.9999	0.9993	0.9972	0.9907	0.9745	0.9408	10
11													1.0000	0.9999	0.9995	0.9981	0.9937	0.9824	11
12														1.0000	0.9999	0.9997	0.9989	0.9963	12
13															1.0000	1.0000	0.9999	0.9995	13
14																	1.0000	1.0000	14

Percentage points of the normal distribution

The table gives the values of z satisfying $P(Z \le z) = p$, where Z is the normally distributed random variable with mean = 0 and variance = 1.

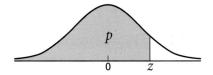

p	0.00	0.01	0.02	0.03	0.04	0.05	0.06	0.07	0.08	0.09	p
0.5	0.0000	0.0251	0.0502	0.0753	0.1004	0.1257	0.1510	0.1764	0.2019	0.2275	0.5
0.6	0.2533	0.2793	0.3055	0.3319	0.3585	0.3853	0.4125	0.4399	0.4677	0.4958	0.6
0.7	0.5244	0.5534	0.5828	0.6128	0.6433	0.6745	0.7063	0.7388	0.7722	0.8064	0.7
0.8	0.8416	0.8779	0.9154	0.9542	0.9945	1.0364	1.0803	1.1264	1.1750	1.2265	0.8
0.9	1.2816	1.3408	1.4051	1.4758	1.5548	1.6449	1.7507	1.8808	2.0537	2.3263	0.9

p	0.000	0.001	0.002	0.003	0.004	0.005	0.006	0.007	0.008	0.009	p
0.95	1.6449	1.6546	1.6646	1.6747	1.6849	1.6954	1.7060	1.7169	1.7279	1.7392	0.95
0.96	1.7507	1.7624	1.7744	1.7866	1.7991	1.8119	1.8250	1.8384	1.8522	1.8663	0.96
0.97	1.8808	1.8957	1.9110	1.9268	1.9431	1.9600	1.9774	1.9954	2.0141	2.0335	0.97
0.98	2.0537	2.0749	2.0969	2.1201	2.1444	2.1701	2.1973	2.2262	2.2571	2.2904	0.98
0.99	2.3263	2.3656	2.4089	2.4573	2.5121	2.5758	2.6521	2.7478	2.8782	3.0902	0.99

Answers

1 Review: collecting and processing data

A Experiment or survey

Exercise A (p 7)

1 Factors such as income, whether they have young children or are single parents, how far from restaurants they live

2 (a) Factors such as amount of light, quality of water, what food is given, how big the tadpoles were in the first place

(b) Place the jars in the same location and use the same water in each jar, put a strict amount of food in each jar each day and make sure that all other factors are kept constant for each jar. Randomly choose 50 tadpoles to go in each jar.

3 (a) Mothers who have recently had babies could be asked about their smoking habits and weights of babies. This would be a quick way of collecting data but the accuracy of results would be doubtful.

(b) An experiment could be set up where a group of smoking mothers and a control group of non-smokers were monitored during pregnancy and the weights of their babies observed. This would be a more accurate method but would take longer to give the results.

B Sampling methods

Exercise B (p 9)

1 (a) This would most likely get a poor response and lead to non-response bias.

(b) Only certain groups of people may visit the public facilities and they are unlikely to be a representative sample. There might be a non-response bias.

(c) This would only work if there was a cross-section of the population in town on Saturday and if the officers used a quota sampling system. Many people do not like answering surveys in the street so this might be an inefficient method with non-response bias.

(d) Steps would need to be taken to ensure that the sample was representative as certain groups might not be at home in the evenings. Now that most people have phones this is a popular method as it is quick way of interviewing people over a wide area.

C Recording and presenting data

Exercise C (p 14)

1 (a)

Class 1		Class 2
1	3	4
	4	5 8
9 8 6 3 1 0	5	1 5 6 8 9
9 6 5 4 2 0	6	2 4 4 8 9
9 8 8 6 6 5 1	7	1 3 3 5 9
7 4 0	8	0 1 3
	9	1

| 3 | 4 represents a mark of 34

(b) The distributions are quite similar but class 2 has a greater spread with more marks in the 40–49 range.

2 (a) 10   **(b)** 10

3 (a) Pie chart of radius 5 cm with these angles:

Fitness suite	96°
Weights room	168°
Swimming pool	64°
Sauna/steam room	8°
Squash court	24°

(b) Pie chart of radius $\sqrt{\dfrac{120}{45}} \times 5 = 8.16$ cm

Fitness suite	162°
Weights room	54°
Swimming pool	75°
Sauna/steam room	15°
Squash court	54°

(c) Pie chart of radius $\sqrt{\dfrac{30}{45}} \times 5 = 4.08\,\text{cm}$

Fitness suite	48°
Weights room	0°
Swimming pool	252°
Sauna/steam room	48°
Squash court	12°

D Averages

Exercise D (p 18)

1 (a) Mean = 55.3 s, median = 52 s
The mean is slightly distorted by one high value.

(b) Mean = 59.95 s, median = 52 s

2 (a)

Time	Cumulative frequency
Up to 2 min	8
Up to 4 min	22
Up to 6 min	45
Up to 8 min	80
Up to 10 min	100
Up to 12 min	104

Median is $6 + \dfrac{52 - 45}{35} \times 2 = 6.4\,\text{min}$

(b) Mean = 6.1 min

(c) The median is unchanged but the mean will increase. However, changing the highest group to, say, $10 \le t < 25$ and using its mid-interval value would be questionable.

E Percentiles

Exercise E (p 21)

1 (a)

Length of stay (days)	Cumulative frequency
up to 5	40
up to 10	98
up to 15	137
up to 20	143
up to 25	147
up to 30	149

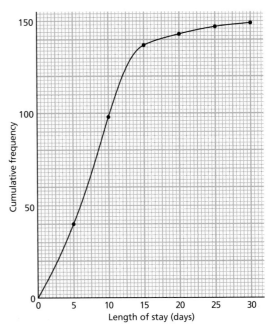

(b) (i) Median ≈ 8 days

(ii) IQR ≈ 11 − 4.5 = 6.5 days

(iii) 12 days

(c)

Length of stay (days)	Cumulative frequency
up to 5	16
up to 10	32
up to 15	39
up to 20	42
up to 25	45
up to 35	48

Median ≈ 7.5 days
IQR ≈ 12.9 − 3.75 = 9.2 days

(d) The average length of stay for men is shorter and the length of stay is less spread out for men.

2 (a) B (b) B (c) A

F Secondary data

Exercise F (p 22)

1 The rates per 10 000 take account of the different number of people in the given groups.

2 It is compiled from court and police records which will be accurate.

3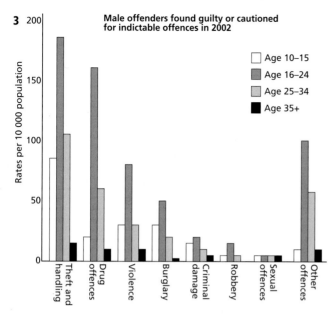

Male offenders found guilty or cautioned for indictable offences in 2002

Mixed questions (p 23)

1 *Smash and Grab*

Age	Frequency density
0–15	1.75
16–24	5.2
25–39	2.1
40–59	0.75
60–80	0.05

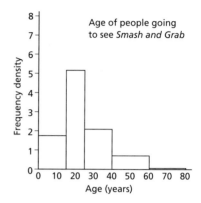

Age of people going to see *Smash and Grab*

4 (a) Pie chart of radius 5 cm with these angles:

Theft and handling	121°
Drug offences	77°
Violence	48°
Burglary	28°
Criminal damage	11°
Robbery	7°
Sexual offences	5°
Other offences	63°

(b) Pie chart of radius $\sqrt{\dfrac{88.6}{391.5}} \times 5 = 2.4\,\text{cm}$

Theft and handling	204°
Drug offences	40°
Violence	39°
Burglary	8°
Criminal damage	6°
Robbery	4°
Sexual offences	1°
Other offences	58°

(Some angles are rounded down to ensure the total is 360°.)

Celtic Dream

Age	Frequency density
0–15	1.81
16–24	5.0
25–39	3.47
40–59	1.85
60–80	1.2

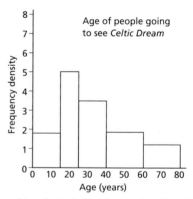

Age of people going to see *Celtic Dream*

2 *Smash and Grab* pie chart of radius 4 cm with these angles:

0–15	81°
16–24	138°
25–39	94°
40–59	44°
60+	3°

Celtic Dream pie chart of radius $\sqrt{\dfrac{187}{123}} \times 4 = 4.9\,\text{cm}$

0–15	56°
16–24	87°
25–39	100°
40–59	71°
60+	46°

(Some angles are rounded down to ensure the total is 360°.)

3 Using linear interpolation:

	Smash and Grab	*Celtic Dream*
Median	22.5	30.8
Lower quartile	16.6	19.6
Upper quartile	33.4	48.1
IQR	16.8	28.5

4

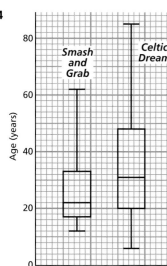

5 Mean for *Smash and Grab* = 24.8
Mean for *Celtic Dream* = 34.1

6 The average age of people going to see *Smash and Grab* is lower than for *Celtic Dream*.
The distribution of *Smash and Grab* is heavily weighted towards a younger audience with half the audience between 12 and $22\frac{1}{2}$ years old.
The distribution for *Celtic Dream* has a wider age range but half the audience are between 20 and 50 years old.
Because of the different overall sizes of the audiences the box plots give the clearest information.

2 Variance and standard deviation

A Measures of spread (p 24)

A1 The lengths of leaves inside appear to have a wider spread.

A2 The deviations are:
0.8, −1.0, 0.1, −1.1, 0.7, 0.4, −0.8, 1.0, 0.2, 0.3, −0.6
The sum of the deviations is zero.

A3 The deviations are:
1.5, −0.6, 0.3, −1.3, 0.1, −0.4, 0.4
and these sum to zero as well. This will always happen since the mean is always such that the total of the deviations from it is zero.
The mean can be thought of as a 'centre of gravity'.

A4 The sums of squared deviations are:
Outside 5.64
Inside 4.72
This is not a useful measure as there is a different number of leaves in each set.

A5 The variances are:
Outside 0.513
Inside 0.674
This suggests the inside group has the greater spread.

A6 The standard deviations are:
Outside 0.716 cm
Inside 0.821 cm

Exercise A (p 26)

1 Mean = 2.7 eggs; s.d. = 1.68 eggs

2 Mean = 9.875 °C; s.d. = 4.28 °C

3 Diet A: Mean = 30.2 g; s.d. = 9.46 g
Diet B: Mean = 32.25 g; s.d. = 18.41 g
The rats on diet B gained slightly more weight on average but the results were much more varied.

B Σ notation (p 26)

B1 Conclusions about how to find the mean and standard deviation on particular calculators

C Calculating the standard deviation

Exercise C (p 28)

1 Mean = 6 peas; s.d. = 2.45 peas

2 Mean = 51 kg; s.d. = 2.19 kg

3 Mean = $\frac{1245}{25}$ = 49.8 kg;

s.d. = $\sqrt{\dfrac{62\,820}{25} - 49.8^2}$ = 5.72 kg

4 (a) Mean = $\frac{85.6}{10}$ = 8.56 cm;

s.d. = $\sqrt{\dfrac{742.96}{10} - 8.56^2}$ = 1.01 cm

(b) Corrected $\Sigma w = 85.6 - 6.8 + 8.6 = 87.4$
$\Sigma w^2 = 742.96 - 6.8^2 + 8.6^2 = 770.68$
This gives the correct mean as 8.74 cm and the s.d. as 0.825 cm.

5 (a) $\Sigma x = 70 \times 5 = 350$

Since variance = $10^2 = \dfrac{\Sigma x^2 - 5 \times 70^2}{5}$

$\Sigma x^2 = (5 \times 10^2) + (5 \times 70^2) = 25\,000$

(b) Now $n = 4$, $\Sigma x = 350 - 80 = 270$ and
$\Sigma x^2 = 25\,000 - 80^2 = 18\,600$
Mean = 67.5 kg; s.d. = 9.68 kg

6 (a) Since $s_x^2 = $
$\dfrac{\text{sum of squared deviations from mean}}{30}$,

sum of squared deviations =
$6.1^2 \times 30 = 1116.3$

(b) For the 20 pears, sum of squared deviations =
$8.4^2 \times 20 = 1411.2$
Total squared deviations for 50 pears = 2527.5
Standard deviation for all 50 pears =
$\sqrt{\dfrac{2527.5}{50}} = 7.11$ g

D Scaling (p 29)

D1 The mean increases by 10 to 14, but the standard deviation is unchanged.

D2 The mean is doubled and so is the standard deviation.

D3 Mean = $\dfrac{ax_1 + ax_2 + ax_3 + \ldots + ax_n}{n}$

$= \dfrac{a(x_1 + x_2 + x_3 + \ldots + x_n)}{n}$

$= \dfrac{a\Sigma x_i}{n}$

$= a\bar{x}$

Standard deviation $= \sqrt{\dfrac{\Sigma(ax_i - a\bar{x}^2)}{n}}$

$= \sqrt{\dfrac{\Sigma(a(x_i - \bar{x}))^2}{n}}$

$= \sqrt{\dfrac{a^2\Sigma(x_i - \bar{x})^2}{n}}$

$= as_x$

Exercise D (p 30)

1 (a) Mean = 54.2 ohms; s.d. = 0.473 ohms

(b) Both increase by 10%
Mean = 59.62 ohms; s.d = 0.520 ohms

2 Mean = 16.0 years; s.d. = 0.25 years

3 Mean = $1.8 \times 12 + 32 = 53.6\,°F$;
s.d. = $1.8 \times 0.5 = 0.9\,°F$

4 (a) $50 = a \times 33 + b$ and $10 = a \times 4.2$
So $a = 2.38$ and $b = -28.54$

(b) $2.38 \times 40 - 28.54 = 66.66$

E Working with frequency distributions (p 31

E1 Mean = $47 \div 20 = 2.35$;

s.d. = $\sqrt{\dfrac{1670}{20} - 2.35^2} = 1.68$

E2 Most scientific calculators with statistical functions allow $x \times f$ then enter to be used.

E3 Before coaching: mean = 11.1; s.d. = 9.2
After coaching: mean = 23.3; s.d. = 12.5

The mean length of rally has greatly increased although there is slightly more variation in the length.

Exercise E (p 32)

1 (a) Using mid-interval values 7, 22, … gives
mean = 28.63 min; s.d. = 16.80 min

(b) There are few groups. A more accurate result could have been obtained using smaller group intervals.

2 (a) Mean = 23.3 words; s.d. = 11.2 words

(b) Most of the sentences are in the middle three groups so the group intervals may be too large. Since the distribution is skewed the data may not be evenly spread in each group.

3 (a) Mid-interval values are:

7.5, 22.5, 37.5, 52.5, 67.5, 82.5, 95

(b) 53 511 000

(c) Mean ≈ 41 years; s.d. ≈ 24 years

(d) The mean age is projected to increase as is the standard deviation. This is probably due to an increasing number of people living longer.

F Choosing measures (p 33)

F1 (a) (i) Median ≈ £20 100

(ii) Mean ≈ £23 860

(b) Both are representative of the data, although the mean is more influenced by the few high earners.

F2 The upper end-point of the last interval, '$h > 120$', is not known.

F3 (a) (i) about 58 s **(ii)** about 38 s

(b) (i) The top end would be stretched to the right.

(ii) They would be unaffected.

(iii) Both would increase slightly.

Test yourself (p 36)

1 (a) Mean = 114.5 mmHg; s.d. = 23.6 mmHg

(b) The boys' blood pressures are on average higher and are also more varied.

2 (a) (i) $\sum x = 71 \times 10 = 710$

(ii) Variance $= 7^2 = \dfrac{\sum x^2}{10} - 71^2$

$\sum x^2 = 10(71^2 + 7^2) = 50\,900$

(b) Corrected $\sum x = 710 - 79 + 97 = 728$

Mean = 72.8

Corrected $\sum x^2 = 50\,900 - 79^2 + 97^2 = 54\,068$

s.d. = 10.3

3 (a) Mean $= \dfrac{2000}{10} = 200\,g$

s.d. $= \sqrt{\dfrac{409\,000}{10} - 200^2} = 30\,g$

(b) Mean cost = 2p × 200 = £4

s.d. = 2 × 30 = 60p

(c) Mean of total cost is £4 + £1 = £5

s.d. = 60p

4 Mean $= \dfrac{2816.5}{37} = 76.1\,mm$

s.d. $= \sqrt{\dfrac{219\,699.25}{37} - 76.1^2} = 12.0\,mm$

5 (a) Cumulative frequency graph of the following data, starting at (20, 0)

Time (seconds)	Cumulative Frequency
up to 39	6
up to 49	14
up to 54	21
up to 59	26
up to 69	35

Median ≈ 52 s; IQR ≈ 16 s

(Strictly, upper limits of 39.5, 49.5 … should be used, but this makes little difference to an approximate technique like this one.)

(b) Mean ≈ 50.4 s; s.d. = 11.9 s

(c) From the graph, median ≈ 53 s

(d) (i) The median, because the mean of all 40 workers who took the test has not been calculated.

(ii) 53 s

3 Probability

A Outcomes and events (p 38)

A1 12

A2 13

A3 From left to right: 30, 9, 10

A4 22

A5 (a) 40   (b) 39

A6 $P(C') = \frac{10}{13}$

$P(C') = \frac{10}{13} = 1 - \frac{3}{13} = 1 - P(C)$

A and A' together account for all possible outcomes.
So $P(A) + P(A') = 1 \Rightarrow P(A') = 1 - P(A)$

A7 (a) (i) $\frac{3}{52}$ (ii) $\frac{22}{52} = \frac{11}{26}$

(b) $P(C) + P(D) - P(C \cap D)$

$= \frac{12}{52} + \frac{13}{52} - \frac{3}{52}$

$= \frac{22}{52} = P(C \cup D)$

(c)
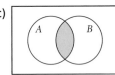

If $P(A)$ and $P(B)$ are added, then $P(A \cap B)$ is included twice.
So $P(A \cup B) = P(A) + P(B) - P(A \cap B)$.

A8 (a) 0   (b) $P(A \cup B) = P(A) + P(B)$

Exercise A (p 41)

1 (a) 1, 1, 1   1, 1, 2   1, 2, 1   1, 2, 2   1, 3, 1   1, 3, 2

2, 1, 1   2, 1, 2   2, 2, 1   2, 2, 2   2, 3, 1   2, 3, 2

3, 1, 1   3, 1, 2   3, 2, 1   3, 2, 2   3, 3, 1   3, 3, 2

4, 1, 1   4, 1, 2   4, 2, 1   4, 2, 2   4, 3, 1   4, 3, 2

(b) (i) $\frac{1}{12}$ (ii) $\frac{1}{3}$

2 (a) 0.3   (b) 0.25

3 (a) $\frac{1}{5}$ (b) $\frac{3}{20}$ (c) $\frac{2}{5}$

4 (a) 0.2   (b) 0.75   (c) 0.55

5 (a) 0.6   (b) 0.45

B Conditional probability (p 42)

B1 (a) $\frac{5}{12}$ (b) $\frac{1}{2}$ (c) $\frac{1}{6}$

B2 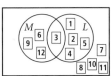 $\dfrac{P(L \cap E)}{P(E)} = \dfrac{\frac{1}{6}}{\frac{1}{2}} = \frac{1}{6} \times 2 = \frac{1}{3}$

B3 (a) The probability that the number is even, given that it is less than 6

(b) $\frac{2}{5}$

B4 (a) $\frac{2}{3}$ (b) $\frac{1}{2}$ (c) $\frac{1}{5}$ (d) $\frac{1}{8}$

B5 (a) 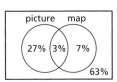   (b) (i) $\frac{1}{5}$ (ii) $\frac{1}{4}$

Exercise B (p 43)

1 (a) $\frac{4}{7}$ (b) $\frac{2}{3}$

2 (a) 0.6   (b) 0.4   (c) 0.28

3 (a)

```
picture   map

  27% (3%)  7%

            63%
```

(b) 0.1   (c) 0.3   (d) 0.63   (e) 0.9

4 (a) 0.4   (b) 0.45 (to 2 d.p.) or $\frac{5}{11}$

5 (a) $\frac{3}{8}$ (b) $\frac{2}{7}$

C Independent events (p 44)

C1 (a) (i) $\frac{1}{3}$ (ii) $\frac{1}{2}$ (iii) $\frac{1}{3}$ (iv) $\frac{1}{2}$

(b) $P(M \mid E) = P(M)$ and $P(E \mid M) = P(E)$

Each conditional probability is equal to the probability without the condition.

Exercise C (p 45)

1 (a) $\frac{130}{200} = 0.65$

(b) $\frac{72}{120} = 0.6$

(c) $P(\text{maths} \mid \text{male})$ and $P(\text{maths})$ are not equal. So studying maths is not independent of the gender.
Alternatively: $P(\text{maths}) = 0.65$, $P(\text{male}) = 0.6$
$P(\text{maths and male}) = 0.36$
As $0.65 \times 0.6 \neq 0.36$, the events are not independent.

2 (a) 0.12   **(b)** 0.58

3 (a) (i) $\frac{1}{3} = 0.33...$ **(ii)** 0.4   **(iii)** 0.4

    (b) (i) W, X

      (ii) V, W; they are not mutually exclusive
because the same member may be female
and adult; they are not independent
because $P(V \mid W) = \frac{5}{24} \neq P(V) = \frac{1}{3}$

D Tree diagrams (p 46)

D1 (a)

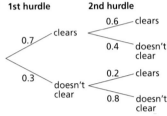

1st hurdle   2nd hurdle

    (b) (i) 0.42   **(ii)** 0.28   **(iii)** 0.06   **(iv)** 0.24

    (c) (i) 0.76   **(ii)** 0.34

D2 (a) $\frac{3}{5}$ **(b)** $\frac{1}{2}$ **(c)** $\frac{3}{4}$

    (d)

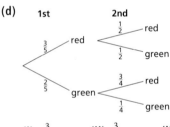

1st   2nd

    (i) $\frac{3}{10}$ **(ii)** $\frac{3}{5}$ **(iii)** $\frac{1}{10}$

D3 (a) $\frac{1}{20}$ **(b)** $\frac{1}{5}$

Exercise D (p 48)

1

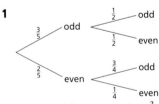

P(one odd, one even) $= \frac{3}{5}$

2 $\frac{4}{5}$

3 (a) (i) 0.27   **(ii)** 0.07   **(iii)** 0.93

    (b) $\frac{0.9}{0.93} = \frac{90}{93} = 0.968$ (to 3 s.f.)

4 (a) 0.882   **(b)** 0.169

5 (a) 0.68   **(b)** $\frac{14}{17} = 0.824$ (to 3 s.f.)

Mixed questions (p 50)

1 (a) (i) $\frac{1}{8} = 0.125$ **(ii)** $\frac{7}{12} = 0.583$ (to 3 s.f.)

    (b) (i) $\frac{19}{714} = 0.0266$ **(ii)** $\frac{50}{357} = 0.140$

    (c) $\frac{125}{1003} = 0.125$

    (d) $\frac{35}{204} = 0.172$

2 (a) $\frac{1}{31} = 0.0323$ (to 3 s.f.)   **(b)** $\frac{1}{961} = 0.00104$

    (c) $\frac{1}{961} = 0.00104$ **(d)** $\frac{870}{961} = 0.905$

Test yourself (p 51)

1 (a) (i) $\frac{13}{95} = 0.137$ (to 3 s.f.)

      (ii) $\frac{65}{95} = 0.684$ **(iii)** $\frac{45}{95} = 0.474$

      (iv) $\frac{13}{45} = 0.289$

    (b) (i) 0.0293   **(ii)** 0.117

2 (a) (i) $\frac{85}{200} = 0.425$ **(ii)** $\frac{164}{200} = 0.82$

      (iii) $\frac{34}{45} = 0.756$ (to 3 s.f.)

    (b) (i) $\frac{90}{200} = 0.45$ **(ii)** 0.0894 (to 3 s.f.)

      (iii) 0.198 (to 3 s.f.)

3 (a) (i) $\frac{1}{3}$ of females study Spanish.
So $\frac{1}{3}$ of 60% of students are females
studying Spanish.
So P(female studying Spanish)
$= \frac{1}{3} \times 0.6 = 0.2$

      (ii) 0.3

    (b) $\frac{2}{3}$

4 Discrete random variables

A Probability distributions (p 52)

A1 FCCC CFCC CCFC CCCF CCCC

A2 (a) 0.2646 (b) 0.0756 (c) 0.0081

A3 1

Exercise A (p 53)

1 (a) P(square) = 0.6 P(triangle) = 0.4

(b) P(S = 1) = 0.48, P(S = 2) = 0.36, P(S = 3) = 0.16

s	1	2	3
P(S = s)	0.48	0.36	0.16

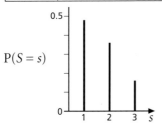

2 (a)

s	0	1	2	3
P(S = s)	$\frac{1}{4}$	$\frac{1}{4}$	$\frac{1}{4}$	$\frac{1}{4}$

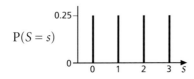

(b) Uniform

3 (a)

1st dice

2nd dice	1	2	3	4	5	6
1	0	1	2	3	4	5
2	1	0	1	2	3	4
3	2	1	0	1	2	3
4	3	2	1	0	1	2
5	4	3	2	1	0	1
6	5	4	3	2	1	0

(b)

d	0	1	2	3	4	5
P(D = d)	$\frac{6}{36}$	$\frac{10}{36}$	$\frac{8}{36}$	$\frac{6}{36}$	$\frac{4}{36}$	$\frac{2}{36}$

(c)

P(D = d)

(d) The game is unfair.
A possible alternative rule is 'I win if the difference is 2, 3 or 4. You win if it is 0, 1 or 5.'

4

s	0	1	2	3
P(S = s)	$\frac{125}{216}$	$\frac{25}{216}$	$\frac{30}{216}$	$\frac{36}{216}$

5 P(X = 1) = 0.1, P(X = 2) = 0.2,
P(X = 3) = 0.3, P(X = 4) = 0.4
0.1 + 0.2 + 0.3 + 0.4 = 1

6 (a) P(X = 1) = k, P(X = 2) = 4k,
P(X = 3) = 9k, P(X = 4) = 16k

(b) Sum of probabilities = 1,
so $k + 4k + 9k + 16k = 1 \Rightarrow 30k = 1 \Rightarrow k = \frac{1}{30}$

B Mean, variance and standard deviation
(p 55)

B1 1.15

B2 (a) The mean score for both games is 1.9.

(b) The distribution for game A is more spread out than that for game B.

B3 Variance = 0.79; standard deviation = 0.89
Game A has the wider variation.
The graph for B is more concentrated around the centre (or less spread out).

Exercise B (p 56)

1 (a) 3.5 (b) 2.92 (to 3 s.f.)

(c) 1.71 (to 3 s.f.)

2 (a) $\frac{70}{36}$ = 1.94 (to 3 s.f.) (b) 2.05 (to 3 s.f.)

(c) 1.43 (to 3 s.f.)

Test yourself (p 57)

1 (a)

x	1	2	3
$P(X = x)$	$\frac{1}{2}$	$\frac{3}{8}$	$\frac{1}{8}$

  (b) $\frac{13}{8} = 1.625$ **(c)** 0.484 (to 3.s.f)

2 (a) (i) 0.5   **(ii)** 2.4   **(iii)** 1.24

  (b) (i) 2.55   **(ii)** 0.4475

  (c) (i) The second   **(ii)** The first

5 Binomial distribution

A Pascal's triangle (p 58)

A1 There are more balls in the middle slots than in the end slots.

A2 There are more ways of getting to a middle slot than to an end slot.

A3 (a) 3   **(b)** $\frac{1}{8}$ **(c)** $\frac{3}{8}$

A4

s	0	1	2	3
$P(S = s)$	$\frac{1}{8}$	$\frac{3}{8}$	$\frac{3}{8}$	$\frac{1}{8}$

A5 4

A6 (a) Slot 0: 1, slot 1: 4, slot 2: 6, slot 4: 1

  (b)

Slot	0	1	2	3	4
Probability	$\frac{1}{16}$	$\frac{1}{4}$	$\frac{3}{8}$	$\frac{1}{4}$	$\frac{1}{16}$

A7 (a) 1, 5, 10, 10, 5, 1

  (b)

Slot	0	1	2	3	4	5
Probability	$\frac{1}{32}$	$\frac{5}{32}$	$\frac{5}{16}$	$\frac{5}{16}$	$\frac{5}{32}$	$\frac{1}{32}$

A8 The student's check

A9 (a) Row 7: 1 7 21 35 35 21 7 1
Row 8: 1 8 28 56 70 56 28 8 1

  (b) (i) 35   **(ii)** 21   **(iii)** 70

A10 (a) If 3 objects are selected from 10, the other 7 objects are automatically selected as well (for rejection). So the number of ways of selecting 3 is the same as the number of ways of selecting 7.

  (b) If r objects are selected from n, the remaining $n - r$ objects are also selected.

Exercise A (p 61)

1 (a) $\binom{6}{4} = 15$ **(b)** $\left(\frac{1}{2}\right)^6 = \frac{1}{64}$ **(c)** $\frac{15}{64}$

2 $\frac{35}{128}$

3 (a) $\frac{1}{32}$ **(b)** $\frac{5}{32}$ **(c)** $\frac{10}{32} \left(= \frac{5}{16}\right)$

  (d) $\frac{10}{32}$ **(e)** $\frac{5}{32}$ **(f)** $\frac{1}{2}$

4 (a) (i) $\frac{1}{64}$ **(ii)** $\frac{6}{64}\left(=\frac{3}{32}\right)$ **(iii)** $\frac{15}{64}$

(b)

h	0	1	2	3	4	5	6
$P(H = h)$	$\frac{1}{64}$	$\frac{6}{64}$	$\frac{15}{64}$	$\frac{20}{64}$	$\frac{15}{64}$	$\frac{6}{64}$	$\frac{1}{64}$

B Unequal probabilities

Exercise B (p 62)

Decimal results are given correct to three significant figures.

1 (a) $\frac{5}{216}$ **(b)** $\frac{15}{216} = \frac{5}{72}$

2 (a) $\frac{90}{1024} = \frac{45}{512} = 0.0879$ **(b)** $\frac{15}{1024} = 0.0146$

(c) $\frac{106}{1024} = \frac{53}{512} = 0.104$

3 (a) 0.276 **(b)** 0.138 **(c)** 0.0369

4 (a) (i) 0.100 **(ii)** 0.267 **(iii)** 0.311 **(iv)** 0.208

(b) 0.114

5

s	0	1	2	3	4	5
$P(S = s)$	0.402	0.402	0.161	0.0322	0.00322	0.000129

C Using the binomial distribution (p 63)

C1

x	0	1	2	3	4	5
$P(X = x)$	0.0778	0.259	0.346	0.230	0.0778	0.0102

C2

x	0	1	2	3	4
$P(X = x)$	0.0016	0.0256	0.154	0.410	0.410

C3 $\binom{n}{x}p^x(1-p)^{n-x}$

Exercise C (p 65)

1 0.0081

2 0.311

3 0.273

4 The weather on one day is not independent of that on other days.

5 (a) 0.18 **(b)** 0.174

D Using tables of the binomial distribution (p 66)

D1 (a) 0.3280 **(b)** 0.9023 **(c)** 0.3529

(d) 0.6471

Exercise D (p 67)

1 0.0193

2 (a) 0.0050 **(b)** 0.1819 **(c)** 0.8131

3 (a) 0.1172 **(b)** 0.7553

(c) The sample size n is not fixed.

4 (a) 0.2375 **(b)** 0.0171

5 (a) (i) 0.0433 **(ii)** 0.4395

(b) p may decrease as Dwight gains experience.

6 (a) 0.1734 **(b)** 0.9245 **(c)** 0.3990

E Mean, variance, standard deviation (p 68)

E1 $\mu = 1.5 \ (= np)$

E2 $\sigma^2 = 1.05 \ (= np(1-p))$

Exercise E (p 69)

1 Mean = 9.6, variance = 5.76, s.d. = 2.4

2 (a)

x	0	1	2	3	4	5
$P(X = x)$	0.2373	0.3955	0.2637	0.0879	0.0146	0.001

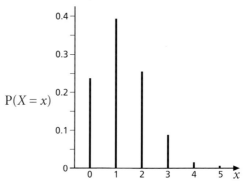

(b) Mean = 1.25, variance = 0.9375, s.d. = 0.9682

3 Mean = 7, variance = 2.1, s.d. = 1.45

4 Mean = 16, s.d. = 2.4

Mixed questions (p 70)

1 (a) 0.0264   (b) Mean = 2, s.d. = 1.26

2 0.2031

3 (a) 0.1099   (b) 0.8801

4 (a) 0.2894   (b) 0.2011   (c) 0.1465

5 (a) (i) 0.5886   (ii) 0.1547

    (b) Random samples

    (c) The number of blue beads on each string is unlikely to be the same, so p is not the same for each 'trial'.

6 (a) 0.1101   (b) 0.8943

7 (a) 0.1712   (b) 0.8139

8 (a) (i) 0.3823   (ii) 0.3669

    (b) Mean = 4, s.d. = 1.55

    (c) (i) Mean = 3.92, s.d. = 3.05

       (ii) The mean is similar but the s.d. much greater than in the model.
The binomial distribution is not a good model.
Siballi's beliefs are not plausible.

Test yourself (p 72)

1 (a) 0.0644   (b) 0.9956   (c) 0.0190

2 (a) (i) 0.979   (ii) 0.2645

    (b) 0.1954

3 (a) (i) 0.0388   (ii) 0.961

    (b) (i) 0.9173   (ii) 0.774

    (c) 0.9117

4 Mean = 1.6, variance = 1.28, s.d. = 1.13

6 Normal distribution

AQA tables are used for these answers.
Other tables may give slightly different answers.

A Proportions (p 73)

A1 (a) 35%   (b) 13%; 14%

     (c) 2%; 1%   (d) 0% above; 1% below

A2

Standard deviations from the mean							
< –3	–3 to –2	–2 to –1	–1 to 0	0 to 1	1 to 2	2 to 3	> 3
1%	1%	14%	35%	34%	13%	2%	0%

The results are roughly symmetrical. There is a large percentage within ±1 standard deviation of the mean. Only a very small percentage are more than 3 s.d.s from the mean.

A3 (a)

< –3	–3 to –2	–2 to –1	–1 to 0	0 to 1	1 to 2	2 to 3	> 3
0%	3.3%	13.3%	33.3%	32.5%	16.7%	0.9%	0%

    (b) The percentages in each section are roughly the same in both tables.

A4 (a)

< –3	–3 to –2	–2 to –1	–1 to 0	0 to 1	1 to 2	2 to 3	> 3
0%	0%	25%	23.8%	28.8%	22.5%	0%	0%

    (b) The proportions are very different from those in the first two tables.

Exercise A (p 76)

1 (a) 16%   (b) 84%   (c) 96%

2 (a) 2%

    (b) 68%

    (c) 69 is 2 standard deviations above the mean. The table says this is 2% of the results.
2% of 80 = 1.6 ≈ 2 people

    (d) 21

3 (a) 2%   (b) 34%   (c) 130

B The Normal probability distribution

Exercise B (p 79)

1 (a) 0.77337

(b) $1 - 0.96784 = 0.03216$

(c) 0.89435

(d) $0.96407 - 0.69146 = 0.27261$

2 (a) Sketch of normal curve;
$0.96407 - 0.5 = 0.46407$

(b) Sketch of normal curve;
$0.99977 - 0.89435 = 0.10542$

(c) Sketch of normal curve;
$0.80234 - (1 - 0.93319) = 0.73553$

(d) Sketch of normal curve;
$(1 - 0.85543) - (1 - 0.99245) = 0.13702$

3 Using the nearest value in the table:

(a) 1.64　　**(b)** 1.28　　**(c)** 2.33　　**(d)** 0.67

4 (a) 0.84　　**(b)** 1.04　　**(c)** −0.25　　**(d)** −0.13

C Solving problems

Exercise C (p 82)

1 $X \sim N(10, 2^2)$

(a) $z = 2.5$, $\Phi(2.5) = 0.99379$
$P(X > 15) = P(Z > 2.5) = 1 - 0.99379 = 0.006$
So 0.6% of batteries fail after 15 hours.

(b) $P(8 \leq X \leq 12) = P(-1 \leq Z \leq 1)$
$\Phi(1.0) = 0.84134$
$P(8 \leq X \leq 12) = 0.84134 - (1 - 0.84134)$
$= 0.68268$
68% of batteries have a lifetime of between 8 and 12 hours.

2 $X \sim N(1.5, 0.01^2)$
$z = 2.0$, $\Phi(2.0) = 0.97725$
$P(X > 1.52) = P(Z > 2.0) = 1 - 0.97725 = 0.02275$
So 2.275% of bolts are rejected.

3 $X \sim N(100, 15^2)$
$z = 2.13$, $\Phi(2.13) = 0.98341$
$P(X > 132) = P(Z > 2.13) = 1 - 0.98341 = 0.01659$
So 1.659% of children have an IQ of 132 or more.

4 $X \sim N(1.5, 0.01^2)$
$z = -2.5$, $\Phi(2.5) = 0.99379$
$P(X < 1.475) = P(Z < -2.5) = 1 - 0.99379$
$= 0.00621$

5 $X \sim N(28, 5^2)$

(a) $z = 0.6$, $\Phi(0.6) = 0.72575$
$P(X > 31) = P(Z > 0.6) = 1 - 0.72575$
$= 0.27425$

(b) $z = -0.8$, $\Phi(0.8) = 0.78814$
$P(X > 24) = P(Z > -0.8) = 0.78814$

6 $X \sim N(500, 4^2)$
For $x = 500.5$, $z = 0.125$, $\Phi(0.125) = 0.55$ (approx)
For $x = 498.5$, $z = -0.375$, $\Phi(0.375) = 0.646$ (appro
$P(498.5 < X < 500.5) = 0.55 - (1 - 0.646) = 0.196

7 $X \sim N(154.2, 5.1^2)$
For $x = 155$, $z = 0.16$, $\Phi(0.16) = 0.56356$
For $x = 150$, $z = -0.82$, $\Phi(0.82) = 0.79389$
$P(150 < X < 155) = 0.56356 - (1 - 0.79389)$
$= 0.35745$

8 $X \sim N(82, 12^2)$

(a) Distinction: $P(X > 110) = P(Z > 2.33)$
$= 1 - 0.99010 = 0.0099$

Credit: $P(90 < X \leq 110) = P(0.67 < Z < 2.33)$
$= 0.99010 - 0.74857 = 0.24153$

Pass: $P(60 < X \leq 90) = P(-1.83 < Z < 0.67)$
$= 0.74857 - (1 - 0.96638) = 0.71495$

Fail: $P(X \leq 60) = P(Z < -1.83) = 1 - 0.96638$
$= 0.03362$

(b) Distinction: $0.0099 \times 90 = 1$ person
Credit: $0.24153 \times 90 = 22$ people
Pass: $0.71495 \times 90 = 64$ people
Fail: $0.03362 \times 90 = 3$ people

D Further problems (p 83)

D1 For the top 5% we require $p = 0.95$ and from the percentage points table $z = 1.6449$.
So the sales figure for a bonus is 1.6449 s.d.s above the mean, or $35\,000 + (1.6449 \times 1500) = £37\,467$.

D2 For a 90% symmetrical interval there should be 5% left at each end. The interval is therefore given by $\mu \pm 1.6449\sigma$, or from
$174 - 1.6449 \times 8$ to $174 + 1.6449 \times 8$, namely from 160.84 cm to 187.16 cm.

Exercise D (p 85)

1 When $p = 0.85$, $z = 1.0364$
Mark $= 47 + 1.0364 \times 12 = 59.4$
so 60 must be achieved

2 When $p = 0.9$, $z = 1.2816$
Mean $= 1 + 1.2816 \times 0.0025 = 1.003\,204\,\text{kg}$

3 When $p = 0.99$, $z = 2.3263$
Minimum $= 1500 - 2.3263 \times 200 = 1035$ hours

4 (a) $z = \dfrac{250 - 265}{10} = -1.5$
$\Phi(1.5) = 0.933\,19$
$P(X < 250) = P(Z < -1.5) = 1 - 0.933\,19$
$= 0.066\,81$

(b) 1 in 200 = 0.005
When $p = 0.995$, $z = 2.5758$
So $\dfrac{250 - 265}{\sigma} = -2.5758$ which gives
$\sigma = 5.82\,\text{ml}$

5 (a) $z = \dfrac{15 - 20}{3} = -1.67$
$\Phi(1.67) = 0.952\,54$
$P(X < 15) = P(Z < -1.67) = 1 - 0.952\,54$
$= 0.047\,46$

(b) When $p = 0.9$, $z = 1.2816$
Time $= 20 + 1.2816 \times 3 = 23.84$ minutes

(c) From the body of the table for $\Phi(z)$, when
$p = 0.9332$, $z = 1.5$
$\mu = 10 - 1.5 \times 4 = 4$ minutes

6 To have a 95% symmetrical interval there must
be 2.5% of values left at each end.
When $p = 0.975$, $z = 1.9600$.
Interval is $80 \pm 1.96 \times 7$, namely from
66.28 cm to 93.72 cm

7 When $p = 0.9$, $z = 1.2816 \approx 1.3$, so $\mu + 1.3\sigma = 70$
When $p = 0.85$, $z = 1.0364 \approx 1.0$, so $\mu - \sigma = 35$
Solving these gives $\sigma = 15.2$ and $\mu = 50.2$

8 $1 - 0.055 = 0.945$ and from the table of $\Phi(z)$,
when $p = 0.945$, $z \approx 1.6$
So $\mu + 1.6\sigma = 165$
$1 - 0.115 = 0.885$ and from the table of $\Phi(z)$,
when $p = 0.885$, $z \approx 1.2$
So $\mu - 1.2\sigma = 140$
Solving these gives $\sigma = 8.93\,\text{g}$ and $\mu = 150.7\,\text{g}$

9 (a) When $p = 1 - 0.16 = 0.84$, $z = 0.9945$
Size $= 224 + 0.9945 \times 4 = 227.98\,\text{mm}$

(b) Since this is 84% of the original distribution
the median (m) is the value such that
$P(X < m) = 0.42$
When $p = 1 - 0.42 = 0.58$, $z = 0.2019$
Median $= 224 - 0.2019 \times 4 = 223.2\,\text{mm}$

Mixed questions (p 87)

1 1 in 1000 = 0.001
When $p = 0.999$, $z = 3.0902$
So quoted weight $= 265 - 3.09 \times 7 = 243\,\text{g}$

2 (a) $P(X < 290) = \Phi\left(\dfrac{290 - 275}{15}\right) = \Phi(1.0)$
$= 0.841\,34$
$P(X < 260) = \Phi\left(\dfrac{260 - 275}{15}\right) = \Phi(-1.0)$
$= 1 - 0.841\,34 = 0.158\,66$
$P(260 < X < 290) = 0.841\,34 - 0.158\,66$
$= 0.682\,68$

(b) $P(X > 300) = 1 - \Phi\left(\dfrac{300 - 275}{15}\right) = 1 - \Phi(1.67)$
$= 1 - 0.952\,54 = 0.047\,46$

(c) If O is the number of jars overflowing, then
$O \sim B(10, 0.048)$
Using the binomial table for $B(10, 0.05)$,
$P(X \le 1) = 0.9139$
$P(X > 2) = 1 - 0.9139 = 0.0861$

3 (a) $z = \dfrac{0.0155 - 0.0158}{0.002} = -0.15$
$P(Z < -0.15) = 1 - \Phi(0.15) = 1 - 0.559\,62$
$= 0.440\,38$

(b) When $p = 1 - 0.26 = 0.74$, $z = 0.6433$.
So $\mu + 0.6433 \times 0.002 = 0.0155$, which gives
$\mu = 0.0142\,\text{mm}$

4 $V \sim N(475, 20^2)$

(a) (i) $z = \dfrac{480 - 475}{20} = 0.25$
$\Phi(0.25) = 0.598\,71$
$P(V < 480) = 0.598\,71$

(ii) $P(460 < V < 490) = P(-0.75 < Z < 0.75)$
$\Phi(0.75) = 0.773\,37$
$P(460 < V < 480) = 0.773\,37 - (1 - 0.773\,37)$
$= 0.546\,74$

(b) $z = \dfrac{500 - 475}{20} = 1.25$

$\Phi(1.25) = 0.89435$

$P(V > 500) = 1 - 0.89435 = 0.10565$

(c) When $p = 1 - 0.001 = 0.999$, $z = 3.09$

$\mu = 500 - 3.09 \times 20 = 438.2\,\text{ml}$

Test yourself (p 88)

1 $X \sim N(901.0, 2.0^2)$

$z = \dfrac{902.5 - 901.0}{2} = 0.75$

$\Phi(0.75) = 0.77337$

$P(X < 902.5) = 0.77337$

2 $W \sim N(25.8, 0.5^2)$

(a) (i) $z = \dfrac{25.0 - 25.8}{0.5} = -1.6$

$\Phi(1.6) = 0.94520$

$P(W < 25) = 1 - 0.94520 = 0.05480$

(ii) $P(25.5 < W < 26.5) = P(-0.6 < Z < 1.4)$

$\Phi(0.6) = 0.72575$, $\Phi(1.4) = 0.91924$

$P(25.5 < W < 26.5) = 0.64499$

(b) When $p = 0.75$, $z = 0.6745$

$w = 25.8 - 0.6745 \times 0.5 = 25.46\,\text{kg}$

3 $D \sim N(135, 12^2)$

(a) (i) $z = \dfrac{111 - 135}{12} = -2$

$\Phi(2) = 0.97725$

$P(D > 111) = 0.97725$

(ii) $P(141 < W < 150) = P(0.5 < Z < 1.25)$

$\Phi(0.5) = 0.69146$, $\Phi(1.25) = 0.89435$

$P(141 < W < 150) = 0.89435 - 0.69146$

$= 0.203$

(b) When $p = 0.9$, $z = 1.2816$

Longest journey $= 135 - 1.2816 \times 12$

$= 120$ miles

4 $X \sim N(32, 2^2)$

(a) $z = \dfrac{30 - 32}{2} = -1$

$\Phi(1.0) = 0.84134$

$P(X < 30) = 1 - 0.84134 = 0.159$

(b) When $p = 1 - 0.025 = 0.975$, $z = 1.96$

$\mu = 30 + 1.96 \times 2 = 34\,\text{mg}$

5 $X \sim N(28, 8^2)$

(a) (i) $z = \dfrac{30 - 28}{8} = 0.25$

$\Phi(0.25) = 0.59871$

$P(X < 30) = 0.59871$

(ii) $P(10 < X < 20) = P(-2.25 < Z < -1.0)$

$\Phi(2.25) = 0.98778$, $\Phi(1.0) = 0.84134$

$P(10 < X < 20) = 0.98778 - 0.84134$

$= 0.146$

(b) Leaving 10% at each end, when $p = 0.9$,

$z = 1.2816$

Limits are $28 \pm 1.2816 \times 8 =$

from 17.7 to 38.3 minutes

6 (a) (i) $L \sim N(1212, 5^2)$

$z = \dfrac{1205 - 1212}{5} = -1.4$

$\Phi(1.4) = 0.91924$

$P(L > 1205) = 0.92$

(ii) 1 in 500 = 0.002

When $p = 1 - 0.002 = 0.998$, $z = 2.8782$

$L = 1212 + 2.8782 \times 5 = 1226\,\text{mm}$

(b) When $p = 1 - 0.015 = 0.985$, $z = 2.1701$

When $p = 1 - 0.019 = 0.981$, $z = 2.0749$

$\mu - 2.17\sigma = 1200$ and $\mu + 2.07\sigma = 1225$

which solve to give $\mu = 1213\,\text{mm}$ and

$\sigma = 5.9\,\text{mm}$

7 (a) $X \sim N(134, 16^2)$

(i) $z = \dfrac{150 - 134}{16} = 1.0$

$\Phi(1.0) = 0.84134$

$P(X < 150) = 0.841$

(ii) When $p = 1 - 0.1 = 0.90$, $z = 1.2816$

$X = 134 + 1.2816 \times 16 = 154.5\,\text{min}$

(b) When $p = 1 - 0.14 = 0.86$, $z = 1.0803$

When $p = 1 - 0.03 = 0.97$, $z = 1.8808$

$\mu - 1.08\sigma = 170$ and $\mu + 1.88\sigma = 200$

which solve to give $\mu = 180.9$ and $\sigma = 10.13$

so mean $= 181\,\text{min}$ and s.d. $= 10\,\text{min}$

7 Estimation

A The sampling distribution of the mean (p 90)

A1 (a) A sample of size 5

(b) The mean from the sample

(c) A set of 30 means

(d) A bar chart of the results, roughly normal

(e) The mean of the sample means should be approximately 173.5 and the variance should be approximately 8.4.

A2 The distribution should be approximately normal.

A3 The distribution should have a mean of approximately 173.5 and a variance of 4.2. The mean of the sample means should be roughly equal to the population mean.

A4 (a) A set of 30 samples of size 10

(b) Yes, the mean of the sample means should still be roughly equal to 173.5.

(c) With samples of size 10 the distribution of the sample means has a smaller variance. So samples of size 10 should give a better estimate of the mean. The distributions are both approximately normal.

Exercise A (p 92)

1 117.25 mmHg

2 (a) 41.87 mm (2 d.p.)

(b) The second estimate as it was calculated from a larger sample

B Reliability of estimates (p 93)

B1 (a) 173.4

(b) 2.12

(c) Yes, the estimates using a sample of size 20 are better as their distribution has a smaller variance.

B2 (a) The table should be approximately

Sample size	5	10	20
Variance of $\bar{X}$	8.4	4.2	2.1

(b) The variance for a sample of size n is the population variance divided by n.

(c) Approximately 1.1

Exercise B (p 94)

1 (a) 1034.3 g

(b) $\sqrt{\dfrac{14\,400}{12}} = 34.64$

2 (a) (i) 1.98 kg (ii) 0.079

(b) (i) 2.41 kg (ii) 0.083

(c) The estimate for breed A is slightly more reliable as it has a smaller standard error.

C Further problems

Exercise C (p 97)

1 (a) (i) 126 mg/l (ii) $\sqrt{\dfrac{25}{6}} = 2.04$ mg/l

(b) $z = \dfrac{80-75}{2.04} = 2.45$ s.e. above the mean

$\Phi(2.45) = 0.992\,86$
so the probability of getting a mean reading greater than 80 is $1 - 0.992\,86 = 0.007\,14$

2 Standard error $= \dfrac{0.4}{\sqrt{12}} = 0.115$

$z = \dfrac{5.7-5.6}{0.115} = 0.87$ s.e. above the mean

$\Phi(0.87) = 0.807\,85$
so the probability of getting a mean length greater than 5.7 cm is $1 - 0.807\,85 = 0.192$

3 Standard error $= \sqrt{\dfrac{1002}{10}} = 10.01$

$z = \dfrac{1000-980}{10.01} = 1.998$ s.e. above the mean

$\Phi(2.0) = 0.977\,25$
so the probability of getting a mean weight greater than 1 kg is $1 - 0.977\,25 = 0.022\,75$

4 (a) Standard error $= \dfrac{3.5}{\sqrt{10}} = 1.11$

$z = \dfrac{98-100}{1.11} = -1.80$ s.e. from the mean

$\Phi(1.80) = 0.964\,07$
so the probability of getting a mean weight less than 98 g is $1 - 0.964\,07 = 0.035\,93$

(b) $z = \dfrac{99 - 100}{1.11} = -0.9$ s.e. from the mean

$\Phi(0.9) = 0.815\,94, \qquad 1 - 0.815\,94 = 0.184$

$z = \dfrac{100 - 100}{1.11} = 0$ and $\Phi(0) = 0.5$

so the probability of a sample of 10 bars having a mean weight between 99 g and 100 g is $0.5 - 0.184 = 0.316$

5 $X \sim N(7.3, 0.078^2)$ so $\bar{X} \sim N\left(7.3, \dfrac{0.078^2}{n}\right)$

95% percentage point of the normal distribution from tables $= 1.6449$

So $z = \dfrac{7.33 - 7.3}{\dfrac{0.078}{\sqrt{n}}} \geq 1.6449$

$n \geq (1.6449 \times 0.078 \div 0.03)^2$

$n \geq 18.29$

so the sample size would have to be at least 19.

6 $X \sim N\left(165, \dfrac{6^2}{10}\right)$

A 90% symmetrical interval would leave 5% out at each end, and since the 95% point of the normal distribution is, from tables, 1.6449, a 90% interval is given by

$$165 \pm 1.6449 \times \dfrac{6}{\sqrt{10}}$$

so the range within which 90% of sample means will lie is given by (161.88, 168.12).

D The central limit theorem (p 98)

D1 (a) The mean of the sampling distribution should be roughly 21.2 and the variance 51.1.

(b) The distribution of the sample means is approximately normal, with mean roughly the same as the population mean but the variance is the population variance divided by 5.

D2 The mean of the distribution of the sample means is approximately normal with mean 50.5 and variance 83.3.

D3 The mean of the distribution of the sample means is approximately normal with mean 50.5 and variance 41.5.

Exercise D (p 100)

1 By the central limit theorem

$$\bar{X} \sim N\left(174.6, \dfrac{6.75^2}{15}\right)$$

$z = \dfrac{180 - 174.6}{\dfrac{6.75}{\sqrt{15}}} = 3.10$

$\Phi(3.10) = 0.999\,03, \qquad 1 - 0.999\,03 = 0.000\,97$

2 (a) By the central limit theorem

$$\bar{X} \sim N\left(4.3, \dfrac{3.2^2}{25}\right)$$

$z = \dfrac{5 - 4.3}{\dfrac{3.2}{\sqrt{25}}} = 1.094$ s.e. above the mean

$\Phi(1.09) = 0.862\,14, \qquad 1 - 0.862\,14 = 0.137\,86$

(b) With a mean of 4.3 and standard deviation of 3.2 a normal distribution would give a large percentage of calls of negative duration.

3 (a) By the central limit theorem

$$\bar{X} \sim N\left(3450, \dfrac{840^2}{20}\right)$$

$z = \dfrac{3000 - 3450}{\dfrac{840}{\sqrt{20}}} = -2.396$ s.e. from the mean

$\Phi(2.40) = 0.991\,80, \qquad 1 - 0.991\,80 = 0.0082$

(b) $z = \dfrac{3500 - 3450}{\dfrac{840}{\sqrt{20}}} = 0.266$ s.e. above the mean

$\Phi(0.27) = 0.606\,42$

$z = \dfrac{3800 - 3450}{\dfrac{840}{\sqrt{20}}} = 1.863$ s.e. above the mean

$\Phi(1.86) = 0.968\,56$

The probability of the mean claim being between £3500 and £3800 is

$0.968\,56 - 0.606\,42 = 0.362\,14$

4 Standard error of the sample means

$= \sqrt{\dfrac{30}{15}} = \sqrt{2} = 1.414$

For only 5% of all mean weights to be less than 250 g, the normal percentage point of 0.95 is -1.6449.

$z = \dfrac{250 - \mu}{1.414} = -1.6449$

$\mu = 250 + 1.6449 \times 1.414 = 252.3$

The mean would have to be set to 252.3 g or higher.

5 (a) $z = \dfrac{5.7 - 5.6}{0.4} = 0.25$ s.d. above the mean

$\Phi(0.25) = 0.598\,71, \qquad 1 - 0.598\,71 = 0.401\,29$

(b) $\overline{X} \sim N\!\left(5.6, \dfrac{0.4^2}{12}\right)$

$z = \dfrac{5.7 - 5.6}{\dfrac{0.4}{\sqrt{12}}} = 0.866$ s.e. above the mean

$\Phi(0.87) = 0.807\,85, \qquad 1 - 0.807\,85 = 0.192\,15$

6 (a) $z = \dfrac{30 - 35}{3} = -1.67$ s.d. from the mean

$\Phi(1.67) = 0.952\,54, \qquad 1 - 0.952\,54 = 0.047\,46$

(b) When $p = 1 - 0.025 = 0.975$, $z = 1.96$

$\mu = 30 + 1.96 \times 3 = 35.88\,\text{g}$

(c) $z = \dfrac{34 - 35.88}{\dfrac{3}{\sqrt{10}}} = -1.98$ s.e. from the mean

$\Phi(1.98) = 0.976\,15, \qquad 1 - 0.976\,15 = 0.023\,85$

(d) When $p = 1 - 0.01 = 0.99$, $z = 2.3263$

$\mu = 34 + 2.3263 \times \dfrac{3}{\sqrt{10}} = 36.21\,\text{g}$

E Estimating the variance (p 101)

E1 (a) Calculation of the variances of 30 samples

(b) Mean of the variances of the 30 samples

(c) The mean of the sample variances should be roughly 34, about $\frac{4}{5}$ of the population value, 42.1.

E2 (a) The variances of 30 samples size 10

(b) The mean of these variances, roughly 38

(c) Yes, the value is closer to the population value.

E3 (a) 41.41

(b)

Sample size	5	10	20
Mean of sample variance	34	38	41

(c) Using a sample of size 100 gives roughly the population variance of 42.1.

E4 The description depends on the calculator. 's' and 'n' or 'σ_n' and 'σ_{n-1}' are commonly used.

Exercise E (p 104)

1 (a) Mean = 32.2 min; variance = 25.7 min^2

(b) Mean = 17 cm; variance = 27.1 cm^2

(c) Mean = 932.4 days; variance = 44\,862.1 day^2

(d) Mean = 1.2652 micrometre; variance = 0.000\,088\,4 micrometre^2

2 Mean = 153.4 g

Variance = $\frac{50}{49} \times 27.4^2 = 766.08\,\text{g}^2$

3 Mean = $60.85 \div 30 = 2.028\,\text{mm}$

Variance = $\dfrac{123.5 - \dfrac{60.85^2}{30}}{29} = 0.002\,62\,\text{mm}^2$

F Using estimated variances

Exercise F (p 106)

1 (a) $\dfrac{39\,920 - \dfrac{1396^2}{50}}{49} = 19.26\,\text{mm}^2$

(b) $z = \dfrac{28.3 - 28}{\sqrt{\dfrac{19.26}{50}}} = 0.483$ s.e. above the mean

$\Phi(0.48) = 0.684\,39$

$P(X > 28.3) = 1 - 0.684\,39 = 0.315\,61$

2 (a) 159.6

(b) When $p = 0.95$, $z = 1.6449$

$\mu = 425 + 1.6449 \times \sqrt{\dfrac{159.6}{30}} = 428.79\,\text{ml}$

Mixed questions (p 107)

1 A parameter is a numerical property of a population.
A statistic is a numerical value calculated from a sample.

2 (a) $z = \dfrac{330 - 334}{5} = -0.8$

$\Phi(0.8) = 0.788\,14$

The probability of buying a can with less than 330 ml is $1 - 0.788\,14 = 0.212$ (3 s.f.)

(b) $z = \dfrac{330 - 334}{\dfrac{5}{\sqrt{10}}} = -2.53$

$\Phi(2.53) = 0.994\,30$

The probability of finding 10 cans with a mean less than 330 ml is $1 - 0.994\,30 = 0.006$ (3 s.f.)

(c) The percentage point for $p = 1 - 0.05 = 0.95$ is 1.6449.

The machine must therefore be set to

$330 + 1.6449 \times \dfrac{5}{\sqrt{10}} = 332.6\,\text{ml}$

3 (a) $z = \dfrac{20 - 22}{\sqrt{\dfrac{15}{30}}} = -2.83$ s.e. from the mean

$\Phi(2.83) = 0.997\,67$

$P(X > 28.3) = 1 - 0.997\,67 = 0.002\,33$

(b) The central limit theorem says that sample means are normally distributed irrespective of the population distribution given a sufficiently large sample size.

(c) Mean = 18.67; variance = 3.20

4 (a) (i) 3.41%   **(ii)** 0.065

(b) $z = \dfrac{3.6 - 3.4}{\dfrac{0.065}{\sqrt{10}}} = 2.47$

$\Phi(2.47) = 0.993\,24$

The probability of the consignment being rejected is $1 - 0.993\,24 = 0.007$ (3 s.f.)

Test yourself (p 108)

1 (a) $T \sim N(20, 6^2)$

Percentage point for $p = 0.8$ is $z = 0.8416$

$z = \dfrac{t - 20}{6} = 0.8416$

$t = 20 + 0.8416 \times 6 = 25.05$ minutes

(b) (i) Standard error $= \dfrac{6}{\sqrt{90}} = 0.632$

(ii) $z = \dfrac{21 - 20}{0.632} = 1.582$ s.e. above the mean

$\Phi(1.58) = 0.942\,95,\ 1 - 0.942\,95 = 0.057$

2 (a) $\dfrac{50}{\sqrt{36}} = 8.33$

(b) $z = \dfrac{490 - 500}{8.33} = -1.200$ s.e. from the mean

$\Phi(1.20) = 0.884\,93,\qquad 1 - 0.884\,93 = 0.115$

(c) For the percentage point $p = 0.95$, $z = 1.6449$

$\dfrac{475 - \mu}{8.33} = 1.6449$

$\mu = 475 + 1.6449 \times 8.33 = 488.7\,\text{g}$

(d) Since the sample size is large and we are looking at the mean of a sample the CLT is appropriate.

3 (a) $\bar{x} = 205,\qquad s = 20.4$

(b) $z = \dfrac{205 - 210}{\dfrac{22}{\sqrt{10}}} = -0.719$ s.e. from the mean

$\Phi(0.72) = 0.764,\qquad 1 - 0.764 = 0.236$

(c) This is a binomial situation where $n = 10$ and $p = 0.5$

$P(1 \text{ or less}) = 0.0107$ (from tables)

(d) The standard deviation of the sample is close to the population value and the sample mean (205) is not surprisingly low. However, (c) shows that the probability of only getting one orange heavier than 210 g is very low; this casts doubt on the random selection by the greengrocer.

(e) Number the oranges 000 to 239. Use a calculator or random number tables to select numbers in the range. 3-digit numbers are chosen and numbers > 239 and repeats are ignored. Repeat until 10 are chosen.

(f) Random sampling is not practical or easy. Customers cannot complain about the size of oranges. The best oranges will go first, leaving less saleable ones.

4 (a) $z = \dfrac{10 - 10.5}{1} = -0.5$

$\Phi(0.5) = 0.691\,46\quad 1 - 0.691\,46 = 0.308\,54$

(b) $z = \dfrac{10 - 10.5}{\dfrac{1}{\sqrt{5}}} = -1.11$

$\Phi(1.11) = 0.8665$

The probability of a sample of 10 sunroofs having mean thickness less than 10 mm is $1 - 0.8665 = 0.1335$

(c) When $p = 0.95$, $z = 1.6449$

$\mu = 10 + 1.6449 \times 1 = 11.645\,\text{mm}$

(d) $S^2 = \dfrac{3359 - \dfrac{317^2}{30}}{29} = 0.323$

(e) $\mu = 10 + 1.6449 \times \sqrt{0.323} = 10.935\,\text{mm}$

(f) Since the variance of the new process is smaller the factory can set the machine to a lower mean thickness to meet the regulation. This will mean a saving in the amount of material used.

5 (a) (i) $z = \dfrac{185-65}{60} = 2.0$

$\Phi(2.0) = 0.97725; \quad 1 - 0.97725 = 0.02275$

(ii) $P(50 < T < 125) = P(-0.25 < z < 1.0)$

$\Phi(0.25) = 0.59871; \quad \Phi(1.0) = 0.84134$

$P(50 < T < 125) = 0.84134 - (1 - 0.59871)$

$= 0.440$

(iii) $z = \dfrac{70-65}{\dfrac{60}{\sqrt{90}}} = 0.791$

$\Phi(0.79) = 0.78524$

$P(T < 70) = 0.785$

(b) (i) The mean is just over one standard deviation above zero. A normal distribution would give a high probability of a time less than zero, which is impossible.

(ii) The central limit theorem says that for a large sample $\overline{X}$ is normally distributed.

8 Confidence intervals

A Estimating with confidence (p 110)

A1 River site: $\bar{x} = 6.13$
Reservoir: $\bar{x} = 7.75$

A2 Since the reservoir has a larger sample and the s.d. is smaller, this result is likely to be nearer the true population value.

Exercise A (p 111)

1 (a) Type A: $\bar{x} = 3.18$, s.e. $= \dfrac{0.4}{\sqrt{9}} = 0.133$

Type B: $\bar{x} = 3.56$, s.e. $= \dfrac{0.6}{\sqrt{12}} = 0.173$

(b) Since the s.e. for type A turkeys is lower, this is more likely to be nearer the true value.

2 (a) s.e. $= \dfrac{0.8}{\sqrt{10}} = 0.253$

(b) Since the value of 4.9 is more than 3 standard errors away from 5.7 it is unlikely that 5.7 is the population value for that area.

3 (a) s.e. $= \dfrac{5}{\sqrt{10}} = 1.58$. The value 45 is 1.90 standard errors away from 48.

(b) It would be reasonable to say that the sample came from the population.

B Confidence intervals (p 112)

B1 Limits given by $7.75 \pm 1.96 \times \dfrac{0.5}{\sqrt{15}}$, so
$7.497 \le \mu \le 8.003$

B2 (a) No, it is very unlikely as the value is well above the confidence interval.

(b) No, there is no overlap of the intervals so there is no value that could be in both intervals.

B3 ± 2.5758 s.e. above and below the sample mean

B4 River site: $(5.153, 7.107)$
Reservoir: $(7.417, 8.083)$

Exercise B (p 116)

1 $\bar{x} = 2377$

Interval given by $2377 \pm 1.96 \times \dfrac{35}{\sqrt{9}}$

(2354.1, 2399.9) ohms

2 Interval given by $80.8 \pm 1.96 \times \dfrac{1.6}{\sqrt{64}}$

(80.408, 81.192) g

3 $\bar{x} = 22.98$

Interval given by $22.98 \pm 2.58 \times \dfrac{2.4}{\sqrt{10}}$

(21.02, 24.94) kN

4 (a) $\bar{x} = 5330.4 \div 12 = 444.2$

Interval given by $444.2 \pm 1.96 \times \dfrac{8.2}{\sqrt{12}}$

(439.6, 448.8) g

(b) It is not likely as 450 g is outside the interval.

5 (a) $\bar{x} = 29.66$;

Interval given by $29.66 \pm 1.96 \times \dfrac{3}{\sqrt{15}}$

(28.14, 31.18) g

(b) Since the population value for a house sparrow is within the interval the flock is most likely to come from this species.

C Other population distributions

Exercise C (p 118)

1 $\bar{x} = 42.39$ newtons

Interval given by $42.39 \pm 1.96 \times \dfrac{1.6}{\sqrt{15}}$

(41.58, 43.20) newtons

2 $\bar{x} = 9.974 \div 10 = 0.9974$ kg

Interval given by $0.9974 \pm 1.645 \times \dfrac{0.03}{\sqrt{10}}$

(0.9818, 1.0130) kg

3 (a) $\bar{x} = 39.1$ thousand km

Interval given by $39.1 \pm 1.96 \times \dfrac{6}{\sqrt{18}}$

(36.3, 41.9) thousand km

(b) Yes, since 40 is within the confidence interval.

4 (a) $\bar{x} = 14.6$ eggs

Interval given by $14.6 \pm 1.96 \times \dfrac{4}{\sqrt{20}}$

(12.85, 16.35) eggs

(b) No, since 17 is outside the confidence interval.

5 (a) $\bar{x} = 98.319\,°F$; (97.96, 98.68) °F

(b) Yes, the interval in (a) is inconsistent with this view.

D Using an estimated variance

Exercise D (p 120)

1 $\bar{x} = 75.2$; $S = 14.214$

Interval given by $75.2 \pm 1.96 \times \dfrac{14.214}{\sqrt{15}}$

(68.0, 82.4) cm

2 (a) $S^2 = 32.56$

(b) $\bar{x} = 99.3$; $S = \sqrt{32.56} = 5.71$

Interval given by $99.3 \pm 1.645 \times \dfrac{5.71}{\sqrt{30}}$

(97.59, 101.01) g

(c) Yes, since 100 g is within the interval, the claim is supported.

3 (a) $7.638^2 = 58.34$

(b) $\bar{x} = 73.93$; (71.64, 76.22)

4 (a) $\bar{x} = 49.97$; $S^2 = 2.11$

(b) Interval given by $49.97 \pm 1.96 \times \sqrt{\dfrac{2.11}{151}}$

(49.74, 50.20) matches

(c) The value 48 is outside the limits; however, the interval suggests the mean is greater than 48 so customers are not being misled.

Mixed questions (p 122)

1 $\bar{x} = 194.5$

Interval given by $194.5 \pm 1.96 \times \dfrac{18}{\sqrt{12}}$

(184.32, 204.68) g

2 (a) $S^2 = 6.25$

(b) $\bar{x} = 17.7$

Interval given by $17.7 \pm 2.58 \times \sqrt{\dfrac{6.25}{50}}$

(16.8, 18.6) km

(c) The central limit theorem states that sample means are normally distributed given a sufficiently large sample size.

Test yourself (p 122)

1 (a) Since the lengths were normal the sample means are also normally distributed.

(b) $\bar{x} = 178$

Interval given by $178 \pm 2.5758 \times \dfrac{3}{\sqrt{16}}$

(176.1, 179.9) mm

2 (a) $\bar{x} = 413$

Interval given by $413 \pm 2.5758 \times \dfrac{3}{\sqrt{12}}$

$(410.8, 415.2)\,\text{g}$

(b) As the interval excludes 410 g it is unlikely to be correct.

3 (a) $A \sim N(10.3, 0.16^2)$

(i) $z = \dfrac{10.5 - 10.3}{0.16} = 1.25$

$\Phi(1.25) = 0.89435$

$P(A < 10.5) = 0.89$

(ii) When $p = 0.75$, $z = 0.6745$

$a = 10.3 - 0.6745 \times 0.16 = 10.2\,\text{cm}$

(b) (i) $\bar{x} = 24.9$

(ii) s.e. $= \dfrac{0.24}{\sqrt{144}} = 0.02$

(iii) Interval given by $24.9 \pm 1.96 \times 0.02$

$(24.86, 24.94)\,\text{cm}$

(iv) Since 25 is not in this interval, it is not possible to agree with the claim.

4 (a) $S^2 = \dfrac{100}{99} \times 2.97^2 = 8.91$

(b) Interval given by $331.28 \pm 2.5758 \times \sqrt{\dfrac{8.91}{100}}$

$(330.51, 332.05)\,\text{ml}$

(c) Since the sample size was large, the central limit theorem applies.

5 (a) $W_\text{I} \sim N(48.1, 0.25^2)$

$z = \dfrac{47.5 - 48.1}{0.25} = -2.4$

$\Phi(2.4) = 0.99180$

$P(W_\text{I} < 47.5) = 1 - 0.99180 = 0.008$

(b) $W_\text{II} \sim N(\mu, 0.32^2)$

When $p = 0.85$, $z = 1.0364$

$\mu = 50 - 1.036 \times 0.32 = 49.7\,\text{g}$

(c) (i) Interval given by

$52.46 \pm 1.96 \times \sqrt{\dfrac{0.1764}{36}}$

$(52.32, 52.60)\,\text{g}$

(ii) The central limit theorem is applicable because n is large so $\bar{X}$ approximates to a normal distribution.

9 Linear regression

A The least squares regression line (p 124)

A1 The scatter diagram shows that as the height of the ramp increases, the distance the car travels also increases in a linear fashion.

A2 (a) A line of best fit on the scatter diagram

(b) An equation close to $y = 4x + 25$.

(c) $\bar{x} = 25$, $\bar{y} = 125$

A3 The line $y = 3x + 50$ plotted on the scatter diagram.

A4

Height	5	10	15	20	25	30	35	40	45
Actual	40	44	106	91	175	138	169	175	187
Predicted	65	80	95	110	125	140	155	170	185
d_i	−25	−36	11	−19	50	−2	14	5	2

$\sum d_i = 0$

A5 $\sum d_i^2 = 5132$

A6

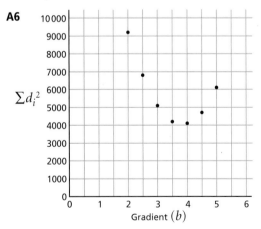

The optimum gradient is about 3.85.

A7 (a) $94.3\,\text{cm}$ **(b)** $40.4\,\text{cm}$ **(c)** $259\,\text{cm}$

Exercise A (p 127)

1 (a)

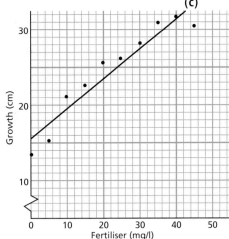

(c)

Yes, linear regression is appropriate.

(b) $y = 15.5 + 0.4x$

(c) Line as above

(d) (i) 24.3 cm   **(ii)** 16.7 cm   **(iii)** 35.5 cm

(e) The first two estimates are reliable as they are within the range of the data. The other value is extrapolated and therefore not as reliable.

2 (a)

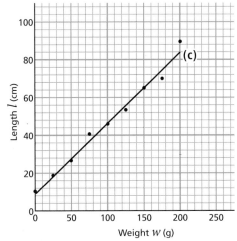

Yes, a straight line is appropriate.

(b) $l = 9.32 + 0.374w$

(c) Line on graph, as above.

(d) (i) 31.8 cm   **(ii)** 121.5 cm

(e) The value 300 g is outside the range of data. The actual value for 200 g is noticeably above the line so predicting for high values may be unreliable.

B Explanatory variables

Exercise B (p 129)

1 (a) $y = 26.2x - 344$

(b) 180 ice creams

(c) The estimated additional ice cream sales for every degree rise in temperature

2 (a) Distance is the explanatory variable.

(b)

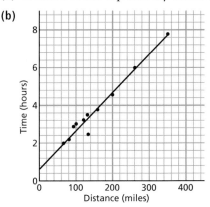

(c) $y = 0.568 + 0.0205x$. Line plotted as above.

(d) Intercept a is a fixed time (just over half an hour) added on to each journey; this might be the time taken to load and unload vehicle Gradient b is the average time taken to travel a mile on the salesman's journeys.

(e) (i) 4.3 hours   **(ii)** 1.6 hours

(iii) 9.2 hours

(f) (ii) is likely to be reliable, but (i) and (iii) ma not be reliable because they are out of the range of the data.

3 $b = \dfrac{2501 - 9\left(\dfrac{32}{9} \times \dfrac{289}{9}\right)}{636 - 9 \times \left(\dfrac{32}{9}\right)^2} = 2.82$

The equation is $(y - 32.1) = 2.82(x - 3.56)$

or $y = 22 + 2.82x$

4 (a)

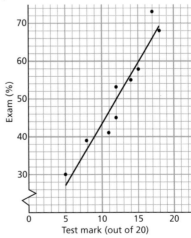

Plot: Wind speed (km/h) vs Atmospheric pressure (mb)

(b) $b = -2.35$, $a = 2437$

The equation is $y = -2.35x + 2437$

(c) b tells you that for every 1 millibar increase in pressure, the predicted wind speed will drop by 2.35 km/h.

(d) (i) 322 km/h   **(ii)** −383 km/h

    (iii) 204.5 km/h

(e) The estimate for 950 millibars is the only reliable one as the others are outside the range of the original data. In fact the estimate for 1200 millibars is an impossible one.

C Scaling

Exercise C (p 130)

1 (a) $y = -130.2 + 3.84x$

(b) $h = 2.54x$ and $w = 0.454y$

So $\dfrac{w}{0.454} = -130.2 + \dfrac{3.84h}{2.54}$

$\Rightarrow \quad w = -59.1 + 0.686h$

D Residuals (p 131)

D1

Car	A	B	C	D	E	F	G
Actual speed	181	159	134	149	124	137	106
Predicted	161.7	152.8	159.1	146.4	133.7	121.0	121.0
d_i	19.3	6.2	−25.1	2.6	−9.7	16	−15.0

H	I	J	K	L	M	N	O
121	117	118	102	101	96	101	90
115.9	110.8	105.7	103.1	108.2	103.1	98.0	95.5
5.1	6.2	12.3	−1.1	−7.2	−7.1	3.0	−5.5

D2 (a) Car A has the highest positive residual, having a high top speed in relation to its engine size.

(b) Car C has the highest negative residual, having a low top speed for its engine size.

D3 (a)

Plot: Exam (%) vs Test mark (out of 20)

(b)

Test	17	12	15	8	11	18
Predicted	64.6	52.5	59.8	42.9	50.1	67.0
d_i	8.4	−7.5	−1.8	−3.9	−9.1	1.0

12	7	5	14
52.5	40.5	35.7	57.3
0.5	20.5	−5.7	−2.3

(c) Not good: some of the predictions are as much as 20 out.

D4 (a) The data pair (7, 61) has the highest residual.

(b) $y = 11.3 + 3.21x$

Plot: Exam (%) vs Test mark (out of 20)

(c)

Test	17	12	15	8	11	18
Predicted	65.9	49.8	59.5	37.0	46.6	69.1
d_i	7.1	−4.8	−1.5	2.0	−5.6	−1.1

	12	5	14
	49.8	27.4	56.2
	3.2	2.6	−1.2

(d) The second line is a closer fit to the data as the residuals are generally smaller.

(e) This data pair represents somebody who did badly in the test but did well in the exam. They may have been ill or unprepared for the test.

Exercise D (p 132)

1 (a)

Temperature	25	26	16	23	24
Predicted	311.7	337.9	75.5	259.2	285.4
d_i	−6.7	35.1	1.5	−97.2	30.6

18	21	18	19	28
128.0	206.7	128.0	154.2	390.4
4.0	−22.7	20.0	23.8	11.6

(b) The data pair (23, 162) corresponds with when the vendor was ill.

2 (a) $y = 17.5 − 0.14x$

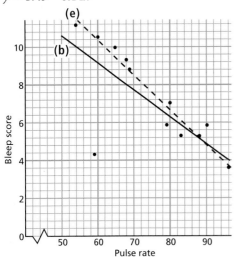

(c) (i) 1.26   **(ii)** −0.64   **(iii)** −4.94

(d) Person D

(e) $y = 21.6 − 0.186x$
Dotted line on graph above

(f) The second regression equation fits the data better. It gives someone with a pulse of 100 a bleep score of 3.0 although this involves extrapolation and is therefore unreliable.

Mixed questions (p 133)

1 (a)

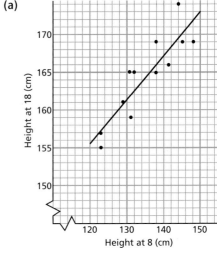

(b) $y = 84.1 + 0.594x$

(c) 173.2 cm. Since this involves extrapolating and the points do not fit closely to the line, the result is unreliable.

2 (a) Engine size is one of the factors influencing fuel economy, but fuel economy does not 'cause' engine size.

(b) $y = 57.2 − 10.2x$

(c)

Car	A	B	C	D	E	F	G
Residual	−2.5	−5.1	1.5	5.4	8.3	−1.6	−3.

H	I	J	K	L	M
3.2	−1.9	−1.9	0.1	0	0

(d) Since they all have positive residuals, cars from this manufacturer have high fuel economies for the size of engines.

Test yourself (p 134)

1 (a)

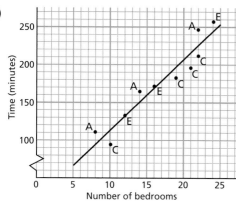

(b) $y = 22.8 + 9.19x$

(c) 188 minutes

(d) 13.7, 13.6, 23.1

(e) Andrew takes on average 17 minutes longer than the others so a better estimate is $188 + 17 = 205$ minutes.

2 (a)

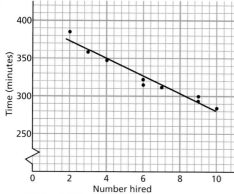

(b) $y = 396 - 11.5x$

(c) a is the time that would be taken if there was no local assistance (although extrapolated!). b is the time that is saved by hiring each extra person.

(d) This would be extrapolating well beyond the bounds of the data and the continuation of a linear relationship is doubtful. The result would give a negative value which is ridiculous. A large number of people would get in each other's way.

(e) The saving in time may be due to other factors such as improved efficiency with more practice.

3 (a)

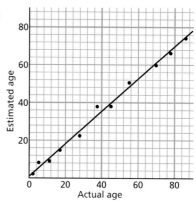

(b) $y = 0.984 + 0.853x$

(c) D: -0.860; I: 5.44

(d) A small residual indicates that the estimate is consistent with the pattern of estimates, but not necessarily that it is a good one. Paulo tends to underestimate age so, despite the small residual, D is not a good estimate. I has a large residual but is in fact a good estimate.

4 (a)

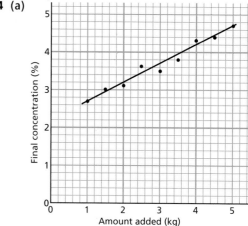

(b) $y = 2.20 + 0.493x$

(c) When $x = 3.0$, residual $= -0.177$
When $x = 3.5$, residual $= -0.124$

(d) Since the data appears to follow a linear relationship quite well, varying the amount of chemical is a good way of controlling the final concentration.

(e) The predicted value for 3.65 is 3.997, which is in the required range. However, the actual value for 3.5 is 0.124 below what was predicted. This suggests that $x = 3.65$ might on occasion give a concentration below 3.9, the lower limit of the required range.

10 Correlation

A Measuring correlation (p 136)

A1 Set 1: snails

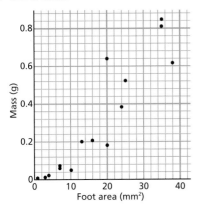

This suggests that snails with larger foot areas weigh more.

Set 2: coins

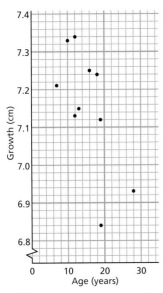

This suggests that generally older coins weigh less, although the relationship is weak.

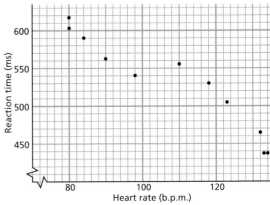

This suggests that with a higher heart rate they generally have a shorter reaction time.

Set 4: blood pressure

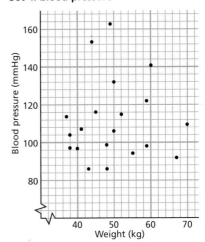

This suggests that there is little relationship between blood pressure and weight.

A2 (a) +   **(b) +**   **(c)   +**

A3 B −, C +, D −

A4 (a) Since all the values will be positive the produ...
     will be a high positive value.

   (b) Since all the values will be negative the product will be a high negative value.

   (c) Since some values will be positive and others negative, they will cancel each other so the product will be close to zero.

A5 (a) (i)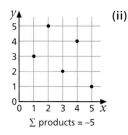

(ii)

Σ products = −5

Σ products = 10

(iii)

(iv)

Σ products = −10

Σ products = 8

(b) When the sum of the products is negative it suggests negative correlation, and when positive, positive correlation. The greater the numerical value, the closer the points are to a straight line. In this case a value of 10 or −10 means the points are on a straight line.

A6 3.19

A7 Coins: covariance = −0.58

This suggests there is a negative correlation.

Reactions: covariance = −1194

This suggests there is a negative correlation.

Blood pressure: covariance = 8.18

This suggests there is a positive correlation.

A8 While 0.345 suggests a positive correlation there is no way of telling how strong the correlation is as the covariance depends on the scale of the data.

A9

	s_x	s_y	$s_x \times s_y$	s_{xy}
Snails	11.850	0.292	3.460	3.194
Coins	5.66	0.154	0.872	−0.576
Reactions	20.8	60.3	1254	−1194
Blood pressure	9.31	20.9	194.6	8.18

A10 (a) The product of the two standard deviations is just slightly higher than the covariance.

(b) The product of the two standard deviations is just slightly higher than the absolute value of the covariance.

(c) The product of the two standard deviations is much greater than the covariance.

A11 $r = 0.923$ (3 s.f.)

A12 $\bar{x} = 3$ and $\bar{y} = 9$

$$s_x = \sqrt{\frac{(1-3)^2 + (2-3)^2 + (4-3)^2 + (5-3)^2}{4}}$$

$$= \sqrt{\frac{10}{4}} = \sqrt{\frac{5}{2}}$$

$$s_y = \sqrt{\frac{(1-9)^2 + (5-9)^2 + (13-9)^2 + (17-9)^2}{4}}$$

$$= \sqrt{\frac{160}{4}} = 2\sqrt{10}$$

$$s_x \times s_y = \frac{\sqrt{5}}{\sqrt{2}} \times 2\sqrt{10} = 2 \times \sqrt{\frac{5 \times 10}{2}} = 10$$

$$s_{xy} = \frac{(-2 \times -8) + (-1 \times -4) + (1 \times 4) + (2 \times 8)}{4} = 10$$

$$r = \frac{10}{10} = 1$$

A13 s_x and s_y are unchanged. In s_{xy} the negative differences are multiplied by the positives giving −10. Hence $r = -1$

A14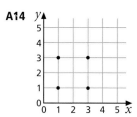

The p.m.c.c. is 0. The means are both 2 so the points are equally spread out in the 4 quadrants.

A15 Coins: p.m.c.c. = −0.662

Weak negative correlation

Reactions: p.m.c.c. = −0.951

Strong negative correlation

Blood pressure: p.m.c.c. = 0.042

No correlation

Exercise A (p 141)

1 (a) $r = 0.958$

(b) There is a strong positive correlation. There is a tendency for cigarettes with a high nicotine content to have a high tar content.

2

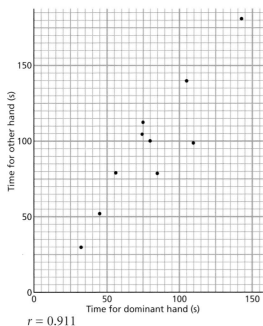

$r = 0.911$

3 (a) $r = -0.824$

(b) Yes, on days where the temperature is high the electricity used is generally less.

4 (a) (i) $r = 0.450$ **(ii)** $r = 0.644$

(b) There is a stronger correlation between weight and blood pressure in the females than in the males.

B Scaling (p 142)

B1 The p.m.c.c. is -0.850 whichever temperature system is used.

C Interpreting correlation (p 142)

C1 No. The two variables are strongly correlated but it is not likely that one causes the other. The older students are likely to be taller and better at general knowledge than the younger ones.

C2 (a) $r = 0.909$

(b) $r = 0.617$

(c) When the teacher's values are included there is strong positive correlation. Without them the correlation is weaker.

Exercise C (p 144)

1 (a) $r = 0.215$

(b)

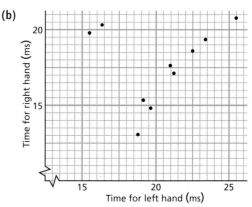

(c) A and H

(d) $r = 0.965$

(e) There is clearly a strong correlation between left- and right-handed reaction times for the right-handed students. The two left-handed students cause the correlation for the group as a whole to be significantly less.

2 The correlation coefficient suggests that towns with large cinema audiences have high crime rates but this does not signify a causal link. Both variables are probably linked to a third variable such as the size of the town: bigger towns are likely to have more cinemas and a higher crime rate.

3 (a) $r = -0.230$

This suggests that there is only a very weak correlation between temperature and the amount of electricity used.

(b)

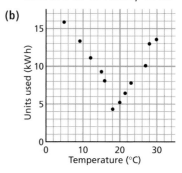

(c) The relationship between the two variables is clearly not linear.

Test yourself (p 145)

1 (a) A 0.9, B 0.7, C −0.4

  (b) Case B, since the relationship is not linear

  (c) Both variables will be linked to the daily temperature. On hot days more ice creams will be sold and more car radiators are likely to overheat.

2 (a) Definitely incorrect. The p.m.c.c. cannot have a value greater than 1.

  (b) Probably incorrect. This implies that there is a weak negative correlation between height and weight, namely that taller people weigh less.

  (c) Probably incorrect. This suggests a strong correlation, namely the more someone is absent the better they will do in tests.

3 (a) $r = 0.151$

  (b) The p.m.c.c. is close to zero so there is very little correlation between verbal reasoning and English scores.

4 (a) (i) 0.929

  (ii) A strong correlation, towns with high numbers of solicitors have a high number of cars stolen.

  (b) This is not suggested by the results. No cause and effect is implied. It may be that with a high crime rate more solicitors are needed or both may be related to the size of town.

5 (a) $r = 0.175$

  (b) Golfers D and J hit the ball further with their right hand in front, whereas all the other golfers hit the ball further with their left hand in front.

  (c) When D and J are included there is very little correlation but if they are excluded there is a strong correlation.

6 This would have no effect on the correlation: it would still be 0.57.

Index

addition rules for probabilities 40
area
    proportions under normal curve 75
    under continuous distribution curve to represent
      probability 86

back-to-back stem-and-leaf diagram 10
bias in data collection 8
binomial distribution 58-69
    calculation of mean, variance, standard deviation
      68–69
    parameters 64
    probability using formula 63–65
    tables 66–67, 148–153
bivariate data 137
box-and-whisker diagram (box plot) 20–21, 24

calculator
    regression function 128
    statistical functions 17, 27, 31
cause and effect 124, 128, 143
central limit theorem 98–100
combinations 60–61
complement of event 39
conditional probability 42–43, 46–48
confidence interval 112–115, 117, 119–120
continuous data 10
continuous random variable 77, 86
controlled variable 124, 128
correlation 136–144
    coefficient (product moment) 139–141
    effect of linear transformation of variable 142
    interpretation in context 142–144
covariance 138–139
cumulative binomial distribution tables 66–67,
  148–153
cumulative frequency graph 16, 19

data collection 6–9
dependent (response) variable 124, 128
discrete data 10
discrete random variable 52–53, 55–56
distribution of sample means 91–96

equally likely outcomes 38–41
estimator of parameter 92

Excel functions 147
explanatory (independent) variable 124, 128

frequency density 11

grouped frequency table 10–11
    mean from 17–18
    standard deviation from 31–34

histogram 11

independent events 44–45
independent (explanatory) variable 124, 128
interquartile range 19, 24, 33–35
interval estimate (confidence interval) 112–115, 117,
  119–120

least squares regression line 124–128
linear correlation 136–144
linear interpolation for median etc. 17
linear regression 124–128, 130–132
linear transformation of variable
    effect on correlation 142
    effect on mean and standard deviation 29–30
    in regression equation 130
    to standardise normal distribution 80–81

mean 35
    effect of linear transformation of variable 29–30
    from grouped frequency table 17–18, 31–34
    of binomial distribution 68–69
    of discrete random variable 55
    of normal distribution 78, 80–81
median 15, 33–35
    by linear interpolation 17
    from cumulative frequency graph 16
modal group 15, 35
mode 15, 35
multiplication rule for independent events 45
mutually exclusive events 40

non-response bias 8
normal distribution 73–81, 83–85
    mean, variance, standard deviation 78, 80–81
    parameters 81
    standardising variable 80–81
    table 78–79, 81, 154

outcomes 38–41
outlier 34, 131–132, 143

parameters
    of binomial distribution 64
    of normal distribution 81
Pascal's triangle 58–60
percentage points of normal distribution table
   83–84, 155
percentile 19
pie chart, proportional 12–13
point estimate 110–111
population mean, unbiased estimate of 92, 110–111
population variance, unbiased estimate of 101–105,
   119–120
primary data 22
probability distribution (function)
    continuous 77–78, 86
    discrete 52–53, 55–56
probability
    as proportion of favourable outcomes 38–41
    conditional 42–43, 46–48
    of independent events 44–45
    of mutually exclusive events 40
    tree diagram 46–48
product moment correlation coefficient 139–141
proportional pie chart 12–13
proportions of areas under normal curve 75

quartiles 19, 24
questionnaire design 9
quota sample 8

random numbers
    to select sample 7–8, 90, 99
    on calculator 8
    use of table 7
random sample 7–8, 90
random variable
    continuous 77, 86
    discrete 52–53, 55–56
range 35
rectangular distribution 86, 99
regression 124–128, 130–132
regression coefficient 125–126, 128
regression equation
    effect of linear transformation of variable 130
relative frequency 52
residual from regression equation 131–132
response (dependent) variable 124, 128

sample
    quota 8
    random 7–8, 90
    stratified 8
    systematic 8
sampling distribution 91–96
scaling of variable
    effect on correlation 142
    effect on mean and standard deviation 29–30
    in regression equation 130
    to standardise normal distribution 80–81
scatter diagram 124–125, 137–138
secondary data 22
set notation for probability 39–41
sigma notation 26
simultaneous equations to obtain normal
   distribution parameters 84
skewed distribution 34
spreadsheet
    for random numbers 8, 99
    statistical functions 27, 147
    to simulate sampling from specified random
      variable 113–114
spurious correlation 143
standard deviation 25–32, 35
    effect of linear transformation of variable 29–30
    from grouped frequency table 31–34
    of binomial distribution 68–69
    of discrete random variable 56
    of normal distribution 80–81
standard error of sample mean 93–96, 110–111
standard normal distribution table 78–79, 81, 154
statistic 92
stem-and-leaf-diagram 10
stratified sample 8
survey 6–7
systematic sample 8

tables
    binomial distribution 66–67, 148–153
    normal distribution 78–79, 81, 154
    percentage points of normal distribution 83–84,
      155
tree diagram for probabilities 46–48
triangular distribution 86

unbiased estimator
    of population mean 92, 110–111
    of population variance 101–105, 119–120
uniform distribution 53, 86, 99

variance 25–27, 35
    from grouped frequency table 31–34
    of binomial distribution 68–69
    of discrete random variable 56
    of normal distribution 80–81
    unbiased estimator 101–105, 119–120
Venn diagram 39